EARLY AMERICAN CINEMA
IN TRANSITION

General Editors
David Bordwell, Vance Kepley, Jr.
Supervising Editor
Kristin Thompson

Film Essays and Criticism
Rudolf Arnheim

Post-Theory: Reconstructing Film Studies
Edited by David Bordwell and Noël Carroll

*Reel Patriotism: The Movies
and World War I*
Leslie Midkiff DeBauche

*Shared Pleasures: A History of Movie Presentation
in the United States*
Douglas Gomery

*Lovers of Cinema: The First American Film
Avant-Garde, 1919–1945*
Edited by Jan-Christopher Horak

*The Wages of Sin: Censorship and the
Fallen Woman Film, 1928–1942*
Lea Jacobs

Settling the Score: Music and the Classical Hollywood Film
Kathryn Kalinak

*Early American Cinema in Transition: Story, Style, and
Filmmaking, 1907–1913*
Charlie Keil

Patterns of Time: Mizoguchi and the 1930s
Donald Kirihara

The World According to Hollywood, 1918–1939
Ruth Vasey

The Magic Mirror: Moviemaking in Russia, 1908–1918
Denise J. Youngblood

EARLY AMERICAN CINEMA IN TRANSITION

STORY, STYLE, AND
FILMMAKING, 1907–1913

Charlie Keil

The University of Wisconsin Press

The University of Wisconsin Press
1930 Monroe Street
Madison, Wisconsin 53711

www.wisc.edu/wisconsinpress/

3 Henrietta Street
London WC2E 8LU, England

1   3   5   4   2

Printed in the United States of America

Library of Congress Cataloging-in-Publication Data

Keil, Charlie.
Early American cinema in transition:
story, style, and filmmaking, 1907–1913 / Charlie Keil.
320 pp.   cm.—(Wisconsin studies in film)
Filmography: p.
Includes bibliographical references and index.
ISBN 0-299-17360-7 (cloth: alk. paper)
ISBN 0-299-17364-X (pbk.: alk. paper)
1. Motion pictures—United States—History.
2. Motion picture industry—United States—History.
I. Title.   II. Series.
PN1993.5.U6 K39   2001
791.43'0973'09041—dc21   2001003112

For Cathy

CONTENTS

TABLES

ACKNOWLEDGMENTS

I first had the idea of writing about the transitional period back at a time which now seems closer to that era than the year I write this. That idea, and my interest in early cinema, were nurtured by several people at the University of Wisconsin–Madison, to whom I feel tremendous gratitude. Principal among them are Don Crafton, my great champion, whose geniality and support were always evident in equal measure; David Bordwell, whose timely interventions and commitment, both intellectual and otherwise, have proven endlessly inspirational; Lea Jacobs, whose expertise and friendship I have always valued; and Vance Kepley, whose keen sense of historiographical method has shaped my own. Others from that time and place who helped me include Tino Balio, Mary Carbine, Beth Corbett, Maxine Fleckner-Ducey, Henry Jenkins III, Jim Moy, the staff of the Iconographic Collection of the Wisconsin State Historical Society, and, especially, Ben Brewster, who will doubtless take issue with much of this book and be the first to alert me of same. Fellowships from the university aided me in my research as well.

Two scholars have played particularly important roles in the development of this book, as their work has proven so influential on my own. Beyond showing me how it is done, Kristin Thompson rode in on a white horse and restored my faith in editors. Her meticulous reading of the manuscript and her rehabilitation of my prose style were icing on the cake. Though he might not realize it, Tom Gunning has been a mentor of sorts, even when we have agreed to disagree. He looms large behind this project and in my thinking about early cinema in general and I salute him for that. Two readers of the manuscript supplied helpful criticisms, and I hope the finished product evinces my respect for their commentary. Beyond that, I want to thank Dick Abel for helping me to see the wisdom of respecting Pathé and for being the definition of an honorable fellow, and Rick Altman for bringing this period to life through his Living Nickelodeon.

Studying early cinema offers the additional benefit of putting one into contact with a host of gracious and committed devotees of this period of film's history. I am grateful that Domitor has existed to bring us together; the published proceedings of the third Domitor conference contains an essay of mine wherein I rehearse a few of the ideas found in chapter 4. And I am elated (on an annual basis) that the Giornate del Cinema Muto has offered us a means to expand our knowledge. Particular thanks to Paolo Cherchi Usai for asking me to participate in the Griffith Project (a version of my analysis of *His Lost Love* from chapter 5 appears in volume 3 of the project). Among the many early cinema scholars and experts who have aided me over the years, memory recalls the following: Eileen Bowser, Scott Curtis, David Francis, André Gaudreault, Antonia Lant, Charlie Musser, Roberta Pearson, Herb Reynolds, Brad Smith, and Yuri Tsivian. Apologies to anyone I have forgotten to include. Two friends whose work I respect immensely, Shelley Stamp and Ben Singer, commiserated with me as we slogged through our respective projects, and generously shared the fruits of our labors.

While researching this book, I was treated especially well by a group of professionals whose efforts transformed their archives into homes away from home. Both the inestimable Charles Silver and, later, Steve Higgins at MOMA went far beyond the call of duty to help me. The team at the National Film Archive in London made my long stay there particularly productive; thanks go to Luke McKernan, Jackie Morris, Heather Osborne, Steve Tollervey, Clive Truman, and especially Julie Rigg. Most of all, I am indebted to Patrick Loughney and the staff at the Library of Congress, but none more so than the wonderful Madeline Matz. I also owe thanks to Eli Savada and Susan Dalton, who helped me with searches while I was in Washington. Others offered lodging, productive discussions, and the comforts of friendship during my research travels: David Weaver in New York, Doug Riblet and Scott and Carole White in Washington, and, most memorably, Murray Smith and Miri Song in London.

Closer to home, I have benefited from the constant and welcome support of colleagues and friends. Staff and faculty at the University of Toronto have helped in numerous ways; I wish to thank Dermot Brennan, Terry Louisy, Alexi Manis, Jean Mutrie, Joe Sokalski, and Cam Tolton from the Cinema Studies Programme at Innis College and Luella Massey and Domenico Pietropaolo from the Graduate Centre for Study of Drama in particular. Most of all, I want to acknowledge the encouragement of my ex-colleague Caryl Flinn and the role of Bart Testa in helping to develop my attraction to early cinema. The staff at the Toronto Metro Reference Library and the University of Toronto's Robarts Library, especially Jane Lynch of Interlibrary Loan, deserve thanks for aiding me in my research. A Connaught fellowship and an earlier grant from the Social Sciences and Humanities Research Council of Canada provided financial assistance.

The process of bringing this book toward publication was eased considerably by the consistently helpful attitude of the editorial and production staff at the University of Wisconsin Press. In particular I would like to thank Carla Aspelmeier, Allen Fitchen, Karen Kodner, Sheila McMahon, Alison Ruch, Jenny Seifert, and especially Raphael Kadushin and Scott Lenz for doing their jobs so well.

Numerous friends and relatives have eased the burden of this project by showing interest and expressing encouragement through the years. Meraj Dhir, Lori Haskell, Melanie Randall, Mary Rella, Rochelle Simmons, and Charles Tepperman were particularly supportive, as were Katie Lynes and Phil Fisher, who provided welcome expertise at key moments as well. Ken Eakin helped with the frame enlargements of *Suspense,* and Marta Braun, my partner in crime, shared her work with me. Family members have managed to blend support with tact when discussing this project with me, and for that among many other things I thank them. Anna Hoad, Harry and Carole Keil, and Bill and Carol Vine deserve special mention. My sister Martha supplied her expert editorial skills on more than one occasion, and her love always. Finally, and most specially, I thank Cathy Vine and our two children, Houston and Emma. The latter have shown a tolerance beyond their years toward a project whose duration has exceeded the span of their lives and I apologize for the time it has kept me from them. Taking up the parental slack has been my partner Cathy; she more than anyone deserves credit for this book reaching completion. In her unflagging support and willingness to help she has defined devotion; to express the gratitude words cannot convey, I dedicate this book to her with love.

EARLY AMERICAN CINEMA
IN TRANSITION

1

Introduction

Our object is to compare type with type, the finished with the finished. Of course, in the strictest sense of the word, there is nothing "finished": all historical material is subject to continual transformation; but we must make up our minds to establish the distinctions at a fruitful point, and there to let them speak as contrasts, if we are not to let the whole development slip through our fingers.

HEINRICH WÖLFFLIN, *Principles in Art History*

As HEINRICH WÖLFFLIN reminds us, the willful act of definition forces historians to abandon the careful balancing act that history writing typically entails. Cautious relativism may reflect sensitivity to the transience of historical phenomena, but indecisiveness will not produce meaningful categories and helpful periodizations. Early cinema historians have proven to be an emphatically decisive bunch. When we confront the seemingly endless changes within cinema's first decades, the trail to classicism resembles a palimpsest, as various historians have marked the territory with their own organizational schema—primitive cinema or cinema of attractions, cinema of narrative integration or prefeature, the welter of definitions reveals a terrain which invites constant redivision. My interest centers on a middle-section within this path, not quite so well worn, beginning with a simultaneous turn to narrative and adoption of the single-reel format and concluding with the advent of the feature film. Having set the boundaries of my study, I will attach my own label as well: the years 1907 to 1913 constitute the period of transitional cinema.

As my periodization derives from specific and proximate factors (changes to production practices, altered industry standards regarding film formats and release schedules, increased monitoring of films by the trade press), I am applying it within a strict national and generic context: this study concerns itself only with American fiction filmmaking. Moreover, my object of study is formal change. Though external forces may motivate the shifting norms I examine, these norms undergo a transformation at the

3

hands of filmmakers experimenting with how to render narrative comprehensible. The films that resulted, the chief laboratory for the formal exploration of the period, remain my primary research resource. By viewing hundreds of examples from these years, I have devised the questions that propel this study: What problems did increased narrative complexity pose for filmmakers at this time? Did all filmmakers construe the problems as similar, and how did this affect the types of solutions they pursued? What particular constraints and potentialities did the medium of film introduce for these filmmakers, and to what degree did solutions derive from the characteristics of the medium? What aesthetic principles shaped the choices made, and what role did the prevailing voices of critical judgment play in guiding filmmakers' decisions?

By proposing these questions in terms of problems and solutions, I am deliberately maintaining a notion of agency within my argumentative framework. Seeing the formal achievements of the transitional period as the outcome of filmmakers' attempts to find ways to become communicative storytellers strikes me as the most methodologically sound approach. If we cannot allow that filmmakers were casting about for solutions to problems deriving specifically from their chosen medium at a crucial stage in its development, how can we produce any but the vaguest of definitions for this period?

Defining Transition: Storytelling at the Crossroads

In effect, to define the transitional period is to define a process of change. As industrial conditions shifted and the single-reel format gained primacy, filmmakers faced the prospect of filling a thousand feet with intelligible, compelling narratives. The brief gags and bursts of action that characterized earlier short films would not suffice as material for longer works, and the presentational model filmmakers had relied upon in the past required revising to facilitate proper storytelling. The advice of commentators stressed the need for filmic narration to supply its own internal explanatory devices, as other mature narrative forms had learned to do: "The acted drama must explain itself. Its story must be unfolded bit by bit, without explanation from a prologue or lecture. The moving picture play should be similarly constructed" (Rollin Summers, "The Moving Picture Drama and the Acted Drama," *Moving Picture World* 3, no. 12, 5 September 1908, 212).

The bulk of this book will devote itself to the task of detailing how filmmakers worked to transform their storytelling technique. However, for the purposes of establishing the "fruitful distinctions" Wölfflin insists upon, let me introduce the nature of the shifts involved with a representative comparison. Using two hypothetical films, typical in their features, if fabricated in their existence, I will outline the ways in which filmmakers would approach a similar story, both at the beginning and end of the period in question. Why play Dr. Frankenstein when so many actual films remain available, none requiring the stitch work I am about to perform? Composite films will allow me to point out parallel differentiating features more economically. However, recall that in each instance, the elements highlighted find their equivalent in existing films from the period.

The first composite film, a ten-shot comedy from 1907 we will call *A Lady's Luck*, places the title character in a series of humorous incidents, all of which end with her narrowly avoiding physical calamity. She walks by a store and immediately afterward the awning collapses; she crosses a busy street, barely sidestepping oncoming traffic; she steps on a sewer cover which is removed a second later; and so on. Only the presence of the central character in each setting connects the disparate collection of locales. At the end of the film, the woman enters a building, passing under a large sign overhanging the entrance that reads "The Lucky Charm Club." The next-to-last shot features her seated among a number of other members, many of them recounting stories. As with all the previous shots, this one is filmed with the camera sufficiently far from the subjects to allow their entire bodies to fill the frame. *A Lady's Luck* ends with an inserted closer shot of the heroine, who shows a rabbit's foot to the person next to her. The background does not match that of the preceding shot, though the positions of the two characters remain roughly similar.

The second composite film, *Lila's Lucky Charm*, from 1913, has more than four times as many shots as *A Lady's Luck*, taken at a noticeably closer range than those of the earlier film. Rather than featuring diverse locales in which a series of linked incidents occur, most of the later film's narrative develops a single event that emphasizes Lila's luck. The depiction of this event comprises the latter two-thirds of the film, with the first third establishing its necessary preconditions. The first portion shows Lila's mother sending her off on an errand. As Lila heads for the store, her devoted boyfriend Fred follows her. (The film's first shot establishes their relationship by depicting them as they enjoy an idyllic afternoon; soon thereafter Lila's mother disrupts the tranquility by requesting help.) On her way to the store, Lila trips in the woods and becomes caught in a bog. Fred witnesses her plight, via an eyeline match, and helps her. After ascertaining that she is safe, Fred gives Lila a good-luck charm, his own rabbit's foot, and they set off together. A title card indicates the passage of a few days, setting up the story's next stage. In this portion, unfriendly Indians lay siege to Lila's farm; in a series of shots, the Indians close in on the house, poised to attack. Just before they burst through the door, Lila remembers her rabbit's foot and waves it outside the front window. Seeing the foot, the attackers grow fearful and disperse. Fred arrives immediately thereafter and comforts Lila while receiving a kiss for the gift of the charm.

Let me underscore some of the salient formal differences between these two films. First, the latter film's larger number of shots complements the increased narrative complexity of its scenario. Greater individuation of character distinguishes the 1913 film from its predecessor: characters now possess names, aspects of the protagonists' relationships receive attention, and closer shot scale helps register pertinent emotional reactions. The earlier conception of space as a series of locales connected merely by similar repeated actions gives way to narratively relevant spatial relationships (as in the Indians' increased proximity to the house). The director of *Lila's Lucky Charm* employs editing patterns to establish these relationships, in combination with cues contained within the *mise-en-scène* (characters' glances, observable props functioning as spatial signposts, etc.). Privileged objects from the *mise-en-scène* acquire altered narrational duties as well: whereas the rabbit's foot of the first film operates as a visual punch-line heightened by the changed shot scale, when the same charm appears in the second example, its presence has become naturalized, as a token representing Fred's love for Lila. Moreover, the recurrence of the rabbit's foot in the latter film points to the scenario's discernible two-part structure. The first section motivates the appearance of the pivotal object, preparing for its narrative usefulness during the climax of the film's second portion.

Though neither of these films actually exists, they can function as "ideal types," aggregate examples of the qualities found in films from the transitional period. In the remainder of this book, I will examine how filmmakers moved from *A Lady's Luck* to *Lila's Lucky Charm*, while insisting on the gradual and inconsistent path of that movement. In common with many who have investigated early cinema's style and narrative, I understand the changes involved in transition as most suitably addressed within a formalist framework. What assumptions animate a formalist approach to film study and what can it tell us about the transitional period? One can find numerous rehearsals of formalism's general precepts elsewhere; I will offer only a condensed overview here, sufficient to anchor this book's orientation. Formalism takes for granted the constructed and deliberately aesthetic nature of its objects of study (if not their concomitant originality). To varying degrees, all artworks promote defamiliarization, a recasting of material derived from the world surrounding the artwork, which results in an entity whose structure and employed means differentiate it from reality. Defamiliarization occurs through the systematic deployment of devices whose functions within individual works help define their uniqueness; at the same time, if those functions recur within a group of works, the resultant norms situate a device's usage historically.[1]

When employed as an approach to analysis, formalism supplies the historian with powerful tools for exploring the process of narration and its articulation through style, as I shall explore in more detail in chapter 3. When applied to the transitional cinema, a formalist approach can aid in explaining more fully the norms that emerge at this time and the ways that constant adjustments to style invariably affect the period's narrational strategies. Formalism encourages the appraisal of specific elements of the medium but always with attention to the functions they perform, the systematic interrelationship of those functions, and their historical relevance. For that reason, I have no interest in merely cataloguing modifications to shot scale or decreased average shot lengths; instead, I enlist such quantifiable changes to prove a changed approach to cinematic storytelling, the radical nature of which renders this period remarkable. As such, my project fits into an ongoing study of the increased narrativization of early cinema that has engaged many scholars of the preclassical years.[2]

The Trail beyond Primitive Cinema

When early cinema entered into its renaissance as an object of scholarly attention, many of its supporters expended considerable energy distancing it from the narrational tenets of classicism, which had condemned the "primitive" era to inferiority. The academic project of retrieving early cinema from its shadowy status as a pre-Griffithian era of minimal interest accounts for why initial revisionist attention tended to focus primarily on film's first decade. As a scholarly enterprise, the study of early cinema received its greatest impetus (and institutional blessing) from the 34th Annual Fédération Internationale des Archives du Film (FIAF) Congress in 1978, commonly known as the Brighton Project. The collective work stimulated by Brighton helped transform perception of the historical

status and formal functioning of early film.[3] Appropriately, this first stage
of early cinema study focused on its earliest years, epitomized by the
Brighton Project's limitation of its purview to the years 1900–1906.

Attention to early cinema as a diachronic phenomenon divisible into
distinct periods emerged somewhat later, with no single event marking this
next stage as symbolically as Brighton had the first. Even so, the Pordenone
Silent Film Festival's retrospective of Vitagraph films[4] in 1987 helped ac-
celerate developments initiated by the pioneering work of Barry Salt and
Kristin Thompson in the first half of the same decade.[5] No longer neglected
as a distinct time frame, the transitional period has served as the backdrop
for a wide range of books on preclassical American cinema published in
the wake of revisionist attention to early cinema's importance. The last decade or so has seen at least three books devoted to Griffith's Biograph period (1908–13) and another to American film history for the years 1907–15,
as well as volumes chronicling the emergence of the star system, the social
problem film, the high-art motion picture, and changing patterns of female
spectatorship over roughly the same time span.[6]

Most of these books acknowledge (and even expand) the terms scholars have employed to explain the distinction between "primitive" and
"classical." Signal differences underlie the approaches devised, but even
so, one can construct a hybrid account of the perceived relationship between the primitive and classical modes that does justice to most of the
contributions involved. As my own examination of transitional cinema in-
tersects with this preexistent heuristic context, I think it worthwhile to re-
count in some detail.

By substituting the term "cinema of attractions" for primitive cinema,
Tom Gunning provided an immensely influential intervention in the
analysis of the opposed features of the primitive and classical. While the
legacy of the attractions model has occasioned some controversy itself,
when Gunning first proposed the concept he stressed a few basic differentiating principles that distinguished the earlier mode from classicism:
the cinema of attractions actively solicits the spectator's attention through
display, as opposed to the classical cinema, which concentrates on telling
a story. For this reason, films from the earlier period maintain a unity of
framing or viewpoint that differs substantially from the deliberately frag-
mented yet analytically cohesive mode of representation dominant later.
The earliest films privilege shot autonomy, which means that the profilmic
event occupying a single space dictates the camera's presence, in direct
opposition to later films, where the camera constantly repositions itself to

offer the ideal vantage point on the unfolding action. In the words of André Gaudreault, "the totality of action unfolding in an homogeneous space" (1983, 322) defines the cinema of attractions, obviating concern for the demands of temporal continuity; the classical system, on the other hand, invokes time constantly as a regulating force, shaping narrative progression.

Classical cinema also brings with it more emphatic modes of closure, a key principle in story construction, indicating a strengthened sense of the force of the diegesis. Emphasizing classicism's dependency on a fortified fictionality, Noël Burch has conceptualized the opposition between the periods in terms of audience address: while the earliest films reinforce the "exteriority" of the spectator's position, eventually this gives way to the envelopment of the viewer within the diegesis (1986, 487). The role of character development proves equally important. Burch cites the dominance of the long shot, the frequently noncentered quality of the image, and the preference for broadly defined character types as contributing to what he terms an "ab-psychological" [*sic*] mode of cinema (1986, 487). Increased attention to character psychology and motivation, abetted by developed strategies of staging and décor, consistently closer shot scales, and shifting performance styles, combine to maintain character as the driving force within the classical narrative. The narrational capacities of the cinema shift to accommodate the importance of character, as the question of character knowledge comes to determine the function of such figures as point of view, previously employed as what Ben Brewster has called the visual "pleasure point" of early films (1982, 7). If the preceding description seems multifaceted, we can discern pertinent tendencies marking the shift to classicism: the changing role and value of time and space; the increased reliance on editing to effect what Burch has termed a distinct form of "linearization"; and the general subordination of individual elements to a narrational program that fosters interdependency and integration, while increasing the power of the diegesis. Overall, these tendencies amplify cinema's powers of narrativization. Prior to 1907, narrational norms favored the adoption of an omniscient stance that operated in a relatively unselfconscious manner, rarely guiding the spectator's attention. What Thompson calls the "neutral and unobtrusive" narrational approach of primitive cinema (1997, 413) eventually gives way to classical cinema's constant guidance of the spectator, shaping and dissecting the representation of narrative action for maximal effect.

Changes to narration clearly remain central when any scholar considers the transitional period. Thompson and Gunning have each elaborated compelling accounts of the narrational transformations involved, with both identifying the advent of storytelling as integral to the shift.[7] (I will consider their respective approaches to narration again in chapter 3.) For Gunning, this new narrational emphasis results in a cinema of narrative integration and a gradual displacement of showing by telling. In his study of D. W. Griffith, Gunning ties the cinema of narrative integration to a more particularized "narrator system" personified by the director's handling of specific devices, such as crosscutting. While this allows Gunning to analyze the features of Griffith's approach to storytelling, it renders many of his findings untested as to their broader application. Thompson, for her part, maintains a less localized perspective when considering how narrational norms change in anticipation of classical practice: she argues that the activity of narration ensures greater clarity by increasing redundancy and developing a range of methods for channeling information to the spectator. Nonetheless, her explanatory energy remains directed at the distinctions that separate primitive narration from its classical counterpart more so than at the process whereby that separation occurs. My efforts in this book involve refocusing attention on transition itself, not because I wish to ignore either the influence of the primitive or classical periods, but because I believe the transitional years constitute a distinct and separable experiment in forming narratives, what Wölfflin might term a "finished type." As Gunning himself has noted, "The transitional period appears to be less a gradual fade into the classical paradigm than a period of ambivalence and contestation" (1998, 266).

Charting My Own Path

Periodizations tell us as much about the historian's understanding of the phenomena under investigation as about the phenomena themselves. Early cinema historians have sliced and diced the years preceding classicism's entrenchment in 1917 into myriad phases. Gunning, for example, identifies three, though he acknowledges the difficulty of assigning dates to the "important [intermediary] period of transition in which the terms (Cinema of Attractions and Cinema of Narrative Integration) represent less two different diachronic periods than different synchronic approaches, often present within the same film" (1987, 231–32); nonetheless, his own statements suggest that the intervening phase separating these two modes lasts from approximately 1904–5 through 1908–9. Thompson has offered up a different tripartite division of the same time span which sees the primitive period falling into two phases (1895–1902 and 1902–8, dominated by one-shot films/documentaries and multiple-shot/staged narratives respectively), followed by a "transitionary phase" extending from 1909 to 1916 (1985b, 159).[8] Obviously, my own periodization diverges from these, not so radically as to suggest a rift but sufficiently to warrant further explanation. In the process of providing a rationale for my study's time frame, I will touch upon issues explored further in chapter 2, so this discussion of periodization will lead logically, if not seamlessly, into an outline of the book's contents.

Widespread scholarly consensus already recognizes a marked shift toward a more emphatically *narrative* cinema beginning in 1907. The dominance of narrative exists not only on the level of sheer output but also in terms of the representational strategies involved.[9] In fact, changes in the industrial sector likely prompted alterations of storytelling techniques. As Charles Musser has argued, "The year 1907 was pivotal for the institution of American cinema. While crises and fundamental changes occurred at almost every level of the industry, perhaps the most important transformations involved the interrelated modes of production and representation" (1983, 4).[10] The reliance on scenario scripts and the breakdown of the collaborative mode of film production indicate a trend toward more regularized industrial behavior.[11] The impact of these altered production practices, combined with narrative films' ascendancy and the proliferation of exhibition venues, spurred filmmakers to initiate changes in filmic representation that would mark a departure from previously established modes.

My decision to see the period as ending in 1913 may strike some as more arbitrary, if only because one can detect a strong continuity between the formal trends evident in films from that year and the principles underlying the classical cinema of four years later. Nonetheless, compelling industrially based reasons justify closing off this study before 1916. First, during the seven-year period from 1907 to 1913, film length conformed to a standardized format of one reel, which remained the accepted norm until the growing dissemination of features, beginning in the United States with some regularity after 1912. The retention of a near-uniform running time for the vast majority of films made during the transitional era provided a stable frame for filmmakers to work out the problems posed by the increased length and complexity of story material. Second, and related to the first, by 1913 one can observe the industry moving into another phase in its structural development, as a series of antitrust law suits precipitated the dissolution of the Motion Picture Patents Company (MPPC). The model of distribution initiated by the MPPC's General Film Company, that of one company circulating the films of multiple manufacturers, became an industrial norm (with Universal and Mutual assuming dominance). This accelerated the trend toward increased consolidation, slowing down the rate of entry into the marketplace by new and inexperienced producers from the highs seen during the early years of the Independent challenge to the MPPC.[12] This, in turn, would promote more uniform development of filmmaking practices in the remaining years until the classical style was in place.[13]

The formal qualities of most American films after 1913 differ from their predecessors in two principal ways. First, scenarists quickly adjusted how they constructed their scripts to accommodate the extended length of the feature: rather than merely expanding the one-reeler, scriptwriters introduced a structure of three or four major sections.[14] Second, by 1913 one can find most of the techniques that collectively constitute the classical style already in use. Up until that date, filmmakers are still experimenting with such techniques, viewing them as innovations to be tested; in the following years, filmmakers engage in a process of refining and honing elements of style they will enlist systematically during the classical period. Whether we should view the years between 1913 and 1917 as a unique entity in the terms I am treating the transitional period remains a matter for a separate study; no matter how we choose to define the achievements post-1913, however, we should bracket them off from what occurs within the transitional years.

The appeal to industrial developments to support my periodizing of a formal study recalls Musser's assertion that the crisis of 1907 reveals the interdependency of production and representation. This belief informs my examination of the period's industrial context in chapter 2. Specifically, I establish how industry structure and production practices could affect representational strategies. Knowledge of the industry's structure permits us to see how filmmakers operated within an atmosphere of sustained competition. In this context, companies attempted to attain a level of quality in order to promote name recognition, such as that established early on by the most dominant American manufacturers of the period, especially Biograph and Vitagraph. By the same token, production procedures encouraged standardization while still allowing experimentation. The rapid pace of production dictated how filmmakers could incorporate innovations. On the one hand, filmmakers would often look to the industry leaders for effective storytelling techniques, and they quickly absorbed easily imitated strategies. However, the same filmmakers might have avoided other approaches requiring a greater degree of planning or expertise, because their production practices would not allow the investment of time or capital.

A symptom of the industry's growing prominence, the burgeoning trade press set itself the task of monitoring and promoting filmmakers' attempts to achieve narrative legibility. The press provided feedback to filmmakers by defining problems and advocating preferred solutions. Critics trumpeted certain aesthetic standards, such as verisimilitude and unity, in an attempt to improve the quality of films. Even so, the occasional contradictions informing trade press advice indicate that commentators could experience uncertainty concerning which solutions would best address the problems of rendering narrative comprehensible. Whatever shortcomings the trade press's aesthetic might demonstrate, it still serves an important function in pointing to the parameters of the problems filmmakers faced and the possible solutions available. By looking at industry structure, production procedures, and trade discourse, chapter 2 establishes how the nature of the industry imposed conditions that bounded and influenced the problem-solving activities of filmmakers during the transitional period.

The next three chapters examine the types of problems and solutions that arose during this period from distinct vantage points, with each chapter addressing itself to a crucial aspect of film form. Chapter 3 offers an extensive look at the changes narrative itself underwent in this period and suggests the different types of narrative structure scenarists employed as a means of organizing story material. This chapter also considers how the move toward increased production of dramatic narratives placed considerable demands upon existing representational systems. In particular, the issue of characterization becomes crucial here, and I examine a variety of character-enhancing devices. Finally, I consider narrational norms, with specific processes (such as titles and inserts) discussed as functions of narration. Tying particular strategies to general concepts in this way allows an investigation of the different methods filmmakers devised to solve the problems of relaying narrative information to viewers.

Chapter 4 addresses how narrative changes occasioned a recasting of the temporal and spatial dimensions of cinema. Particular problems arose—such as conveying temporal duration, manipulating temporal order, and suggesting spatial contiguity or distance—which led filmmakers to formulate different solutions, some more durable than others. In particular, the demands of time and space led to a renewed investigation of the potential of editing, which proved instrumental (if not always easily manageable) as a tool for creating spatiotemporal connections.

Editing figures in chapter 5 as well, where I discuss the various properties of the medium, grouped under the broader categories of *mise-en-scène* and cinematographic properties, in addition to editing. The development of stylistic norms emerges haltingly, shaped by filmmakers' mounting ability to elicit emotion, create atmosphere, and guide viewer attention. Prevailing aesthetic standards, voiced by the trade press, also exert an influence: at times critical opinion encouraged stylistic shifts, as when commentators' desire for increased verisimilitude led them to advocate changes to staging and décor; at other times, however, the press functioned as a conservative force, militating against emergent trends, such as crosscutting and closer shot scale.

Chapter 6 synthesizes the observations of the three preceding chapters through extended analyses of six sample films. These films substantiate the changes that resulted from the pursuit of various solutions throughout the transitional years. The analyses demonstrate both the range of stylistic options employed during this period as well as their changing narrational purposes. Collectively, they embody the nature of transition as a diachronic phenomenon, while also exemplifying how the transformation of norms occurs gradually and in an inconsistent fashion.

Based on the particulars of transition traced out in the body of the book, chapter 7, the conclusion, charts the broad tendencies evident within this period. This provides another opportunity to demonstrate how the problem-solution model functions within the parameters of the established industrial context. However, the conclusion will also suggest how historians might explore the nature of transition beyond the realm of early cinema. While the examples I provide in this study derive from a particular period of transition, the issues I raise are applicable to historical change in general.

Historical Poetics and Roads Not Taken

At the beginning of this chapter, indulging in some metaphorical overload, I compared the trail running through early cinema to a palimpsest, bearing the traces of numerous scholars pursuing their own research agendas. Let me heap excess upon indulgence by extending the metaphor one final time. Inevitably, some of those previously chosen paths will intersect with mine; occasionally I will retrace terrain someone else has already covered. Just as certainly, I cannot (or choose not to) pursue other roads at all, as logical as their connection to this project may seem to the informed observer. I will pause here to justify what I consider the most regrettable of these exclusions, before making a final case for the value of my overall approach.

First, though I am studying only American cinema during the transitional period, this restriction ignores the reality of the marketplace circa 1907, when national boundaries proved far more porous in response to imported films than they would just a few years later. French films, particularly those of Pathé, dominated American screens in the first few years of the transitional period, much as they had for several years previous. Pathé supplied so many more films than its competitors during cinema's surge in popularity after 1905 that it virtually monopolized the market. As Richard Abel, the authority on Pathé's fortunes during this era, has written, "by stimulating and then exploiting the nickelodeon boom in the United States, Pathé sharply defined the issue of who would exercise control over the cinema market, and how" (1999, 87). Pathé's preeminence in this period extended to include innovations in standardizing production procedures, regulating print delivery, and marketing the company's reputation as a reliable trademark. For all these reasons, we must consider Pathé the industry leader at least for the first two years of the transitional period, until American producers wrested control back from the French company by setting up the MPPC.

Of what specific relevance is Pathé's domination of the American market to any consideration of domestic filmmaking in the transitional period? First, Pathé's economic centrality translated into (and doubtless sustained) formal preeminence as well. Many of the features I discuss in relation to the first half of the transitional period appear in Pathé films, often at least a few years earlier. Pathé developed many if not all of the formal innovations American companies eventually adopted by 1910. Second, given Pathé's privileged position within the industry up until 1908, we can reasonably assume that its stylistic and narrational achievements influenced complementary (if delayed) developments within American films. Obviously, I cannot disregard Pathé's influence, but the singularity of this company's achievements (and the fact that production of its films occurs in another country, within a distinctly different industrial context) renders incorporation of its films into my study problematic. Because Abel has already provided an exhaustive account of the formal features of early French cinema (including Pathé's films) in *The Ciné Goes to Town,* I see no purpose in replicating his work. I do acknowledge Pathé's importance throughout the book, however; whenever influence seems likely, I cite corresponding innovations in the company's films as endnotes.

The second omission looms even larger: I have chosen to marginalize issues of exhibition, audience, and reception within this study, mentioning them only in passing. With my own stated emphasis on the relevance of proximate influential factors still ringing in their ears, readers must think me either obtuse or capricious. Factoring in the tremendous interest this area of early cinema study currently holds for the academic community, some might choose to add "misguidedly out-of-step" to that list as well. My decision to invoke exhibition only rarely derives primarily from a conviction that as fascinating as study of exhibition practices and reception might be, it will serve my own work poorly.[15] As research in this area has grown, we have learned we still have much to learn. Not only have scholars failed to reach consensus on the class constituency of nickelodeon audiences in key cities like New York,[16] but regionally based studies indicate wide-ranging distinctions obtain depending on the size of city, its geographic location, its population's ethnic makeup, and so on. Similarly, the vagaries of exhibition practice only become amplified by the wide range of theater types that emerged during this period. With so many variables at play, can one usefully employ transitional-era exhibition or audiences as a proximate factor in forging a portrait of broad-based changes? My own approach invokes exhibition factors on occasion but also accounts for filmmakers' efforts as motivated by the desire to create films understandable to any audience without the aid of exhibitor-supplied supports.

For many scholars, questions of exhibition practice and audience data pale in comparison to the cultural significance of the supposed shifts the post-nickelodeon era introduced for viewing patterns and social behavior. Leaving aside the difficulties any such generalizing would engender when the audience in question has proven so diverse, I hesitate to enlist any correlations between formal change and large-scale social observations because the conclusions reached strike me as too tenuous to be helpful. Even astute analysts of transitional issues have inadvertently revealed the limitations of this approach. For example, in his exemplary book on the narrational strategies evidenced by D. W. Griffith's early Biograph films, Tom Gunning proposes a culturally based meaning for the director's favored device, parallel editing:

An urban and industrial working-class audience might find this race
against the clock and rhythmic division of time strangely familiar. . . .
The syncopated rhythms of ragtime and the mechanically produced
sensations of speed and force in amusement park rides reproduced the
new and often repressive experiences urban workers encountered and
transformed them—temporarily—through play. . . . Likewise, Griffith's
parallel editing invokes the split-second timing of industrial production
and workers' enslavement to an oppressive temporality. (1991, 105)

Gunning goes on to say that parallel editing both works to encourage
worker accommodation of novel and industrially imposed temporal
rhythms while also offering liberation from the "unbearable oppression of
clock time." In this way, "Griffith's parallel editing, like much of contemporaneous popular culture, clothes a new experience of time and labor
in the forms of fantasy and desire" (1991, 106).

Viewing Griffith's formal response to the demands for more precisely
articulated temporal relations in cinema as operating on a continuum with
other rhythmically distinctive popular entertainments, Gunning sees all
these forms as a response to the redefinition of time by industrialized
labor. Or, more particularly, he argues that exposure to such types of labor
conditioned how sectors of the audience reacted to this aspect of parallel
editing. But what prompts such a connection? Is it merely the rhythmic
qualities of the editing, or the fact that parallel editing combines a rapidity of cutting with a compression of time, in a manner indebted to the capacities of a mechanized medium? If the former, one could make the same
kind of argument for the chase or, before it, the motion films promoting
kinesthetic pleasure that proved popular in cinema's earliest years. The
latter suggests that parallel editing attracted the working-class portion of
the audience because they alone could relate editing's potential for radical temporal alignment to their own experience. It then makes little sense
to argue, as Gunning does elsewhere, that Griffith's formal innovations
were designed to attract bourgeois audiences and appease the complaints
of reformers troubled by cinema's appeal to the base instincts of the lower
classes.

Gunning's claims concerning the resonance of parallel editing fail to
persuade because of his insistence that this form of cutting acquires
greater affective power due to its placement within a cultural constella-
tion of class-based temporal oppression. Does this mean that the formal
means devised by filmmakers to answer the demands of narrative and

verisimilitude can never possess meanings beyond those dictated by functionality of the kind I will outline? Of course not. What it does mean, I believe, is that we must be careful not to overburden formal features devised for particular reasons with the weight of the culture that surrounds them. For that reason, I will keep audience issues on a short leash in this book, preferring to concentrate on those proximate forces whose affect on form I can specify with more assurance.

My qualms about cultural determination aside, the general approach of this book conforms to that adopted by many currently working within the field of early cinema study. David Bordwell has labeled such work "[the manifestation of a] gradual emergence of a self-conscious poetics of film" (1989b, 269). The self-consciousness of the enterprise compels me to adopt the label "historical poetics," despite the controversies that have grown up around it. In his efforts to sketch out a model for a historical poetics of cinema,[17] Bordwell has suggested that it "produces knowledge in answer to two broad questions: 1. What are the principles according to which films are constructed and by means of which they achieve particular effects? 2. How and why have these principles arisen and changed in particular empirical circumstances?" (1989a, 371).

In the case of this study, I will establish the narrative and stylistic norms of the period under investigation by analyzing a large body of representative films with an eye to the emergent formal trends. A parallel examination of the constraints and options offered up to filmmakers by selected proximate forces will establish how these norms constitute solutions to the problems of storytelling the period entailed. My study will reveal filmmakers forming films to tell stories through an analysis of how a problem-solving process produces a set of changing formal properties.

Two final points remain. By opting to extend the work of various prominent early cinema scholars in this field and by including myself as engaging in a historical poetics of cinema, I do not necessarily accept the attendant criticism of all work that does not fit within its mandate.[18] While I agree that the historical-poetical approach can best help us learn much of a basic nature we still need to discover about this period (and others), I would not discard out-of-hand insights gleaned from other methodologies. Even if I question some of the premises and conclusions that inform such work, it strikes me as too valuable to ignore. And while my study pays scant attention to the social dimension of this period, scholarly research still coming to light from the likes of Shelley Stamp (2000) and Ben Singer

(2001) amply demonstrates the continued merits of carefully reasoned cultural history.

By the same token, I hope the findings this book provides may help other scholars refine their own positions regarding early cinema. Work on the relation of films from the transitional years to overarching cultural phenomena still requires grounding in the formal operations of this period. Without a thoroughgoing sense of how such films function, one cannot speculate in any but the loosest of fashions on how to position transitional cinema within a larger cultural framework. If I leave that work for others to do, I do so not because I think it either inadvisable or unworthy, but because I wish to accord the issues I treat here priority. When subsequent scholars pick up my path as they negotiate their own way through early cinema study, I trust learning about the nature of transition will prove valuable to them in one way above all others: it teaches we can only provide the larger answers by responding satisfactorily to the smaller questions.

2

"Boom Time in the Moving-Picture Business": Industrial Structure, Production Practices, and the Trade Press

> Three years ago there was not a nickelodeon, or five-cent theater devoted
> to moving-picture shows, in America. Today there are between four and
> five thousand running and solvent, and the number is still increasing rapidly.
> This is the boom time in the moving-picture business. Everybody is making
> money—manufacturers, renters, jobbers, exhibitors. Overproduction looms
> up as a certainty of the near future; but now, as one press agent said
> enthusiastically, "this line is a Klondike."
>
> JOSEPH MEDILL PATTERSON, *Saturday Evening Post*
> (23 November 1907)

THE PERIOD 1907–13 was a tumultuous one for the American film industry, as the exhibition landscape was transformed by the proliferation of small nickelodeon theaters, often converted storefronts. This nickelodeon boom, which began in 1905 and stretched into 1908, revolutionized the exhibition sector and led to a significant upsurge in demand for films.[1] Domestic producers eventually met the demand but only after industrial restructuring. The Motion Picture Patents Company (MPPC), incorporated in September 1908, merged the interests of the most prominent producers and set out conditions aimed at standardizing print manufacture and delivery. The rate of market growth outpaced the MPPC's attempts at controlling it, however, and after 1909, a growing number of new producers appeared, aligned with the so-called Independent movement. At the same time, production extended beyond the established New York–Chicago hub to include other locales, California in particular. Finally, a trade press grew up around the burgeoning industry, reflecting and communicating the changing status of an increasingly prominent entertainment form.

One could hardly expect the films made at this time to emerge untouched by the dramatic changes occurring within the institutions that produced them. Even so, I am not interested in demonstrating, say, how one can draw a direct line from the emergent consolidation of manufacturing power to the increased reliance on continuity practices after 1909. Instead, I substitute for such a dubious model of causality a more reasonable proposition: industrial conditions encouraged production trends that fostered efficiency and centralization; these trends, in turn, facilitated the development of the form of cinema unique to this period. Nowhere is the signaling of these trends more evident than in the pages of the trade press of the day. The trade press functioned as the industry's mouthpiece, prescribing aesthetic rules, describing formal tendencies, and voicing objections to perceived transgressions of acceptable norms. Though many industrial forces played a role in shaping the distinctive formal features of the transitional period, I have elected to concentrate on three exemplary mediating influences in this chapter—the structure of the industry, dominant modes of production and production practices, and the trade press and its discourse. Each influence exerted pressure on the period's film form, but none did so in a manner that ensured predictable results.

Within each area discussed herein, contingencies tend to block any prospect of outright determination. Did changes to industrial structure ensure that leading producers would be at the vanguard of formal change? Yes, if one examines the 1908 output of Biograph, one of the key agents in the formation of the MPPC in that year; no, if one studies chief rival Edison's films instead. Why do Biograph's films undergo a marked transformation when Edison's do not? Features unique to each company—personnel changes, varying production practices, and differences in managerial approaches—apparently overrode the similar role both companies played in the restructuring of the industry.[2] Trade organizations and the trade press consistently trumpeted the virtues of harmonizing interests and standardizing production methods by 1909, but film companies still resisted the message. The exigencies of a shooting situation could compound a company's unwillingness or inability to adhere to prescribed norms of filmmaking practice. Finally, trade press advice, while easily proffered, was not always followed; moreover, commentators in the press often found themselves in disagreement with one another, or notably out of sync with the affinities of the filmmakers that they monitored. Nonetheless, these complications to a straightforward model of direct influence should neither surprise nor concern us unduly. (In fact, a history predicated only on patterns of clear-cut determination strikes me as far more suspect.) In a period marked by flux, where the most consistent feature *is* contingency, the resultant portrait of proximate influential forces inevitably lacks the comforting predictability of paint-by-numbers history.

The Film Industry, 1907–1913: Conflicts and Consolidation

By 1907, tremendous growth in the United States exhibition sector influenced producers to meet mounting demand by increasing productivity, standardizing film manufacture, and rationalizing distribution.[3] Disputes between Thomas A. Edison and those companies that Edison claimed had infringed upon his possession of certain patented technologies kept the industry in a state of constant disruption, causing it to lag behind its European counterparts (particularly the French) in terms of productivity and international market share.[4] When court decisions appeared to give credence to Edison's charges of patent violations in 1907, the affected manufacturers agreed to a licensing arrangement that would permit them to continue operating. It is testimony to the substantial growth of the market by 1907 that Edison took this opportunity to negotiate such agreements rather than force the rival companies to cease operation. Clearly, the Edison Company stood to make more from harnessing the manufacturing power of its competitors than it did by operating in isolation, attempting to serve a market too large for its production capacity. When Biograph, the sole holdout on the strength of its own patents, joined with the Edison combine in late 1908, one centralized body stood poised to control American film production.

The drive for increased manufacturer profits propelled consolidation efforts, culminating in the MPPC's formation in 1908, the aim of which was twofold: to gain oligopolistic control of the industry (hence its nickname, "the Trust") and to wrest power away from exchange operators (i.e., distributors) and exhibitors. More specifically, Trust initiatives would redirect more revenue to affiliated manufacturers by regulating and standardizing the industry's operations. Once organized as a unified body, the MPPC had a far greater chance of enforcing its policies. The Trust targeted for elimination those distribution practices that both cost producers money and perpetuated a negative image of the industry—including duping, selling previously purchased prints among exchanges, and circulating prints past their prime. Edison, Biograph, and the other participating companies possessed the combined manufacturing weight to enforce all of the policies they introduced. Reforms to the distribution system affected exhibitors as well, because now when manufacturers leased prints to exchanges for a set time and charged higher prices per reel, the expense was passed on to theater owners. Moreover, exhibitors paid the royalties imposed on projectors directly to the Trust.

The MPPC's control of the industry accelerated when the Trust moved to absorb affiliated exchanges in 1910 via the General Film Company. This increased control, in conjunction with a steady source of income from exhibitors, helped lend stability to the production schedules of the manufacturers within the MPPC. Not only could manufacturers spend more on their films, but they could also increase output, knowing that the films they had already made would be removed from the marketplace after a fixed length of time.[5] Regularly scheduled release dates helped organize the flow of product and ensured that manufacturers would produce films in a more efficient manner (or at least one geared to increased rates of production).[6]

Resentment toward Trust policies mounted, and those in dissent allied to create the Independent movement. Its eventual success thwarted the MPPC's plan to control the industry from the manufacturing base.[7] The number of Independent companies grew as the market continued to expand, and Independent production depended less on imports once it had established a more stable manufacturing base by 1910. Despite the Trust's formation of the General Film Company as its own distributing arm in 1910, the strength of the Independents persisted throughout the remainder of the period. By 1913, the Independents and the Trust enjoyed virtually identical status in terms of number of reels released and the production values of their respective films.[8] The stability achieved by 1913, once the Independents had settled into forms of organization quite similar to those of the Trust, marked the end of a period of industrial growth. The subsequent era witnessed the advent of feature films and revised methods of distribution, the construction of larger and more luxurious theaters, and the increased consolidation of producing/distributing enterprises.[9] The onset of World War I helped to curtail the presence of foreign films within the domestic market, though the industrial initiatives undertaken in the years immediately preceding the war had worked to weaken imports anyway.[10]

During this period, the developing industry structure moved toward a model of greater consolidation but still promoted competition, particularly between the MPPC and the Independents. Moreover, the split between these two factions accelerated the drive for quality already fostered by the terms of the MPPC's dominance. It was assumed that all manufacturers within the Trust used technology based on patents held by Edison and Biograph. Thus, the manufacturers were differentiated primarily based on the quality of the films they produced. Once the Independents established themselves, the emphasis on brand-name identification became even more crucial. Within certain constraints, many exhibitors could choose which manufacturer's films they would project, which only encouraged filmmakers to balance the aping of trends with attempts at innovation and the upgrading of their films to attract renters.[11]

In many ways, company identification outstripped other forms of promotion during this period. Stable genre categories do not figure prominently within company advertising, partly because firms promoted their films as products of quality, and genre labeling could reduce the distinctiveness of individual films. Nonetheless, both advertising and trade press commentary do discriminate between comedies and dramas. The western (and offshoots, such as Indian films and Civil War dramas) emerged as the single most important new genre, especially after 1908.[12] As Eileen Bowser (1990) has indicated, a principle of balance defined most exhibitors' programs, so companies attempted to produce films of different types in order to satisfy the needs of theaters. Even so, companies became associated with certain specialties, and those firms accorded the most trade press respect, such as Vitagraph and Biograph, were known for their dramatic productions.

Regardless of their generic orientation, Trust films stand out as markedly superior, particularly during the early years of the Independents' existence.[13] This makes sense for a number of reasons. First, many of the Trust members were established companies, several of which had been in existence since the 1890s. Second, MPPC companies had a fixed source of revenue from which to estimate production expenses, resulting in greater financial security and the means to improve production values. Third, because of their position within the industrial hierarchy, the more senior production companies had the greatest chance of attracting experienced personnel, particularly writers and actors from other disciplines such as theater. Recollections from the period, by Trust and Independent employees alike, substantiate that established companies like Biograph and Vitagraph were most likely to set the standards of quality and that Independent companies deliberately copied the successes of these firms. Billy Bitzer, Griffith's usual cameraman at Biograph, avers that "the little independent companies would quickly copy anything we did that the public seemed to favor" (1973, 52). In addition, Allan Dwan, a director at American, confirms the Independents' reliance on the Trust for aesthetic guidance: "I had to learn from the screen. I had no other model. We picked up and manufactured what technique we could, watched the other fellow. The only man I ever watched was Griffith, and I just did what he did. . . . I'd see his pictures and go back and make them at my company" (Bogdanovich 1971, 24).

However, because the Independent producers led a more tenuous existence, they tended to be more aggressive in their approaches to competition, which resulted in attempts to lure Trust-aligned personnel to their companies. Actor defections are the most prevalent, and one can track the career decisions of actors like Arthur Johnson (from Biograph to Reliance to Lubin) or Mary Pickford (from Biograph to IMP to Majestic and back to Biograph again) merely by watching a cross-section of films from the period. However, the history of the Independents is constructed upon the crossing over of a variety of former Trust employees, from technicians to directors (including Edwin S. Porter, who worked at both Defender and Rex after leaving Edison).[14] While many creative personnel enjoyed extensive tenures at one company (Griffith at Biograph, or Van Dyke Brooke and Larry Trimble at Vitagraph), sufficient turnover existed to militate against attributing too fixed a company identity to all but the most established of manufacturers.[15] Moreover, the Independents' ready willingness to steal away talented employees from established companies provided a quick way of improving the quality of their output, though without guaranteed results.

As the Independents gained in strength, they increased in number. Many companies came and went in quick order, but almost as many proved fairly durable. The first films of the Independent Moving Picture Company (IMP), Powers, and the New York Motion Picture Company (responsible for releases under the "Bison" trademark) came out in 1909. By 1910, Nestor, an offshoot of the pre–MPPC Centaur Company, began manufacturing films for distribution, followed by Thanhouser, Atlas, Yankee, Defender, Champion, Reliance, American/Flying "A," and Solax, to name the most prominent. Between 1911 and 1913, Rex, Majestic, Crystal, Broncho/Kay-Bee/Domino, Keystone, and Victor started production as well. This proliferation of Independent companies after the first year of the Trust's existence not only signals the Trust's failure to keep the market closed to competitors but also reveals the ongoing demand for more films. In keeping with the steady growth in number of Independent producers, the release rate of the companies increased as well. From an estimated seven reels that domestic Independent producers supplied in November 1909, production figures jumped to near twenty by September 1910. Combined domestic release rates (both Trust and Independent) reached sixty by September 1911 and 200 by mid-1913.[16] These numbers indicate dramatic changes in the manner in which films were made. The transformation of production practices would, in turn, affect the form of the films produced.

Changing Production Practices: Shuffling toward Standardization

Faced with added pressure to deliver more films according to an established release schedule, manufacturers responded by changing their modes of production. What form did these changes assume and when were they implemented? Janet Staiger (1985b) has argued for a typology of film production that starts with a cameraman system, in place until 1907, supplanted by a short-lived phase wherein a director system dominated (1907–9). After that, a director-unit system was instituted for the following five years until it was replaced in turn by a central-producer system in 1914. Disputing Staiger's portrait of succession, Charles Musser (1991b) offers a far more streamlined model of American production practices, claiming that a collaborative mode of production persisted until 1907–9, at which point the central-producer system took hold. Looking beyond the differences between these two accounts, one can discern a shared insistence on a trend toward increased centralization.

According to Musser, by 1909 manufacturers began devising methods to guarantee "accountability and efficiency through specialization, the regularization of production, and vertical organization" (1991b, 54). Rationalizing the production process could involve calculating predictable expenses, putting personnel on salary, establishing hierarchies within departments, and placing much of the control with a single figure, often the producer. Nonetheless, a company's individual circumstances determined how control was meted out: both Allan Dwan and Fred Balshofer have painted portraits of their early days shooting Independent productions in California, attributing near-total control to the director and indicating scarcely any division of labor.[17] Recollections such as these validate Musser's and Staiger's assertions that films shot in a locale far removed from the company's base of operations restricted a central producer's ability to oversee a director's decisions, thus promoting directorial autonomy, albeit by default.

Overall, the adoption of a centralized production system bespeaks a desire to regulate production and, by extension, the product. Regulation could translate into the upgrading of film quality through improvement of narrative clarity; at the same time, regulation represented a drive to guarantee a consistency of output, which often resulted in repetitiveness and imitation. The methods adopted during this period precluded neither instances of unrestricted directorial autonomy nor production of nearly incomprehensible films; nonetheless, companies did take measures to eliminate the chances of either occurring with any regularity.[18] Promoting continuous, efficient production became the primary goal and led to manufacturers implementing scenario scripts (and later, continuity scripts) and constructing studios along the lines of maximal organization (Staiger 1985b, 124–27, 142–53).

Changes in distribution were developed in concert with these modifications to production practices. One alteration of distribution policy in particular precipitated a substantial shift in approaches to constructing the fiction film. With the increase in demand for films, methods of formatting and pricing film required standardization in order to simplify delivery of prints. Around the end of 1908, manufacturers adopted a uniform length of approximately 1,000 feet for a single-reel subject; this definitely affected the manner in which films were made.[19] Stories had to be fashioned to fit a prescribed length, which entailed devising predictable procedures to shape narrative structure. As Staiger has argued, "Here is an instance in which economic practices (the one-reel limit) influenced film style" (1985b, 126). Moreover, the restrictions imposed by a uniform length encouraged industry-wide adherence to particular formulas of narrative construction and representational strategies. The adoption of such principles was not left to chance, even with the establishment of more rigorously controlled production practices. During this time, the industry stepped up efforts to secure self-improvement and enhance its image as a cultural institution, while the trade press helped to set standards for a formal system in development.

The Trade Press: A Forum for Feedback

The nickelodeon boom initially spurred the trade press's interest in cinema, and with industrial consolidation this interest escalated. Journals devoted to other forms of entertainment, such as *Variety* and *New York Dramatic Mirror,* expanded their coverage to include cinema by 1908, much as *Billboard* and the *New York Clipper* had done earlier. Even more significantly, following the debut of *Views and Film Index* (later *The Film Index*) in 1906, *Moving Picture World, Show World, Motion Picture News,* and *Nickelodeon* (later *Motography*) started up between 1907 and 1909, all focused primarily on film.[20] Finally, a steady stream of how-to manuals, many devoted to the crafts of acting and scenario writing, emerged in the years to follow, cementing cinema's claim to maturity as a medium.

Because it directed itself to members of the industry and not the public at large, the trade press shared the concerns of the film community to a greater degree than regular newspapers. Its intended audience also required diverse types of information; for that reason, most trade journals offered not only reviews and editorials but also technological advice on projectors and cameras, tips to theater owners and accompanists, profiles of actors and manufacturing executives, letters from readers, and instructions for prospective scenarists. One also finds pages devoted to advertisements and (highly complimentary) preview layouts of upcoming films. Collectively, these assorted articles, service items, and ads help indicate what the industry wanted to learn more about, what it valued, and what it may have believed about itself.

Cheerleader and critic, voice of conscience and apologist, the trade press functions neither as a detached commentator on the film industry nor as a print version of a publicist. Instead, the trade press attempts to advance the cause of the industry while also shaping and dictating that agenda. For that reason, the rhetoric of trade press writers occasionally may seem overtly prescriptive or condemnatory, while at other times it may strike the reader as uncritically supportive. Its often contradictory nature aside, the trade press still must be approached with some trepidation by the historian wishing to use it as a gauge of contemporaneous industry practice. In many instances, the trade press's reportage is the most comprehensive evidence we have concerning the industry's own beliefs or prevailing aesthetic norms. However, we must remember that trade press coverage *is* reportage, and thus subject to the editorial biases and sociocultural constraints of the time.[21]

Still, I believe the trade press played a signal role in aiding filmmakers to develop solutions to their problems. The function of the trade press extended beyond any demonstrated expertise in various areas of filmmaking practice; whether filmmakers actively listened to all trade press advice or responded to it in the same way seems beside the point.[22] The mere presence of the trade press provided an established avenue for film-makers to receive criticism regarding their strategies. If we understand trade press reaction in terms of feedback, it helps amplify our sense of how filmmakers continued to craft solutions to the problems posed by more complex narratives. The trade press could help identify problems and suggest possible solutions; filmmakers, in turn, would continue to devise their own approaches and wait to see how the press responded. This would entail some degree of mediated integration of trade press advice on the part of filmmakers. In certain cases, encouragement of a particular ap-proach might motivate other filmmakers to adopt the praised strategy; in others, harsh criticism might convince filmmakers that a device was un-desirable. Acclaim within the trade press could produce tangible benefits, because it would increase the status of the company within the industry and possibly influence exhibitors to screen its films. From this, I do not assume that filmmakers blindly followed the dictates of the press, nor that the trade press was a consistently reliable arbiter of preferred solutions. In fact, as Noël Burch has pointed out, journals like *Moving Picture World* were "the sites of struggle between the two systems of representation [and often offered] 'false solutions'" (1991b, 133). The lack of guaranteed con-sensus among trade press commentators amplified the potential for con-flicting advice. In what follows, I will highlight several of the often-contested guiding principles that the trade press relied upon in its attempts to shape industry practice.[23]

Aesthetic Norms: The Quality of Realism

> The real uplift of the motion picture . . . is the uplift of quality—
> photographic, producing, artistic, narrative quality. With all these at their
> best, there will be no need to talk about uplift: the goal will be reached.
> "The Usual Thing," *Moving Picture World* (8 October 1910)

The trade press had ample reason to promote increased quality of product within the industry, even as late as 1910. Ideally, improved standards would bolster the medium's popularity, which could only benefit the press (through increased ad revenues, for example); better films would draw "better classes," and if the large middle-class audience could be attracted to films without any loss of the client base that currently existed, cinema's status and profitability would be enhanced.[24] Advocating improved quality of product communicated exhibitor wishes to manufacturers, helping to align the trade press's editorial stance with the aims of its primary readership—theater owners and managers. Positioning itself as an arbiter of taste helped justify the trade press's existence and affirmed its value to the industry. Because negative reviews of films could anger the very clients who purchased advertising space, trade press critics would repeatedly rationalize their views, explaining how improved standards would better the industry as a whole.

In editorials and reviews, the trade press formulated an aesthetic, wherein it specified the attributes of a well-made film. Over time, the priority placed on various features changes, and inconsistencies occasionally emerge, but still one can discern how the press defines "quality" filmmaking. Moreover, many commentators supported their calls for improvement by invoking audience reactions (which typically confirmed the writer's complaints). An appeal to the audience possessed obvious tactical advantages: first, it proved that the trade press had developed a superior sense of what audience members wanted by listening directly to their comments; second, it lessened the gap between viewer and critic, the latter being no more than a voice for collective responses.[25] The critic might go so far as to identify himself as one of the crowd, thereby elevating the audience member to the position of critic: "I make no claims to be an authority—I am just one of the mass of people who pay my little nickel—and what I see and criticise, the other people are apt to see and criticise, also" (C. H. Claudy, "It 'Went Over,'" *Moving Picture World* 8, no. 5, 4 February 1911, 231). Nonetheless, using the audience as a means to justify criticisms often invited complications, as when evident audience support for despised genres and hackneyed plots caused the critic to distance himself from the "common" viewer and adopt a position of superiority.[26] In these instances, the critic would be forced to lecture both viewer and manufacturer, claiming that the inferior products of the latter degraded the taste of the former. The critic could frame his comments in terms of industry improvement and argue all the more vociferously for the benefits of enhanced standards.

Those standards derived from criteria shared by many of the critics, regardless of their journal affiliation:

> [in reference to Selig's *Chinese Slavery*] . . . we have no hesitation handing out our highest praise to this film on the three principal grounds we always

keep in view when writing of moving pictures. First of all, it is a grand piece of photography, it is a splendid dramatic production, magnificently staged, and . . . it tells a good story in a clear, intelligible, and interesting manner, and these are the things that make for notable films of the week. ("Notable Films of the Week," *Moving Picture World* 4, no. 19, 8 May 1909, 593)

A great film [involves] the story first; art in the interpretation of the story by good players, second; and the photography, third. (H. Kent Webster, "Little Stories of Great Films," *Nickelodeon* 1, no. 3, 1 January 1910, 13)[27]

Arguably, *Moving Picture World* was slightly more attentive to issues of photographic excellence, though the emphasis on that aspect gradually diminished, perhaps as a reflection of improvements in film stock, processing procedures, and the like. By 1911, reviewers were far more likely to mention a film's acting, suitability of subject matter, or seriousness of purpose; the phrase "truthfulness to life" became a preferred catch phrase. Even as the interest in a film's relative visual clarity abated, however, the medium's roots in photography continued to influence the trade press's aesthetic values.

Most writers shared an implicit belief that cinema's reliance on photography promoted an aesthetic predicated on both reproductive realism and believability. Commentators readily acknowledged that cinema's ability to replicate the world as it existed provided it with a visual advantage over comparable forms, particularly the theater. However, the cinema could not content itself with merely providing copies of nature, as it had done in those years before the demands of narrative had taken over. If cinema's photographic base imposed a realist mandate upon the medium, it encompassed whatever film represented as much as the means employed. The demand that film provide access to a believable fictional world became the dominant strain in most trade press criticism, especially from 1909 onward.

The medium's indebtedness to photography dictated this fidelity to realism on the visual level. The camera registered falsity and shoddy representation with immediacy, especially if the film's photography and processing had been expertly done. (Ironically, the more technically adept filmmakers became, the more they would be taken to task for deficiencies of "stagecraft.") Accordingly, commentators objected to closer shot scales in part because these shots revealed too much, including the evident application of makeup to actors' faces.[28] Rarely did commentators consciously link the issue of believability with cinema's photographic origins; nonetheless, the preference for location shooting and realistic sets evident in so many reviews demonstrates an affinity with the more explicitly articulated position of Edward R. Higgins: [29] "In scenic arrangement the average director is manifestly deficient. More or less he is groping blindly for his effects. Stagecraft, with its traditions, set pieces, painted scenery and stereotyped effects is the bane of the picture. The photoplay is a series of pictures—not a stage. The rules of composition and balance, arrangement of light and shade, etc. are essential to a perfect picture" ("Possibilities of the Film," *Moving Picture World* 9, no. 8, 2 September 1911, 611). One sees in this argument a dual conception of photography's role in filmmaking: it exposes artifice while remaining subject to its own rules of artistic enhancement.[30]

Sometimes, the attempt to apply criteria derived from photographic aesthetics to cinema reveals a failure to distinguish what differentiates the two. A notably misguided analysis of cinema as still photography occurs when columnist Lux Graphicus chooses photographs from three producer advertisements and criticizes them for their compositional flaws. In one of the more revealing sentences from his critique, he proclaims, "I am applying these criticisms just in the same manner as I have done for years to thousands of stationary photographs" ("On the Screen," *Moving Picture World* 8, no. 5, 30 July 1910, 241). The columnist treats these stills as though they were images from the film, forgetting that cinema always incorporates movement, so that the compositional "flaws" notable at one particular moment may be undetectable the next. He compounds the problem by leveling his criticism at production stills and thus at images which might never appear in the finished film. Striking a blow for visual literacy, *Moving Picture World* reacted to its critic's error by announcing only two weeks later that it was lodging a (rather improbable) "protest now and forever against the use of still photos as illustrations or advertisements of the motion picture. That is, unless it is taken with a special camera at the same time and from the same point of view as the motion picture was made. Specifically posed still pictures or moving picture scenes do not interest us. An enlargement from the film itself always does" (7, no. 7, 13 August 1910, 352). [31] Graphicus's attempt at compositional criticism indicates an understanding of the importance of *mise-en-scène* but an inability to conceptualize it in cinematic, as apart from purely photographic, terms.

The question of whether cinema's roots in photography resulted in any inherent artistic benefit sometimes produced diametrically opposed responses. In the mind of the trade press, photography was either a tool to be used properly or a base from which the filmmaker created art, ever mindful of the medium's demands:

> Photography, like printing and engraving, is but the handmaiden of the other arts. It should be considered in motography as merely the means for placing before the audience the thoughts of the author of the picture as embodied in changing scenes, the art of the picture being developed fully in the scenes themselves before the motion picture camera is called upon to record them. . . . Art in a motion picture must exist prior to the photographing of the picture. (David S. Hulfish, "Art in Moving Pictures," *Nickelodeon* 1, no. 5, May 1909, 139)

> It is open to any manufacturer to-day to devote such attention to the work that he could give his pictures their own pictorial individuality. One maker might go for delicate grays; one might go for razor-edge definition; that is, fine focusing and a well-stopped down lens; others again might diffuse the lens slightly. . . . There is, in fact, a wide field open for individuality of expression in the photographic end of moving picture making. Again we say we are leaving out of consideration the acting and scenario ends. We are dealing with the moving picture as a picture. ("The Qualitative Picture," *Moving Picture World* 6, no. 25, 25 June 1910, 1090)

Hulfish sees photography as but a means to an end, the art assumed to lie outside the realm of the recording medium, whereas the second writer understands aspects of photographic artistry as distinct from the material being recorded.[32] Photography, whether artistic or not, could not be divorced from issues of realism or of narrative intelligibility, as the statements above indicate.

Typically, when a photographic aspect threatened a reviewer's sense of realism, the critic would reestablish the terms of photography's proper employment emphatically. The debate over closer shot scale provides a telling example: objections to these "enlarged" views involved claims that the representation of the human form exceeded "life size," thereby violating cinema's claims to verisimilitude.

> Many beautiful scenes are marred by showing these enlarged figures, with the head touching the very upper part of the frame, and the feet missing. Some pathetic scenes, some love scenes, etc., would be far better without enlarged figures, as the surroundings, either in furniture or natural

> scenery, would give depth to the picture and add some charm, some
> closer resemblance to the natural. . . . The greatest success of motion
> pictures over the regular playhouse is that they show natural scenery,
> real water falls, trees, gardens, etc., instead of painted scenery. Yet
> with all these advantages to please the eye some manufacturers are
> willing to ruin the effects to show us what they call facial expression.
> ("The Size of the Picture," *Moving Picture World* 8, no. 10, 11 March
> 1911, 527)

In this case, the believability attached to constancy of screen size overrode the actual capacity of cinema to present enlarged views. In keeping
with its observance of the "natural," cinema was to avoid such excesses
at all costs.

Generally, writers in the trades equated "realism" with verisimilitude.
For some, the photographic heritage clearly prevails, and realism entails
providing images drawn from actuality, as when J. P. Chalmers states, "If
the picture does not tell a strong enough story to hold the interest undi-
vided, the public at least look for realism. Studio scenes of outdoor subjects, however well done, rarely impress. In other words the moving picture artist must go to the scenes of his plot and get the atmosphere and
realism" ("'Genre' Motion Pictures and an Example," *Moving Picture
World* 6, no. 18, 7 May 1910, 725). Others supplied a more nuanced sense
of the term, seeing realism as a necessary counterbalance to the conventions imposed by fiction:

> Don't for a moment think that this is a plea for excessive naturalism in
> the moving picture play. We all recognize that these things must be made
> more or less according to formula. . . . You can never get away from this
> formula in a moving picture plot; the public won't let you. They insist
> upon their plays being made according to formula. And liking formula
> they necessarily demand the observance of conventions. In other words,
> whilst the form of the moving picture play must take a certain shape or
> design, there must also be a certain plausibility or verisimilitude in the
> piece. It all comes to this: that the things that are set to happen on the
> moving picture screen are reasonably likely to happen in real life. (Lux
> Graphicus, "On the Screen," *Moving Picture World* 7, no. 24, 10
> December 1910, 1291)

Here, Graphicus understands that the audience requires both realism and
the formulas it offsets. In effect, the one demands the other.[33] If conven-

tions provide comfort, realism allows the audience to believe such stories could really happen. As George Rockhill Craw expressed it, "A drama is an illusion, and the more perfect the illusion, the better the drama" ("The Technique of the Picture Play—Structure," *Moving Picture World* 8, no. 4, 28 January 1911, 178).

Increasingly, the trade press would emphasize the value of preserving the necessary illusion underpinning successful fiction filmmaking, often tying it to the sustenance of emotionally involving drama. Audience belief and emotional investment became the twin hallmarks of a commendable film, and critics assessed films in terms of their ability to cultivate such responses from their viewers. C. H. Claudy put it in these terms: "The reason so many photoplays fail utterly in getting across is due to one thing—unnaturalness . . . we don't thank you, Mr. Producer, we motion picture audiences, for forcing down our throats, the knowledge that this is only a screen and a picture—we want to think it's the real thing" ("It 'Went Over,'" *Moving Picture World* 8, no. 5, 4 February 1911, 231–32). Accordingly, even excessive realism could be a violation of proper verisimilitude if it overwhelmed the qualities of drama it was meant to underwrite: "Realism, as an integral part growing directly and naturally out of the plot, is much to be commended. The silent stage has a great advantage in being able to tell a story with natural settings. Realism for the sake of realism and the subordination of the plot to some feat of realism, is to be rejected and can be safely left to outdoor vaudeville" ("Facts and Comments," *Moving Picture World* 9, no. 7, 26 August 1911, 520).

As attention to the purely photographic aspect of cinema diminished, concern for the story grew. However, the issues of realism that had informed discussion of photography persisted in the criticism of narratives, suggesting that the fundamental question remained one of believability; the oft-repeated phrase "truthfulness to life" demonstrates the centrality of verisimilitude to the trade press aesthetic. Trade press critics understood audience comprehension and involvement to go hand in hand, always predicated on a film's sustained cultivation of verisimilitude: "The story is dramatic because it is simple and easily understood. After all, the strongest and most affecting dramas are those that represent something which might happen. This picture is so much like life that it assumes an importance it would not otherwise possess" (*Moving Picture World* 7, no. 26, 24 December 1910, 1480). The increasing emphasis on the audience's emotional investment in believable stories led reviewers to implement criteria of developed characterization and adequate motivation in their reviews.[34] In turn, this shift in the trade press's aesthetic focused attention on the scenario to an unprecedented degree, with the belief that a properly crafted scenario was the key to an effective film.

Perfecting the Scenario: The Value of the Story

From 1910 onward, the trade journals began to devote themselves to the improvement of scenarios with the conviction of the converted. One finds a steady stream of articles devoted to criticizing flaws in story construction. Prospective scenarists were advised how to avoid these errors in articles bearing titles such as "The Rejected Manuscript"; and multipart series by writers like George Rockhill Craw and Epes Winthrop Sargent examined the principles of crafting a successful scenario in painstaking detail. What occasioned this marked increase in attention to scenario writing? Changes within the industry, particularly the acceptance of the standardized 1,000-foot length for most film narratives, in combination with the previously cited trend toward production efficiency, led manufacturers to create permanent positions within their organizations for scenario editors and staff writers.[35] Janet Staiger has estimated that "by at least 1911, firms had a story reading/writing department with a head, readers, and writers" (1985b, 146). Companies responded to the considerable demand for useable stories by relying on professional writers (drawn from the ranks of journalism, literature, and theater) and by soliciting scripts from novices.[36] Because most writers had virtually no experience crafting scenarios, there was a ready market for advice, which the trade press (and numerous how-to manuals shortly thereafter) rushed in to serve.

A 1911 entry on "Scenario Construction" provides a wealth of background on the topic, including an informal history of its development and information concerning the operations of the scenario department:

> To go back to the beginning of the moving picture scenario, we find that it
> has not been so very long ago that the directors wrote and staged all the
> scenarios, week in and week out. Then came the two-a-week releases
> which has much to do with the changing of the system, inasmuch as it
> overtaxed the directors' creative ability, and took from him time necessary
> to proper directing [*sic*]. This in turn, necessitated the advertising for
> moving picture plots, and employment of scenario editors to consider
> the reams of manuscripts that began to pour into the offices from
> unsuccessful playwrights and short story writers. . . . Out of these has
> evolved the modern scenario. . . . Slowly, but surely the amateur and the

novice are being weeded out of the scenario competition game through the medium of discarded manuscripts, their exeunt giving place to the modern newspaperman and magazine writer, who, when paid an honest price for his work, does not hesitate to submit it for moving picture production. More would enter the field if their names appeared on the films. The only companies to comply with their aspirations have been the Edison, and the Paris studio of the Pathe Freres [*sic*]. Of the better-known writers writing for moving pictures may be mentioned: Richard Harding Davis (a novelist and short story writer of international reputation), Rex Beach, John Luther Long, Carolyn Wells, Elbert Hubbard, Roy Norton, Opie Reid, Hal Reid, and a score of lesser-known literary lights. Does anyone for an instant imagine that these experienced novelists, playwrights, and short story writers of national and international reputation, write for the "10–20–30" prices paid by some of the film companies (Licensed included)? . . . The qualifications and abilities of scenario editors vary. . . . Many of them are men and women who have had many years of theatrical experience. Not a few are retired newspapermen. . . . Several of the larger Independent companies receive in excess of one thousand manuscripts monthly, while several Licensed companies receive double and treble that number. . . . Those [manuscripts] that possess possible merit are read and laid aside for further consideration, and eventually are considered by the director whose judgment is final. The scenarios that are accepted, according to the authority of the various editors, does [*sic*] not exceed one per cent! (R.V.S., *Moving Picture World* 8, no. 6, 11 February 1911, 294)

Aside from providing practical information on proper manuscript formatting and reminders of various limitations that necessarily shape scenario content (e.g., budgetary constraints, censorship restrictions, the generic specializations of various companies), many articles also complain about the poor remuneration for accepted scenarios. Demands for improved pay rates typically accompany such complaints, addressed directly to the manufacturers, whose Scrooge-like behavior is charged with preventing improvement in scenario quality. The argument for publicizing the authors of selected scenarios runs along the same lines: "In the field of the spoken drama, the author of a piece is fully recognized on posters, programs and in its advertising, no matter how little known or obscure he may be at the time his play is produced. It is this policy that has given to the spoken drama some of its most brilliant authors. It would do the same thing for the picture play" (George Rockhill Craw, "The Technique of the Picture Play," *Moving Picture World* 8, no. 3, 21 January 1911, 127). Craw's entreaty asserts a principle of authorship for the scriptwriter: the film's scenarist should be valued on a level commensurate with the theater's playwright.

In fact, critics routinely assigned sole authorial status to the script-writer.[37] Nonetheless, belief in the scenario's supremacy, promulgated by the scriptwriting columns, found itself challenged when writers in the trades began to consider whether the story or its telling determined a film's effectiveness. Sentiments such as one finds in a 1908 letter writer to *Moving Picture World*—"a perfectly thought out plot, well put together, should tell its own story" (2, no. 8, 22 February 1908, 143)—became more difficult to champion as acknowledgement of the director's role gained credence in reviews after 1910: "The greatness of a picture depends more upon the art of the producer than upon the author of the plot" (*Moving Picture World* 9, no. 6, 19 August 1911, 465). An oft-expressed corollary to this held that the director owed it to his or her material to provide the script with its ideal expression, to develop it "in a way which graphically interprets the thought of the author" (*Moving Picture World* 6, no. 1, 8 January 1910, 16).

Regardless of whether plot or production should be accorded primacy, advisers to prospective scenarists consistently promoted the necessity of sustaining believability. However, they also began preaching the virtues of organicism, wherein each part of the script contributes to the whole. Epes Winthrop Sargent, for example, advocated a strongly connected plot, wherein "the occurrence of some incident . . . gives rise to a series of intimately connected events which lead to some definite conclusion. . . . The story should move naturally and simply toward its climax, unhampered by the introduction of a lot of action, possibly interesting of itself, but which does not advance the story" ("Technique of the Photoplay," *Moving Picture World* 9, no. 4, 5 August 1911, 281–82). If executed expertly, a script obeying the proper rules of structure would efface the marks of same, thereby reinforcing the work's believability: "The play goes smoothly on without any markings of the structural divisions upon which we have built it. The very adherence to structural rules hides the evidence of the author's craftsmanship, and the illusion is perfected in accordance with the proper use of them" (George Rockhill Craw, "The Technique of the Picture Play—Structure," *Moving Picture World* 8, no. 4, 28 January 1911, 178). In terms of a developing aesthetic, authorities like Craw definitely were steering scenarists toward central features of classicism: organicism, verisimilitude, and self-effacement.[38]

The structural needs of the film script received attention as early as 1909, when reviewers began to comment upon climaxes within film plots;

not long after, scenario experts schooled their readers on how to engineer climaxes properly, moving from introduction through climax to denouement.[39] Arguing that audiences "like to see the plot move consistently with a swing toward its climax," Thomas Bedding accounted for the appeal of such a properly calibrated "dramatic moment" in terms of its effect upon viewers: "Moving picture audiences, like other audiences, are influenced very much by the mood of the moment. A moving picture audience may be likened to a delicate musical instrument upon which the executant, in the shape of the moving picture, plays with greater or less effect. If the executant is an accomplished musician, then the effect obtained is bound to be satisfying, esthetically and emotionally" ("The 'Dramatic Moment,'" *Moving Picture World* 6, no. 10, 12 March 1910, 372).

Believability, strong characterization, proper structure—for a scenario to engage its audience fully, it could not lack any of these attributes. Yet, as many commentators readily acknowledged, demands upon the film included the struggle for intelligibility as well. Cinema's supporters could claim, as Bedding does at the conclusion of "The 'Dramatic Moment," that "the moving picture play . . . is just like any other stage play, or, indeed, a novel," but Bedding knew that the moving picture play lacked the resources of language upon which the other two forms relied. As often as appeals might be made to the other arts, particularly theater, for bases of comparison, filmmakers had to confront cinema's singular lack—the absence of speech. Measuring film's aesthetic norms against those evident in the theater became a preferred way of defining the medium.

"The Silent Stage": Contrasting Film and Theater

> The proper work of the photoplay is to give life as life really is, at its chosen, dramatic moments, and I believe that we shall find that all the well-known theatrical makeshifts, so effective on the stage, will be less effective in a photoplay than the simplicity of every-day life is. Photoplay producers will find that they will have to discover new and original tricks of their own.
>
> HANFORD C. JUDSON, "What Gets Over," *Moving Picture World*
> (15 April 1911)

When casting about for aesthetic role models, trade press commentators often relied upon comparisons with the more established arts, either to elevate cinema's status through the association with a respected art form or simply to affirm that cinema observed similar rules. In either case, such comparisons operated as a form of "uplift," placing cinema on a cultural continuum with those forms already granted social approval. Moving beyond these comparisons—which were more rhetorical than substantive—commentators began to grapple with the question of what rendered cinema unique. What debt did it owe to the other arts? How did it differ? These questions acquired particular pertinence when trade press writers related cinema to theater, the art form preferred for comparison purposes. The two forms shared obvious similarities, such as use of performers to enact stories and reliance on comparable narrative structures. Film companies had forced the issue of affinity by actively attracting personnel from the theater as a means of improving cinema's aesthetic standards. Forced to live in the shadow of theater, film (through its representatives in the trade press) developed a predictably ambivalent attitude toward its chief rival and influence.

Trade press commentators allowed that cinema's silence (more so than, say, its abbreviated length) most distinguished it from the stage. The limitations that this muteness imposed on film's storytelling capacities became evident in the crucial period of 1907–8, the very years when the industry adopted a wide array of approaches to offset cinema's inability to tell stories in the absence of sound.[40] At least initially, the industry gravitated toward aids to intelligibility that relied upon exhibitor involvement, such as lectures and "talking pictures" (placing actors behind the screen to provide helpful dialogue).[41] However, the size of the market and the difficulties of ensuring consistent and economical means of facilitating comprehension at the exhibition level dictated that solutions originate from the producers themselves.[42] As of 1909, cinema was engaged in a struggle to promote intelligibility by relying chiefly on the resources of the filmic text itself; but at this stage, the image of cinema as an adjunct to the theater had already been established, as Charles Musser has explained: "The rise of talking pictures . . . coincided with an initial influx of theatre-trained directors like J. Searle Dawley, D. W. Griffith and Sidney Olcott. It occurred as cinema was taking over legitimate theatres for exhibitions and as a theatrical newspaper like the *Dramatic Mirror* began to review films. In 1907–09 these elements defined cinema as a kind of theatre—superior to the traditional stage in some respects (diversity of locale) though deficient in others (sound, colour and three-dimensional space)" (1983, 8). Cinema's legacy as a "kind of theatre" weighs heavily in most trade press comparisons between drama and film, where the latter's status as a "silent art" often entailed recasting an apparent limitation as a virtue.

Commentators argued, with seeming conviction, that film's inability to speak could operate as a more powerful form of communication than the speeches of theater. Clayton Hamilton would claim that "in abolishing dialogue the moving-picture show relieved the cheap drama of its weakest element: it could suggest character with less obvious falsification than the actual popular drama; and it could easily excel it in the projection of incidents, both on the score of variety and on the score of vividness" ("The Art of the Moving Picture Play," *Bookman,* January 1911; repr. in *Nickelodeon* 5, no. 2, 14 January 1911, 52). In a preview of Vitagraph's *A Discarded Favorite* (released as *Jealousy*), Louis Reeves Harrison argued that the film's silent depiction of the protagonist's torment is a superior rendering, preferable to what the stage could offer:

> The whole play is a silent communication of the spirit, and, according to Maurice Maeterlinck, speech never communicates the real and inmost thoughts. If "we do not know each other we have not yet dared to be silent together." According to this great poet the pictorial drama must be destined to take high place in the arts, as he believes that we talk to fill up the blanks of thinking and never to reveal our true selves. The discarded favorite, being alone, has the courage to let the truth be told in her countenance and movements. The audience gazes into the mystery of a human soul. ("Superior Plays," *Moving Picture World* 9, no. 5, 12 August 1911, 361)

Harrison's argument transforms cinema's imposed silence into a purity of expression, neither wanting nor needing words.

When Harrison asserts film's superiority as an expressive medium, his arguments rest heavily on the actor's capacities, evidenced again when he describes cinema's suitability in portraying suspense: "A moral crisis can be depicted on the screen when theatrical attempts to show physical danger can only cause . . . amusement. . . . This form of drama lends itself more than any other to development on the screen because mere figures of speech can never delineate either high emotion or that of suppressed nature as well as can facial and gestural expression" ("Plots," *Moving Picture World* 8, no. 26, 1 July 1911, 1494).[43] Critics like Archer McMackin would enlist cinema's silence as a measure of the screen actor's skill: "The perfect motion picture play is harder to evolve than the drama of words. When one realizes that the story must be told entirely by the 'business' or actions of the actors, that not a word can be spoken to help convey the story . . . one readily sees the task is not an easy one" (*Nickelodeon* 2, no. 6, December 1909, 171).[44] As trade writers realized that actors might be forced to carry much of the responsibility for film's intelligibility, attention to the role of performance increased from 1908 onward; as Harrison conceded, "In carrying the thought from the screen to the audience, the actor is the essential medium of transmission" ("Eyes and Lips," *Moving Picture World* 8, no. 7, 18 February 1911, 348). Ideally, screen performers would become guides to narrative comprehension while maintaining the desideratum of believability. Accordingly, Epes Winthrop Sargent advised the actor to "convey his emphasis by making prominent the vital actions. This should be done not by violent ranting, but by pointing up the action; by dwelling upon it, until the spectator assimilates the point" ("The Technique of the Photoplay," *Moving Picture World* 9, no. 7, 26 August 1911, 525).

When arguing that "the power of good pictures to convey the phases of emotion by the facial expression of the actor is greater than that of the actual stage," Rollin Summers goes on to point out that cinema enjoys this advantage because of its capacity to shoot at "close range" whenever "shades of emotions are to be expressed" ("The Moving Picture Drama and the Acted Drama," *Moving Picture World* 3, no. 12, 19 September 1908, 213). Unlike most commentators, Summers speaks to film's formal uniqueness when comparing cinema to theater, as does Clayton Hamilton, marveling in *Bookman* that "the new art of the moving-picture play is the only one of all the many arts of narrative which makes it possible for the observer to follow with the actual eye the passage of a character through a mile or more of space. . . . This fact offers to the artist who devises a scenario for the kinematograph many possibilities of narrative which lie far beyond the range of the writer for the restricted stage of the ordinary drama" (repr. in *Nickelodeon* 5, no. 2, 14 January 1911, 51). Such observations remain in the minority, and for the most part, the trade press rarely demonstrated sufficient formal ingenuity to advise filmmakers on how to deploy style to solve narrational problems. I raise this issue not to chide the press for lacking prescience in these matters; rather my observation confirms that the trades typically embraced a conservative aesthetic, adhering to tenets of verisimilitude and emphasizing reliance on actors and well-crafted scenarios. Ironically, their aesthetic derived more from the prevailing norms of bourgeois theater than these commentators might have been willing to admit. As much as the trade press helped to establish a variety of principles for an emerging industry and art form, the contours of its proposed aesthetic were still rigidly circumscribed by the writers' own limitations.[45]

What, then, is the nature of the trade press's influence on the formal development of American cinema during this period? Primarily, I think that the trade press functioned as an arbiter of taste, emphasizing certain tenets of classicism that would be absorbed over time. Moreover, the trade press did provide expertise in particular realms (such as narrative construction) that helped to establish certain norms. Finally, writers and critics within industry journals helped map out some of the possible options for filmmakers at this time and conveyed a mediated version of public response to developing formal tendencies. If the critical positions of the trade press vary in reliability and consistency, that stance parallels the development of the industry and production practices at this time. In each case, attempts were made to improve a system, but only with intermittent and partial success. The MPPC did not achieve full control of the market, production methods were not sufficiently standardized to ensure the efficiency and quality control desired, and the trade press sent out conflicting messages regarding how filmmakers might achieve narrative legibility through medium-specific means.

Nevertheless, the effort expended did translate into a radically different industrial and aesthetic environment for filmmakers by 1913. Market demands pushed for changes in film form at the same time as the industrial context promoted it. However, an increasingly oligopolistic industrial structure could not ensure such formal changes alone, any more than a more standardized set of production procedures could. And to whatever degree the trade press critics exerted influence—with expanded reviews and increasingly detailed aesthetic prescriptions—they could not provide filmmakers with solutions to all of their problems. In fact, they might even have added to these problems by prodding filmmakers to consider issues beyond those of viewer comprehension, such as verisimilitude, photographic composition, and emotional effectiveness. In other words, as much as forces within the industry provided the means to identify and address problems, they could also complicate the filmmakers' situation by introducing conflicting demands or compromising constraints. Thus, while the trade press identified narrative legibility as an issue of concern, it could also advocate maintaining camera distances that kept actors' expressions from registering. Similarly, by streamlining production practices, a studio could speed delivery of improved scenarios; however, if this increased efficiency translated into a more rapid rate of production, rushed directors would find their efforts to develop novel storytelling methods impeded. Hanford C. Judson's prediction, cited earlier, that "photoplay producers will find that they have to discover new and original tricks of their own," aptly describes the predicament facing filmmakers during the transitional period. But the linked demands of narrative legibility, spatiotemporal articulation, and verisimilitude, among others, forced directors to engage in a problem-solving process more complex and protracted than Judson's description implies. Having defined the industrial forces shaping that process, I will now turn to the problems that filmmakers encountered and the solutions they devised.

3

"A Story Vital and Unified in Its Action": The Demands of Narrative

MARKET-BASED DEMAND for films of increased length and narrative complexity created interlocking problems for filmmakers of the transitional period. Scenario writers had to determine what types of stories and narrative structures best suited the one-reel running time. Once directors had these scenarios in hand, they needed to devise appropriate storytelling methods. Increased narrative complexity further challenged filmmakers to develop methods to ensure viewer comprehension. The crafting of coherent and legible narratives introduced problems of characterization, motivation, and causality that had not concerned filmmakers in earlier years.

In fact, narrative scarcely figured at the point of cinema's origins. The protocinematic realms of photography, motion toys, and projection rarely incorporated a storytelling function and as such did not bestow a legacy of narrativity upon the new medium. Dominant figures in cinema's initial development, such as Edison and the Lumières, demonstrated little regard for cinema's narrative potential.[1] Scholars typically refer to the first few years of cinema's existence as the technological or novelty phase, highlighting cinema's early status as a visual phenomenon.[2] Producers capitalized on the camera's ability to record diverse views; accordingly, the first films were either records of vaudeville acts or some type of *actualité* (documents of newsworthy occurrences, everyday events, or visually distinctive locales, the latter occasionally rendered as a "panorama" view with the camera mounted on a moving vehicle).[3] One can trace the origins of these representational options back to cinema's predecessors: visually defined replications of the outside world derive from photography, the sensation of movement from motion toys, and non-narrativized entertainment, such as displays of prowess or exoticism, from vaudeville. In other words, the defining features of film's precursors, none of them narratively oriented, shaped cinema's formal tendencies in the medium's earliest years.

45

Length imposed another obvious limitation. Given the extremely brief duration of the first films' running times, originally dictated by technological constraints, filmmakers found it difficult to engage in narrative representation.[4] However, even as film length increased, the realization of cinema's narrative potential resided more with exhibitors; they could craft a series of single-shot views into an evening's entertainment, held together by music, a lecturer, and stereopticon slides. With the advent of the multi-shot film, responsibility for investing cinema with a narrative dimension shifted back to the producer, and the success of "story films" demonstrated narrative's commercial possibilities.[5] From 1900 onward, films cease to be merely fictional and unnarrativized (as in the recordings of vaudeville scenes); instead, filmmakers attempt storytelling in the forms of fairy-tale films (also known as *féeries*), films of humorous episodes, and, eventually, chase films.[6]

As Tom Gunning has argued, one can define the earliest "genres" in relation to cinema's developing mastery of "filmic space and time" through editing, apart from the distinct types of subject matter involved (1984, 105). The structural simplicity of the humorous episode and the *féerie*, then, recommended them as early versions of multishot narratives. Filmmakers gravitated toward the chase format in 1904, and the appeal of the genre resided in how well the medium's formal capabilities fit with the chase's easily reproduced narrative formula (i.e., an agent of disruption being chased and eventually caught and, perhaps, punished). One finds in the chase film an early version of film narrative that fuses a compelling narrative situation with its ideal (cinematic) articulation: conflict is conveyed through action spread over a variety of locales, linked by editing. This logic of narrative progression would assume considerable influence within filmmaking circles, as evidenced by Eustace Hale Ball's advice to aspiring scenarists a decade later: "The keynote of all dramatic construction (a truth which cannot be too strongly emphasized) is STRUGGLE. Remember this whether you are writing comedy, drama, tragedy or romance" (1913, 45).

Building on Tzvetan Todorov's suggestion that narrative patterns emerging out of conflict conform to set patterns, Edward Branigan has sketched out how "narrative in its most basic form is a causal 'transformation' of a situation through five stages: (1) a state of equilibrium at the outset; (2) a disruption of the equilibrium by some action; (3) a recognition that there has been some disruption; (4) an attempt to repair the disruption; (5) a reinstatement of the original equilibrium" (1992, 4). Insofar as these requirements do not exist in an arbitrary relationship, we can define narrative as much by the principles underwriting the *arrangements* of its elements as by those elements in and of themselves. Causality propels narratives based in conflict, wherein an asserted first cause produces a subsequent effect that will, in turn, exist as the motive for subsequent reactions, and so on. Stated another way, one can understand Branigan's five stages as producing the following causal chain: (2) causes effect (3), which in turn becomes the cause for effect (4), which similarly leads to the final result of (5). This binding force of causality also patterns the elements' arrangement, such that they can only appear in the order they do. Moreover, the elements possess a particular relationship to one another: (5) mirrors (1) in the same way that (4) inverts (2). So, one might say that a narrative of this nature involves a patterned relationship of transformation and restitution, predicated on causality holding elements together in a temporally specified fashion.[7] As a response to the demands of causality-based narrative, the chase film provided pretransitional filmmakers an opportunity to develop storytelling skills.[8]

Enter Running: Chasing after Narrative

Chase films enjoyed a fairly extensive vogue, lasting at least until 1908. Undoubtedly the most popular of early story films, the chase was also the most influential model of narrative construction. By singling out the chase film, I am not denying the importance of other notable story films produced around the same time, particularly some of Porter's films for Edison or Méliès's initial successes. But Méliès stages elaborate scenes operating as blocks of action independent from those which follow; in so doing, Méliès focuses more attention on narrative within a shot-as-scene and not on the process of sustaining narrative across shots, as did the chase film.[9] Whatever influence Méliès exerted on subsequent narrative developments would manifest itself more obviously within certain tendencies in European early cinema. As for Porter, one can make a case for films like *Life of an American Fireman* and, even more evidently, *The Great Train Robbery* as early examples of the chase film, before its constituent elements became distilled.[10]

Why privilege the chase film when charting the development of early film narrative? Unlike earlier films featuring extended motion, the chase film provides an instance of specified action. This action typically finds motivation, however weak, in the desires and/or needs of the person at the center of the chase. In this way, the intertwining of character and narrative begins: a reason for the pursuit of the protagonist must be supplied, else there can be no chase. Providing such an excuse involves the construction of a persuasive pre-chase scenario that develops—no matter how perfunctorily—the protagonist's culpability. Initially, these character-based rationales scarcely extended beyond the reliance on types (e.g., mischievous boys, philandering husbands, maladroit unfortunates). However, as the chase genre persisted, filmmakers elaborated on the chase's motivation and developed the characters at the center of the pursuit in order to sustain interest in the main action.

At the same time, the articulation of the chase was also undergoing a transformation. The earliest chase films simply feature the protagonist running through a designated space, followed quickly thereafter by a rampaging group of angry pursuers. Biograph's *Personal* and Edison's *Maniac Chase*, both from 1904, exemplify this tendency. However, soon a principle of aggregation began to inform the logic of the chase, wherein an increasingly larger body of pursuers chases the protagonist in each successive shot. One can note this development as early as Biograph's *The Lost Child* in 1904, but it becomes more prevalent in later years, as exemplified by *Jack the Kisser* (Edison 1907) and *The Curtain Pole* (Biograph 1908). The principle of aggregation lends a sense of narrative necessity to the introduction of each new shot/space. The protagonist enters a new locale because he is being chased. His presence, in turn, causes some calamity to befall a character already present in that new locale. That character now has a reason to want to chase the protagonist as well, and he joins in the chase, which will spill over into another locale with the next shot. Little differentiates the reasons for the participants' involvement in the chase, but narrative action does dictate the shot order, thereby distinguishing chases subject to the logic of aggregation from their predecessors. In this way, the chase film extends causality's role in narrative construction.[11]

This admittedly underdeveloped causal logic stands as one of the chase film's central contributions to the early development of narrative principles in cinema.[12] Progressing from a randomly connected series of frantic actions across disparate locales to a logically advancing trajectory through causally connected spaces, the chase film offered up a model of how to shape a story in such a way that individual shots added up to more than the sum of their parts. But the single-reel format's running time of approximately eighteen minutes would push filmmakers to consider ways of formulating the central components of narrative (desire-driven characters engaged in a causally connected set of actions) other than those established within the chase film.

The Dominance of Drama
and the Problem of Comprehension

As helpful as aggregation had proven in developing the narrative potential of the chase format, it possessed limited applicability as a structuring principle within dramas, which became the dominant type of film produced by the American companies as of 1908. To understand the problems faced by producers of dramatic films circa 1907, I will analyze a characteristic example, Edison's *The Trainer's Daughter*. This film, subtitled *A Race for Love,* is loosely derived from Theodore Kremer's 1904 play *A Race for Life,* wherein the victory of a race horse ensures the "wealth, health, and happiness" of a young couple.[13] As Charles Musser has indicated, the Edison version would make little sense to a viewer unfamiliar with the basic outline of the Kremer play, unless exhibitors employed extradiegetic means during projection to facilitate comprehension of the narrative (1991a, 407). This speaks to the pronounced difficulties that filmmakers confronted at this point in cinema's history: the demands of the marketplace encouraged increased output, dictating standardized production methods; at the same time, external pressures for moral uplift and the hope of luring an audience comprised of more affluent, middle-class spectators pushed for more emphasis on dramatic material.[14] But replicating the methods of the stage— for example, by mounting extended tableaux of gesticulation by actors shot from a considerable distance—could only result in audience incomprehension. In the case of *The Trainer's Daughter,* the narrative's relative complexity outstrips the representational system employed to mount it. *The Trainer's Daughter* features what Edward Branigan has termed the "double causal structure" (1992, 30), which the classical cinema later would perfect. It appears in a fairly undeveloped form in this 1907 film, though its advantages are apparent even here: the couple's romance and the intrigue surrounding the horse race depicted in the film's central section intertwine so as to become interdependent. Accordingly, the doubling of causal mechanisms reinforces the motivation of the central character. In *The Trainer's Daughter,* the double causal structure ensures that the outcome of the horse race will also determine who becomes the husband of the eponymous female character.

Narrative stage:	Equilibrium	Disruption	Recognition	Repair	Reinstatement
First causal strand	romance (shot 1)	romance (shot 1)	romance (shot 2) leads to bet	romance and race/bet (shots 15–18)	with race's completion, romance allowed its resumption in shot 20
Second causal strand	race/bet (shot 2)	race/bet (shots 7–8)	race/bet (shot 11)		

Figure 3.1. Narrative outline of *The Trainer's Daughter* (1907).

In brief, the plot is as follows: Jack and the trainer's daughter are in love (established in shot one), but the trainer does not approve. A rival suitor for her hand (also the owner of a stable) enters into a wager with Jack concerning the outcome of a race in which they both have horses competing. The trainer's daughter agrees to marry the man whose horse wins the race (shot two). Once the stable owner determines that his horse cannot beat Jack's (shots three through five), he bribes a stable boy to dope Jack's horse, a plan Jack's jockey overhears (shot six). When the jockey attempts to intercede, the stable owner and stable boy overcome him (shot seven) and remove him from the stable (shot eight). Even though the jockey subsequently escapes (shot ten), he is not in any condition to ride, so the trainer's daughter offers to takes his place (shot eleven). Despite intense competition from the stable owner's horse, the trainer's daughter perseveres, and emerges the victor (shots fifteen through eighteen). She and Jack have won the race and each other (shot twenty).

The plot warrants attention both as an exemplar of Todorov's formula for narrative construction and as a revealing instance of an early film drama whose structural components overwhelm its representational strategies (though in an intriguingly inconsistent fashion). Let us examine these in turn. First, figure 3.1 indicates how the plot of *The Trainer's Daughter* corresponds to Todorov's general outline.

This analysis indicates that the dovetailing of the two causal lines derives from two moments of "correspondence." The first occurs in shot two, when recognition of the romance's disruption leads to establishment of the bet, which will in turn supply the motivation for the bulk of the film's narrative action. The second is the outcome of the race itself, which resolves the two narrative strands simultaneously. Interestingly, the "object" of the wager, the trainer's daughter, becomes the agent of the wager's completion when she replaces the jockey; in occupying the literal position of the jockey, the daughter replicates the doubling process that the narrative structure itself enacts.

As stated earlier, filmmakers would increasingly rely upon the double causal structure exemplified by *The Trainer's Daughter* with the advent of the classical era. However, in 1907, the availability of the structure did not ensure narrative legibility. At various points in the film, often in those shots whose duration is the longest, clear communication of narrative information breaks down. A case in point is shot two, which establishes the wager: one must glean from this shot that both Jack and the stable owner have a horse competing in the same race. Employing a single shot, with characters filmed from a considerable distance, the filmmaker fails to convey the involved nature of the information. However, to indicate the superiority of Jack's horse, the filmmaker relies on a different approach, using a three-shot unit comprised of shots three to five. This involves two framing shots of the owner looking through binoculars, separated by a masked point-of-view shot of Jack's jockey riding his horse. Unlike the depiction of the waging of the bet, this articulation of the action presents it as a character's view and ties together viewer and character knowledge. Moreover, this strategy also manages to introduce (and rather effortlessly, at that) the jockey, a character of value for the second strand of the doubled narrative action.

We can draw two points from this: first, narrative information of a more obviously visual nature lends itself to more effective communication than does verbal or aural information. A seeming exception, which only confirms this hypothesis, is shot twelve, one of the film's briefest, which shows a bugle being sounded. The immediately understandable nature of this coded sound allows it to function on the level of action, as a visual sign. Filmmakers had to find ways to render the verbal in visual terms, and they would devote much of the following five years to establishing such methods. Rollin Summers's advice from a 1908 article entitled "The Moving Picture Drama and the Acted Drama" indicates as much: "All necessary facts in a moving picture play must be visibly presented" (*Moving Picture World* 3, no. 12, 19 September 1908, 212).

Second, narrative elements defined by their qualities of action found a more suitable home in cinema than those defined by intellect or emotion. Hence, one finds the figure of the jockey (and later, his structural substitute, the trainer's daughter) deployed whenever the dispersal of action across multiple shots articulates the narrative. The first instance (shot four) involves the previously discussed point-of-view shot of Jack's horse, while the last is the race itself, depicted over a number of relatively brief shots at film's end. The other occurs in the middle of the film, after the owner has spirited the jockey away, hiding him in a shed (this action conveyed by one of the film's two pans). After an intervening shot where the trainer's daughter meets up with the owner (shot nine, representing the possible resumption of the romance narrative), there is a cut to the jockey escaping from the shed. The actual interruption of the action initiated in the previous shot (belonging to the romance) by this one (belonging to the bet/race) mirrors the function of the jockey's presence in the film's larger narrative pattern: by escaping and then implicating the owner, the jockey will convince the trainer's daughter that she needs to act as his substitute in order to ensure the wager is decided in her favor. In other words, his insertion into the romance facilitates the merging of the two lines of action, and the only moment in the film which implies simultaneity (i.e., as the owner and the daughter converse, the jockey escapes) signals that point of convergence.

The Trainer's Daughter's reliance on extended long shots (such as shots two, five, and six, which collectively constitute over one-third of the film's running time) renders much of its crucial narrative action incomprehensible. Even so, its moments of increased narrative legibility point to the strategies that filmmakers will avail themselves of in the near future. In films a few years hence, filmmakers will adopt the narrative structure from examples such as this one, but they will devise methods to convey significant information with more consistent success.[15]

Narrative Dilemmas: Shaping a Story

As the examination of the trade press discourse in chapter 2 has indicated, concern over proper narrative structure as well as improving the quality of narratives remained paramount throughout the transitional period. The adoption of the standardized 1,000-foot-reel length coincided with producers' thoroughgoing commitment to construct filmic narratives that audiences could comprehend regardless of the extratextual supports exhibitors might provide. This placed the onus on filmmakers to furnish stories that would prove compelling to audiences without confusing them. Operating with a fairly limited supply of narrational tools, filmmakers often decided to keep their narratives simple to avoid undue complications in their telling. However, given the rapid rate of production at this time, one could hardly expect manufacturers to provide an endless array of suitable source material. Moreover, external forces limited their options. Reform groups, the clergy, and municipal politicians exerted pressure to regulate film content, while the trade press exhorted producers to deliver more respectable films. Accordingly, producers borrowed from preexisting sources with regularity, and they also copied story ideas from their own previously successful films.

Nonetheless, some stories fit the prescribed length better than others did. Though novels and plays were frequent sources for single-reelers, these forms were rarely felicitous choices given the expansiveness of the originals. More appropriate were vaudeville playlets and short stories, forms also limited by length. Eventually, the number of original scenarios would increase as production companies hired writers to devise workable narratives. Concurrent with this development (fully evident by about 1910), experts on scenario construction began filling the pages of the trade press with advice on how to write the successful single-reel scenario.

Within these articles, one can discern a preference for a story structure that involves the establishment of a state of affairs, followed by its development, complication, and resolution. Ideally, unity would bind together the stages of the narrative's progression.

Repeated adherence to similar narrative formulas probably reinforced the tendency toward unity promoted by the preferred story structure. Advice such as that proffered by John Nelson in his 1913 scenario writing guide, *The Photo-play*, recognized unity and structure as mutually supportive: "Each scene [i.e., shot] should be associated with its purpose, which is to say that the outline of a play should comprehend: First, 'cause' or beginning; secondly, development; third, crisis; fourth, climax or effect; fifth, denouement or sequence" (quoted in Thompson 1985b, 175). As early as 1909, David S. Hulfish was stressing unity and simplicity, while prescribing a virtually identical narrative model:

> In literature, the drama, and in pictorial art, the masterpieces consist mostly of simple stories simply told. Singleness of purpose, simplicity in plan, skill in execution; these make a masterpiece in any art. The art of making motion pictures is no exception, cannot be an exception, to the principles which underlie all arts. The artist who manifests his art in the making of motion pictures must select a simple story. . . . It should reveal the features of introduction of characters, development of plot, culmination, climax and resolution of plot. (*Nickelodeon* 1, no. 5, May 1909, 37)

The notion of simplicity extolled by Hulfish typically translated into directives concerning a narrative's temporal duration and number of plot lines. Notions of unity underwrote this advice as well, which frequently pointed to the short story and vaudeville drama as exemplary instances of narrative economy. Archer McMackin explicitly invokes limitations imposed by the single-reel length when discussing "How Moving Pictures Are Written" in 1909: "We are told by our masters in short story writing and in drama writing that we must have one theme and one theme only. . . . The period of action in a motion picture play is not restricted although it is best to follow the arrangement as depicted in the vaudeville drama. A single episode or incident which might occur within the length of time it takes to run the film is better than dragging the tale through twenty or thirty years" (*Nickelodeon* 2, no. 6, December 1909, 171). The scenarist of the one-reeler, then, capitalized on the fit between the format's limitations and the economy of the single-plot narrative. As a result, the canonical narrative described by Nelson and Hulfish flourished. A *Moving Picture World* review of Selig's 1910 *The Ranch King's Daughter* identifies the main features of the canonical plot and underscores its typicality: "Here is a love story, with jealousy as the influence which causes the disappointed lover to seize the girl and carry her away to an Indian stockade, a thrilling rescue with a running fight and finally safe arrival home" (6, no. 5, 5 February 1910, 169).

The canonical plot dominated single-reel scenarios, primarily because it offered the twin virtues of economy and unity. However, other options were available, including the double-plot variant exemplified by *The Trainer's Daughter*.[16] Given trade press allegations of padding once the 1,000-foot reel became the standard,[17] one could argue that a doubled line of narrative (or extended characterization) would help to stretch the film to the requisite length. But not all films proved equally adept at developing narrative action to incorporate the double plot. The problems encountered by *The Renegade* (Kalem 1908) demonstrate that unity was a principle more easily desired than acquired. Employing a military backdrop, the film attempts to tie together the loss of love with professional disgrace: the protagonist, Jack, faces court-martial for striking the rival for his sweetheart's affection. He achieves reinstatement by rescuing a major's young daughter, but she is not introduced until two-thirds of the way through the film, and her endangerment remains unrelated to any other narrative incident presented in the film's first half. Not having provided a way to ensure the interconnectedness of Jack's reinstatement and the regaining of his love, the film's script must rely on *deus ex machina* to restore him as a hero.

Had the scenario writer observed the desideratum of unity, she or he would have placed Jack's fiancée in harm's way, fusing the functions of love interest and means of reinstatement. Similarly, at an early stage in the scenario, the writer would have linked the agent of her undoing to the triangle depicted in the opening shot. Finally, relevant traits of Jack's character might have been established to tie together his striking the rival suitor and performing a heroic rescue. Instead, Jack virtually disappears from the film while the actions precipitating the rescue are set up. *The Renegade*'s failure to develop pertinent aspects of Jack's character at the outset demonstrates how inadequate motivation can produce structural deficiencies.

Narrative Strategies: Building a Character

The narrative awkwardness of films like *The Renegade* pointed to the need for a more focused and concise approach to characterization. In particular, scriptwriters had to establish characters' goals as soon as possible to build in causal logic. For that reason, quickly setting forward preconditions for the central narrative incident became a pertinent feature of single-reel narrative structure. Filmmakers had to supply salient motivational material rapidly and efficiently, or else the structure of the film would become unbalanced. Sometimes the rush to provide such material causes these narratives to begin *in medias res,* since so little time is allowed for establishing the setting or introducing characters. The single-reel narrative often launches the central arc of action as close to the outset as possible, permitting a resolution by the film's conclusion without undue abruptness. In other words, the film's relatively constricted running time means that the middle of the film corresponds to its narrative center, with the introduction and conclusion worked in to accommodate what occurs between.[18]

Similarly, the devising of a protagonist's goals can lead directly to the central narrative action at a film's core. In *Back to Nature* (Vitagraph 1910) a chauffeur finds his romantic overtures constantly rebuffed by his employer's daughter, but he has a chance to prove his worth when the family is shipwrecked during a cruise to Australia; in *Path of Duty* (Lubin 1910) a young customs officer wants to marry a fisherman's daughter, but forces himself to perform his duty when he sees a note indicating smuggling activity which he (mistakenly) attributes to her father; in *Not Guilty* (Thanhouser 1910) a devoted son, wrongfully imprisoned, successfully escapes in order to be reunited with his mother when her health fails—communicating these situations at the outset permits the ensuing action to take place immediately thereafter.[19] Whatever opposition the protagonist's desires might meet is virtually contained within the description of his predicament (or springs "naturally" from his occupation, as in *Path of Duty*). Thus, the script need not provide further impediment to the achievement of the protagonist's goals, as the film's running time won't allow protracted disruption of the narrative's drive toward completion. An extension of the dilemma that derives from the narrative's original set-up might occur (as in *Not Guilty*, when the son must attempt to elude the police once he has reached his mother's home), but new predicaments rarely surface midway through the narrative for fear of needlessly complicating the planned trajectory.[20] Note how the wager concocted in *The Trainer's Daughter* arises out of the professional involvements of the main characters and how the jockey's being incapacitated, though a relatively late narrative development, is easily solved.

Narratives of this type also avoid introducing new characters after establishing the story's situation in the initial moments; similarly, they seldom provide new information about the characters (or develop unrevealed traits) past that point.[21] As Eustace Hale Ball advises, "the first scene is the key-note of the photoplay . . . and should be in the midst of activity, introducing as many of the leading characters as possible" (1913, 51). For this reason, most one-reelers possess a highly developed aura of inevitability, since the outcomes of the narratives often seem preordained.

In fact, with narrative structure and characterization so clearly circumscribed, most one-reel dramatic narratives rarely deviate from the Todorovian model of an initial problem posed, experienced and struggled against, and eventually overcome.[22] Though this formula rapidly became the norm, a recurrent variation involved the introduction of a destabilizing narrative event after a sizeable temporal gap, exemplified by Selig's *A Tale of the Sea* (1910). In this film, the protagonist, jealous of his friend's marriage, goes away for five years. When he returns, his friend has become a father, which leads to a reconciliation. The friendship is put to a test when a fishing accident leaves the two alone in a lifeboat with only enough drinking water for one. The once-jealous man now sacrifices himself so that his friend has a chance to return to his family. Here we have a pattern of equilibrium and disruption, followed by restitution

Figure 3.2. The valued object in *An Alpine Echo* (1909) . . .

Figure 3.3. . . . cues character recognition.

after a gap, only to have disruption occur again immediately thereafter.[23] But note how narrative events (and the engine of causality) emerge directly out of established character traits of the protagonists, simple yet particularized.

Developing characterization not only provided adequate motivation for story events but also contributed further to a narrative's unity. As Ben Brewster (1991a) has noted, one of the favored ways of ensuring unity in the single reeler involved employing an object of shared interest to connect characters and draw together plotlines.[24] In *An Alpine Echo* (Vitagraph 1909), the object of reunification must work to override gaps of both space and time once the two protagonists are separated. The plot develops as the male of the couple, Antoine, falls in love with a visiting tourist and goes off to America in pursuit of her. Years later, Antoine and his abandoned sweetheart, Marie, are inadvertently reunited when she brings a music box from their youth to the antique shop where he works (figs. 3.2 and 3.3). In some ways, the valued object in films like *An Alpine Echo* shares a function with the recurring item in the linked vignette, a comic form particularly popular from 1905–7 (see, for example, *The Stolen Pig* [Vitagraph 1907]). Whereas in its earliest variation, the recurring object merely functioned as an excuse to link shots via the object's trajectory through disparate spaces, in its later modification it became a causal skeleton for the actual narrative. Hence, in Vitagraph's *The Forgotten Watch* (1909), the titular object serves as the motivation for all the comic complications that ensue. Unlike comical films, which merely posit the object's importance, dramatic films connect object to character by making it part of the protagonists' shared history or identifying it as a personality-defining prop.

Beyond that, the valued object can serve a further narrative purpose as well, often signaling a moment of character recognition. Hence, the music box in *An Alpine Echo* works as both a symbolic representation of something less tangible (Marie and Antoine's idyllic life together in Europe) and also as the mechanism for physically bringing Marie into Antoine's shop, as she means to sell it as an antique (reinforcing its ties to the past). D. W. Griffith, in particular, would often wrest such objects away from their obvious function as narrative expedients and embellish them so that they became a tool of characterization first and foremost. In this way, the valued object could also serve as a performance-enhancing prop, an aspect of use I will discuss in chapter 5.

One can discern the valued object's centrality to many narratives in the later phase of this period by acknowledging the increasing number of times that objects form the basis of films' titles: *Romance of the Umbrella* (Vitagraph 1909), *White Roses* (Biograph 1910), *Daisies* (Vitagraph 1910), *The Gambler's Charm* (Lubin 1910), *The Bandit's Mask* (Selig 1910), *The Crippled Teddy Bear* (IMP 1910), *The Black-Bordered Letter* (Edison 1911), *The Totem Mark* (Selig 1911), *The Lost Freight Car* (Kalem 1911), *The Rosary* (Essanay 1911), *The Forged Dispatch* (IMP 1911), and so on, through the period. As much as the valued object promoted unity, it also revealed character traits or past affiliations unknown to one or the other of the protagonists. In this way, the object becomes the site of character (and hence viewer) knowledge and serves as a powerful tool of narration as well as narrative structure. It is to the issue of how narration functions during this period that I will now turn.

Shifting Narrational Norms

In their attempts to render character-centered stories comprehensible, filmmakers learned that specifying character desires increased narrative legibility and provided dramatic impetus. Eustace Hale Ball reminded aspiring scenarists "that 'want,' whether it be wanting the love of a woman, of a man, of power, of money or of food, is the steam of the dramatic engine. The fight to satisfy this 'want' is the movement of the engine through the play" (1913, 50). Character actions required motivation, and for that reason, how to provide causally significant information became an ongoing concern. Put another way, filmmakers had to devise ways to let audiences know what characters knew. No longer could cinematic narration presuppose and maintain a stable level of audience knowledge. Now, viewer ignorance would have to be redressed (or preserved) at pivotal moments as narration provided (or suppressed) new story information.

One model of filmic narration has proposed that story information within films is meted out in ways determined by the range and depth of that information, as well as the degree of communicativeness and self-consciousness the narration demonstrates. A film's narration can choose to disseminate information in such a way that the knowledge displayed closely adheres to that possessed by only one of the characters, or it can operate in a seemingly omniscient fashion. Similarly, the narration can choose to explore character subjectivity in some depth, allowing access to both the perceptual and mental subjectivity of the protagonists depicted. Communicativeness involves the narration's demonstrated willingness to share the information it possesses. A film's narration may possess omniscience and reveal all relevant information readily, or it may suppress vital aspects of story information at crucial junctures. Finally, a film's narration may display itself quite openly, revealing story information in a particularly ostentatious fashion (one thinks here of Hitchcock's celebrated, insistent forward-tracking shots), or it may choose to do so in a manner that does not call attention to the process at work.[25]

As narration is a process, it will constantly reestablish itself according to the outlined parameters. In other words, narration may offer an instance of perceptual subjectivity that we can define as restricted, uncommunicative, and self-conscious at one moment; it may then shift a few moments later to a relatively objective mode that strikes us as comparably unrestricted, communicative, and substantially less self-conscious. Even though fluctuation can occur both within and across the properties defining narration as a process, a somewhat predictable set of choices within the options available helps to define a particular mode of cinematic practice.

As narrational norms are historically determined, the way films within a defined time period typically negotiate narration in terms of range and depth of knowledge, communicativeness, and self-consciousness has significant bearing on how one defines an individual film's narrational strategies. As Kristin Thompson has proposed, early cinema prior to 1908 rarely manipulated story information so as to regulate audience knowledge. Insofar as story information comes presented "in a block," as Thompson has labeled the method, the viewer is left pretty much cue-less: "the narration would stage a shot's action with almost no further guidance to help him or her sort out the phases of the action" (1987, 246). The principle of restriction scarcely applies: the range of story information provided supersedes that possessed by the characters and fluctuates very little.

Similarly, because of the limited access to character psychology available at this stage, depth of knowledge remains a non-issue, despite the ongoing interest in presenting various types of "points of view" in a wide range of optical films, peephole scenarios, and dream films of the 1900–1905 period. Tellingly, a simple fascination with looking holds sway in such films and rarely a concern for the narrativizing potential of the view. At most, as in dream films, the return to consciousness simply reinforces the disparity between the dream world and the waking one, the point emphasized by a shot transition that often serves as the punch line to what constitutes a three-shot joke. This stands in stark contrast to films of the transitional period, where a delineated dream state provides access to a character's thought processes, helping to propel the enveloping narrative.[26] Narration in the pre-transitional period rarely functioned to block or suppress story information deliberately, but, because of a relative poverty of means, narration often emerged as inadvertently uncommunicative.[27] Finally, given the limited attempts at obtrusive handling of devices such as titles prior to 1908, we can label early cinema's narrational stance unselfconscious.

In summarizing the gap between primitive and classical narration, Kristin Thompson has indicated that the former rarely promotes ease of viewer comprehension: "Primitive narration on the whole lacks the redundancy and the break-down of the action into a linear chain of causes and effect that make the classical narrative so easy to follow. . . . These principles of redundancy and clarity guided the formulation of a classical approach to narration" (1997, 414). At the outset of the transitional period, the demands of dramatic narrative, combined with a need for enhanced clarity, set the stage for a changed approach to narration without indicating preferred strategies. Faced with the prospect of retooling cinema's narrational capacities, filmmakers experimented before eventually favoring particular devices—intertitles, inserts, and narrativized views, among others. In what follows, I will call upon the categories of range and depth of knowledge, communicativeness, and self-consciousness to chart this refashioning of narrational norms.

Titles and Inserts as Narrational Aids

Titles (both expository and dialogue) and inserts (close-up shots of portions of texts, photographs, or other simple carriers of narrative information) provided the easiest and most relied upon methods to convey story information during the transitional period.[28] Previously, filmmakers might have been able to depend on lecturers to explain story information that confused the viewer, but industry standardization meant solutions had to emerge from the filmic text. Titles could expedite the communication of an involved narrative point (such as explaining a character's motivation or signaling an important plot turn), but at the same time, they interrupted the flow of images. Inserts, while not as versatile, seemingly emerged from the diegesis of the film and, in the case of letters and newspaper reports, conveyed story information by delivering text as image. Embraced by filmmakers who viewed them as an easy way to communicate a wide range of complicated story information, titles and inserts were labeled a narrational crutch by a trade press committed to more inventive solutions. Everett McNeil's "Outline of How to Write a Photoplay" is representative in its cautionary stance: "Use sub-titles [*sic*] or leaders sparingly—only when necessary to the proper understanding of the play. Make the action in the pictures tell the story as nearly as possible. Never use a note or letter, unless the action absolutely demands it" (*Moving Picture World* 9, no. 1, 15 July 1911, 27). Whether in response to advice such as McNeil's or not, filmmakers continued to modify how they deployed titles and inserts. This speaks not only to changing narrational norms but also to the shift in values attached to these devices (involving such issues as overtness of narration, degree of verisimilitude, ease of comprehension, etc.). However, from 1909 onward in particular, titles and inserts functioned as an integral but compromised solution for addressing problems of narrative legibility (table 3.1).

Expositional Titles

Titles came into use in cinema as early as 1903. Typically, these early titles summarized the narrative action to follow: the subsequent shot served as an illustration of the description preceding it. The function of titles begins to shift around 1907–8, though the evidence remains tenuous, not only because of the unrepresentative sampling of extant films made in these years but also because so many prints exist without their titles intact.[29] Nonetheless, based on the limited number of films available from 1907, titles start to serve diverse narrational purposes at this time. Examples range from markedly episodic films like *Trial Marriages* (Biograph 1907), which designates each separate (and separable) example of the series of

Table 3.1. Intertitle use, 1907–1913

YEAR	TOTAL NUMBER OF FILMS	TOTAL NUMBER OF EXPOSITIONAL TITLES	TOTAL NUMBER OF DIALOGUE TITLES	TOTAL NUMBER OF INTERTITLES	AVERAGE NUMBER OF TITLES PER FILM
1907	40	62	1	62	1.55
1908	48	63	1	64	1.33
1909	52	202	12	214	4.11
1910	92	399	79	454	4.93
1911	92	619	107	723	7.85
1912	121	775	136	909	7.51
1913	51	339	144	482	9.45

Note: I have included in the sample for this table only those films whose intertitles appear to be original. In some films one finds individual intertitles which incorporate both expositional and dialogue functions; for that reason, the combined total of the two columns tallying instances of the distinct types of intertitles may exceed the figure for total number of intertitles in a given year.

marriages depicted with a pithy title, to more elaborate narratives that even include temporally specific titles (e.g., *The Mill Girl* [Vitagraph 1907], whose only title reads, "Next Day—discharged"). If a film relies consistently on titles, suspension of titles may signal a change in the articulation of narrative action, as in Biograph's *The Hypnotist's Revenge* (1907), which follows a one-title-per-shot pattern before erupting into a chase at shot six, and then abandons further titles until the chase is terminated at the end of shot eleven.

The employment of expositional titles becomes more uniform by 1908,[30] but comparing two films from that year indicates how disparate the function of titles could still be: *The Renegade* (Kalem) introduces each shot but its first and last with a separate title, whereas Biograph's *The Guerilla* employs only five across forty-nine shots. Though neither film offers titles of substantial length, those of *The Renegade* are composed in considerably less developed prose, which typically telegraphs information in the summarizing style of the previous years ("Jack a renegade. Marauding Indians." or "The Major's child. A desperate situation.").[31] In its more sparing use of titles, *The Guerilla* points to later practice, with titles primarily used to indicate pertinent narrative actions.[32]

By 1909, trade papers began warning against the possible damage to narrative continuity inflicted by over-reliance on titles: "Too many notes and subtitles interrupt the story and detract from interest. The story which requires the least number of explanatory subtitles or notes is always more compelling in interest" (*Nickelodeon* 2, no. 6, December 1909, 171). At the same time, commentators conceded that titles could create narrative economy, as in this assessment of Biograph's *Cricket on the Hearth:* "Some of the scenes might have been shortened or eliminated to make room for subtitles that would have made the story clearer" (*New York Dramatic Mirror* 61, no. 1589, 15 June 1909, 15).[33] Trade reaction to titles indicates most critics viewed them as a necessary evil, superior to incomprehensible gesticulation, but still a jarringly overt form of narration that threatened to disturb the careful creation of verisimilitude a film was meant to sustain.[34]

Ambivalence concerning title use suggests critics promoting narrative legibility believed at the same time that storytelling should emerge effortlessly from within the diegesis. The trade press grappled with the same problems confronting filmmakers, and criticized inadequate solutions to reinforce aesthetic standards. If critics grudgingly accepted titles, they did so in the face of films' continued narrational deficiencies, demonstrated in this instance by Nestor's *Elda of the Mountains:* "This photoplay is so meagerly explained in the sub-titles that the plot escapes comprehension and the pictures become a sort of guessing contest as to what the action means. . . . Terse, sententious sub-titles, such as 'The Other Girl,' 'The Other Man,' 'Disowned,' etc. are all very well if the play explains itself, but this play does not" (*Nickelodeon* 5, no. 5, 4 February 1911, 138).[35]

Despite the variety of warnings issued by the trade press and screenwriting manuals, reliance on titles persisted throughout the transitional period. If anything, their narrational capacity expanded from 1909 onward to incorporate moralism, as demonstrated by the title "As Ye Sow," in Lubin's *The Two Cousins* (1909). The potential role of titles to provide commentary, reveal characters' emotions or describe their traits, or, most pertinently, establish hierarchies of knowledge, arose in tandem with their increased length but developed unevenly. A title from Biograph's *To Save Her Soul* (1909) offers insight into character motivation while also establishing that the viewer knows more than the heroine: "Crazed by jealous love, he would kill her that her soul may remain pure." The same company's *The Gibson Goddess* (1909) lets us in on the eponymous character's joke on her fickle band of admirers via the title "A New Way to Get Rid of the Troublesome Pests." We learn that she has fabricated a physical imperfection to dissuade the men, which also allows us to appreciate the irony of a subsequent title: when one man perseveres despite the revelation of the false infirmity, our laughter at "None but the Brave Deserves the Fair" consolidates our sense of superior

Figure 3.4. Florid expository intertitle from *Victims of Fate* (1910).

knowledge (which exceeds that of the unwanted suitors). Not all omniscient titles invited laughter intentionally: a narrational voice could succumb to the temptations of purple prose, such as one finds in the final title from Vitagraph's *Victims of Fate* (1910): "Father, mother, sister and sweetheart, all sacrificed through murderous lust of blood and passion" (fig. 3.4).

The occasional tendency to editorialize via titles notwithstanding, most filmmakers avoided using them to engage in narrational commentary. This reluctance renders even more striking the direct address adopted by the title card from Edison's 1911 *A Stage Romance,* which asks the question, "Will the maid notice the real bullets?" Here, the title draws our attention to our superior knowledge while also promoting suspense from said knowledge. Exploitation of the obvious comic potential of titles (evident in humorous films in later silent periods) rarely occurs, save for idiomatic dialogue titles (such as one finds in Nestor's *Mutt and Jeff* series of 1911).[36] Perhaps the persistent cautionary tone of the trade press convinced filmmakers not to exploit the overt narrational capacity of titles. This might also explain the desirability of dialogue titles, which by depicting characters' actual speech naturalized their narrational role to a greater degree.

Dialogue Titles

Some of the earliest inventive titling variants involve dialogue. A number of films from 1906–7 play with the potential uses of dialogue as text in particularly self-conscious ways: word balloons communicate dialogue in two 1906 Biograph films, *Nurse Wanted* and *Si Jones Looking for John Smith;* a string of words moves across the screen from one talking party to another as a means of depicting a telephone conversation in Edison's *College Chums* (1907). The sheer novelty of dialogue titling itself at this point probably explains the adoption of such innovative approaches, defined by visual gimmickry.

After this brief phase of experimentation, dialogue titles settled into their role as highly communicative narrational devices incorporating a broad range of knowledge. They appear with some regularity in 1909. Six of the nineteen Lubin 1909 films I have seen feature them, as do two of the four Edison films from the same year. While dialogue titles become more plentiful from 1909 onward, little consistency informs their placement or formulation. If filmmakers demonstrated a preference for placing dialogue titles in advance of the shot featuring actors mouthing the equivalent dialogue, rather than in the middle of the shot or after it, they probably did so to prevent disruption of continuity.[37] Such anticipatory placement also might have cued musical accompanists, indicating what they could expect from the subsequent shots.[38] Once cue sheets began to be distributed to exhibitors, the need for this practice would diminish.[39] Whatever the reason, cutting dialogue titles into the action at the point when the characters speak gains credence by the end of the transitional period.

Around 1910, some filmmakers began experimenting with the form of dialogue titles again, though less self-consciously than in 1906–7. On the limited evidence available, it appears this variant, the joint title, which marries a summarizing function with dialogue, briefly enjoyed popularity as a novelty form of title. Both *An Italian Sherlock Holmes* (Yankee 1910) and *A Touching Mystery* (Atlas 1910) rely almost exclusively on such hybrid titles throughout. (Examples include: "The loss discovered / 'My necklace is gone, but don't tell the guests'"; "The attempted hold-up / 'The charm has some good qualities after all.'") Beyond their novelty value, these joint titles could mitigate the overt nature of expositional titles by combining them with lines of dialogue; they also present information more economically, eliminating the need for two separate titles. Eventually, title writers would find ways of incorporating expositional material into characters' dialogue, thus naturalizing the process further. (The first example, wherein the loss of the necklace is expressed through dialogue, renders the opening exposition redundant.) However, dialogue titles did not become a popular means of expanding characterization until the final year of the transitional period when their rate of use increases significantly; before that date, this task had been taken up by inserts, if at all.

Inserts

As a narrational device, inserts occupy an unsettled middle ground between the potentially overt intertitle and the fully diegetic actions of actors. Robert Grau's description of them as "disillusionizing" (see endnote 34) indicates that some critics of the day saw them as no less obtrusive

Figure 3.5. Fully narrativized insert in *The Army Surgeon* (1912).

than titles. Filmmakers found ways to contextualize inserts more fully, possibly in order to address such criticisms; for example, they framed inserts with actors' thumbs, or photographed them within the décor employed for the film's dramatic action rather than against a blank background. No such conventions govern the early use of inserts. In Selig's *The Cattle Rustlers* (1908), when the filmmaker wishes to provide information from a poster detailing the terms of a reward, he simply cuts in to show a character from the preceding shot looking at the poster, which is now fully legible. The presentational logic of an earlier mode of narration prevails in this instance, with an on-screen reader showing the viewer what to notice. The insert's proximity to the cut-in becomes more pronounced in a few films from later in the period, when inserts are shot to emulate an established point of view, or framed over the shoulder of the sender/receiver, as in *The Army Surgeon* (Kay-Bee 1912). The unique nature of the message's medium in this example (the stretched-out top of a drum) might have militated against the comparably unindividuated form a letter insert could assume. Even so, the attempt to integrate the insert more fully into the visual flow of the narrative looks forward to the principles of classical narration as surely as the example from *The Cattle Rustlers* points back to the primitive era (fig. 3.5).

Dependence on inserts, dialogue titles, and summary titles using expanded text increases by 1909, indicating a consolidated effort by filmmakers to explore different narrational options.[40] Even by 1908, one can find inserts in various productions from industry leaders Biograph and Vitagraph. One film in particular, Vitagraph's *Nellie, the Beautiful Housemaid*, though it only exists in fragments, relies on three different letters to forward its narrative action. Lubin uses inserts in fully half of the nearly twenty films I viewed from 1909, and every one of the eight production companies represented in my sampling has at least one film employing an insert. Occasionally, multiple inserts occur within a single film, indicating the device soon became something of a narrational crutch.[41] (For further confirmation, look to the December 1909 date of the *Nickelodeon* piece warning against undue reliance on inserts, quoted on pp. 62–63.)

At the same time, filmmakers expanded the range of inserts used, moving beyond the preferred letters and notes to incorporate newspapers, telegrams, business cards, social announcements, and legal documents as well. Once inserts became a dependable narrational device, filmmakers also experimented with their form: *Three Thanksgivings* (Edison 1909) actually mobilizes an insert, as it shows a hand coming

Figure 3.6. Restricted narration via an insert in *The Preacher and the Gossips* (1912).

into the frame to sign a bill of sale, while a receipt for $120,000 passes in front; Essanay's *A Ranchman's Rival* (1909) uses a photo as an insert; and in Lubin's *The Unexpected Guest* (1909), the narrative hinges on someone tampering with a letter insert, an act that we are aware of from the time it occurs, placing us in a position of greater knowledge than either the letter's original sender or recipient.

Conversely, narration can withhold knowledge via an insert, as in a later Lubin film, *The Preacher and the Gossips* (1912), where the plot turns on a letter, only a portion of which the viewer can read initially. In that section available for the viewer to read, the letter seemingly implicates its writer, the preacher, in a scandal, but the full version reveals him to be innocent. The diegetic reader of both versions of the letter, the preacher's landlady, possesses knowledge the viewer does not: though we are made privy to the contents of a folded version of the letter at the same time she is (via a shot of the letter which angles it for her), we must wait to learn of the contents of the full letter until she opens it for others to read (fig. 3.6). As filmmakers began shaping the viewer's response to the narrative, they modified the degree of communicativeness exhibited by transitional-era narrative devices, titles and inserts alike. For that reason, inserts are particularly prevalent in genres that deliberately restrict knowledge, such as the mystery/detective film. A *Nickelodeon* review of an early detective film, *The Livingston Case* (Edison), suggests as much: "Part of the film consists of reading matter which the detective is supposed to write in his note book. It is very important that this be clearly shown, as a great many of these notes carry the plot of the play. . . ." (2, no. 3, 15 February 1910, 95). Edison's *The Black-Bordered Letter* (1911) relies on inserts of all types in such a varied and insistent manner that it virtually exhausts the insert as a device; one particular example, a message gradually revealed as the ink bleeds through, models the way inserts could manipulate the flow of story information to both characters and viewers.

Exploiting the insert's narrational potential also provided filmmakers with a convenient way to develop characterization. Because identified characters within the diegesis often write the text of letter inserts, these letters can help identify the characters' salient traits. Accordingly, such letter inserts may be written in a distinct script and employ a well defined "voice," as in this example from Edison's 1909 western, *The House of Cards:* "Little One. I am dead gone on you - Never wrote a love letter in my life - but take my word for it - this is one. You just say the word and I will marry you in a week. My life ain't worth much, but it's yours - sure, Rattlesnake Jim, Sheriff of Cedar Gulch." Beyond establishing a character's motivations, a detailed letter insert like this could allow the writer's own thoughts and expressiveness to emerge through words and verify his or her suitability as a confidante, mate, or messenger.

Certain films even thematize the reading of character out of letter inserts. In Essanay's *The Corporation and the Ranch Girl* (1911), the owner of a corporation needs to convince a female ranch owner, Ann, to sell her land to him. He sends his son Gerald to seduce her and thereby ensure the successful completion of the deal. Even though Gerald really does fall in love with Ann, she becomes disillusioned when she reads a note from his father, which reveals the plan. Gerald must convince her that love and not money is his sole motivation; he does so inadvertently when Ann reads a letter he means to send to his father, which states his true feelings. The letters in this film, more than Gerald's actions, act as signifiers of truth, and are finally converted from a medium of commerce to one of love.

Selig's *Pals of the Range* (1910) renders the notion of letter writing as a test of character explicit by building an entire narrative around it. In it, two suitors, both conveniently named Jack, write a joint letter to Clara, asking her to choose which she will marry. When she selects Jack number one (via letter of course), Jack number two, who manages to receive his letter first, switches his negative response for the other Jack's acceptance letter from Clara. Jack number one decides to go off prospecting when he believes he has been rejected, but he writes a gallant letter conceding his loss to Jack number two before leaving. This letter unintentionally reveals Jack number two's treachery while also vindicating Clara's choice of Jack number one as her husband. In a narrative that arises out of the contrast of two disparate character types (putting the noble and trusting Jack number one at the mercy of the duplicitous Jack number two), *Pals of the Range* must depend to an inordinate degree on letters as plot devices, signaled most baldly by having an incriminating letter stick out of Jack number two's pocket at one point.

Letter inserts established character motivations and psychology effectively, not the least because of their concrete visual nature. They allowed other characters (and the viewer) to "read the thoughts" of their authors. But as Epes Winthrop Sargent suggested in 1911 when writing about titles and inserts, even more compelling ways existed to visualize character motivations: "When the erring wife confronts her wronged husband and he is seen to take her back, the vision of a dead child will explain his reasons" (*Moving Picture World* 9, no. 5, 12 August 1911, 363). Filmmakers would opt for visions, dreams, and flashbacks constantly throughout the period as a means of expanding their arsenal of devices for exploring character psychology.

Showing Thoughts: Visions as a Window on Psychology

It is only in handling the element of character that the new art is at a disadvantage in competing with the novel and the drama. The many expedients that the dramatist and the novelist may use for delineating character are reduced, in the moving picture play, to one. What people are may be suggested only by what they do: by their deeds, and only by their deeds, we know them.

CLAYTON HAMILTON, *Bookman*

As Hamilton suggests, devotion to a principle of action defined transitional cinema, which created problems for allowing viewers access to a character's thoughts and feelings. Without such access, the viewer was bound to find films emotionally uninvolving. As Louis Reeves Harrison asserted in 1911 (in an article entitled "Characterization"), "The right incident and situation to bring out character and build up a play that will reach out to the people is [too] rarely provided" (*Moving Picture World* 7, no. 17, 29 April 1911, 937).[42]

Filmmakers could always rely on actors to telegraph the appropriate emotions, but notions of acceptable performance styles and proper camera distances remained in flux during this period, which militated against placing too much responsibility on the performers' emotive capacities. Besides, even the most skilled actor might have trouble showing that his or her character was beset by the guilt of a past wrong without the aid of additional narrational cues. A 1909 review of Edison's *The Coward* accurately summed up the dilemma for filmmakers attempting to convey psychological states: "It is certain that many near the writer did not understand this picture and wondered what it all meant. The delineation of the mental processes of a man who becomes a coward when contemplating an approaching duel requires exceptional ability and a thorough knowledge of artistic possibilities. . . ." (*Moving Picture World* 5, no. 8, 21 August 1909, 254).

In order to ensure adequate viewer access to character psychology, filmmakers had to find ways to render the mental concrete. This could mean presenting characters' dreams, fears, or thoughts as actual images or investing the valued object (mentioned on pp. 57–58) with sufficient meaning that it could operate as an objective correlative for a prior state. Reviewing Biograph's *A Wreath of Orange Blossoms,* a *Nickelodeon* critic alludes to the prevalence of this latter practice before adroitly articulating its functional advantages:

> A type of drama that is much favored by the film makers. Somebody is on the verge of yielding to temptation when they catch sight of some object associated with better moments of their past life, which reacts morally on their wavering mental state and prompts them to resist the present temptation. It provides a good dramatic expedient, particularly adaptable to the requirements of the motion picture in that the moral reaction is rendered visual through the agency of the material object. (*Nickelodeon* 5, no. 6, 11 February 1911, 170)

Some films went so far as to combine the valued object with the vision, thus compounding the effect, and supposedly ensuring the viewer would understand the increased depth of subjective knowledge. In these films the object functions as a trigger, motivating the character's vision, while also reinforcing the object's own emotional centrality.

One such example occurs in *A Baby's Shoe,* an Edison film from 1912, wherein a recently unemployed chauffeur, about to steal from his former boss, finds his baby's shoe in his pocket (while placing a stolen item inside), which convinces him to curtail his plans. The shoe does not operate in isolation, however. Even before the would-be thief discovers the shoe, a vision of his wife and child has appeared in the room. Only when he touches the shoe in his pocket and places it on a table does the vision

become apparent to him. Appearing
as a superimposition frame right,
the vision actually interacts with
the chauffeur, which intensifies its
emotional force and fully justifies
his decision to abort the planned
theft (fig. 3.7).

Kristin Thompson has suggested
filmmakers explored character psychology via visions and dreams only
"occasional[ly]" during this period,

Figure 3.7. The combination of valued
object and vision in *A Baby's Shoe* (1912).

probably because the "compressed structure of the one-or-two-reeler
was . . . an inhibiting factor in the use of subjective effects" (1985b, 179).
However, I would say the incidence of such devices is fairly high, particularly because the short length allowed filmmakers to structure entire
films as dreams. Those films tend to be comedies, whereas an isolated
dream (typically depicted in a single shot) most often occurs in a dramatic
context, much as a vision would, and possesses the same narrative function. While films relying on a dream structure usually do so as a means of
playing a joke on the dreamer (and providing one for the audience), films
with an overarching flashback structure operate as a serious variant, treating the memories of the recalling figure as sacrosanct.[43] Dream films also
refer to the central narrative mechanism explicitly in their title, unless the
dream is meant to be a surprise to the audience as well, as in *The Princess
in the Vase* (Biograph 1908) and *A Touching Mystery* (Atlas 1910). In both
the examples cited, the dream provides a rationale for the fantastic events
that occur but does not function as some form of wish fulfillment, a far
more common occurrence if the dream is signaled explicitly from the outset. Some typical dream films from the period include: *Terrible Ted*
(Biograph 1907), *The Dream Pill* (Lubin 1910), *The Politician's Dream*
(Vitagraph 1911), *The Dream* (IMP 1911), *A Western Dream* (American
1911), *Bobby's Dream* (Edison 1912), and *The Tankville Constable* (IMP
1912).

In the pre-1907 period, both dreams and visions operated primarily as
gimmicks; later, as narratives relied on expanded characterization, the vision vignette in particular became fully integrated into the film's narrational system, explaining a character's state of mind and subsequent (i.e.,
consequent) actions.[44] One cannot deny that an early transitional film such
as Edison's *Fireside Reminiscences* (1908) exists primarily to stage a series

Figure 3.8. A vision supplies motivation   Figure 3.9. A vision supplies motivation
in *Not Guilty* (1910).   in *Leaves in the Storm* (1912).

of recalled moments (and a final, temporally coexistent vision) as a pageant of pictorially distinctive "attractions" (enacted within the fireplace of the title as superimposed vignettes). Nonetheless, the final vision (in conjunction with the previous memories) serves equally to motivate the protagonist's change of heart at the film's conclusion, providing a reconciliation and narrative closure.[45]

In the following years, visions would become more plentiful, particularly by 1912, when approximately 10 percent of the films from the sample contain visions or dreams. They occur in films other than purely "psychological" dramas at this point, including westerns (*Kid Canfield, Notorious Gambler* [Champion 1912]; *Broncho Billy's Love Affair* [Essanay 1912]) and even comedies (*Buck's Romance* [Selig 1912]). Their growing popularity may relate to the increased emphasis on psychology in films by 1912, as other ways to develop characterization (including more nuanced acting, cutting in to closer shots, and reliance on point-of-view structures) gained acceptance as well. Still, the vision retained special status, as its appearance often marked the turning point in the plot, signaling a change in a character's thinking (e.g., *Not Guilty* [Thanhouser 1910], where the protagonist's vision of his ailing mother motivates his decision to escape from jail [fig. 3.8]; *His Mother's Hymn* [Solax 1911], where an errant son returns to his righteous ways after seeing a vision of his devoted mother; *Leaves in the Storm* [Rex 1912], where an unfaithful wife's vision of her recently deceased daughter prompts her to leave her lover [fig. 3.9]; and *The Girl in the Arm-Chair* [Solax 1912], where a son who has robbed his father's safe has a dream reinforcing his guilt, which precipitates his confession).

By 1912, filmmakers' exploration of the capacity of visions to intensify depth of knowledge could result in complex representations of subjectivity. *'Twixt Love and Ambition* (Lubin 1912) uses two visions to tell the story of a

Figure 3.10. A shot of the remembering party in *'Twixt Love and Ambition* (1912) . . .

Figure 3.11. . . . followed by a shot of his vision.

couple, John and Marie, whose relationship suffers because of her opera career. The first vision is a standard rendering of John's desire for Marie after they have parted, executed as a two-shot series. Its first shot depicts John at frame left, looking at "mementoes of lost love" by the fire, followed by a longer-scaled shot of the same composition with a vision of Marie superimposed on the fireplace in the right-hand side of the shot (figs. 3.10 and 3.11). The second, more complicated vision entails numerous shots:

Shot one: (interior, Marie's home)
Marie slumps into a chair, slow dissolve to . . .

Shot two: (interior, John's home)
John is reading.

Shot three: (insert)
News item relating Marie's success as an opera singer.

Shot four: (as shot two)
Dissolve back to . . .
(fig. 3.12)

Shot five: (as shot one)
Marie revives.

Title:
"Memories of the old love"

Figure 3.12. Dissolve from one remembering party to another in *'Twixt Love and Ambition* (1912) . . .

Figure 3.13. . . . who then beckons to a vision.

Shot six: (as shot five)
The image is now altered so that an opening exists beside Marie for a
     vision of John (superimposed at frame left) to which she beckons.
(fig. 3.13)

Shot seven: (as shot four)
John is still despondent.

At its simplest level, this second vision scene merely serves as a companion piece to the first, demonstrating that John occupies Marie's thoughts, as she had his. But in the complexity of its representation, this second vision blurs the distinctions between one character's thoughts and another's. First, though Marie's reverie initiates the sequence, it is not filtered entirely through her consciousness (the narrative establishes later that John has indeed read the newspaper as indicated). Instead, the ambiguity of the dissolves suggests that Marie and John's actions are linked, both by her desire/remembrance and by causality. The sequence begins with a brooding Marie but ends with John in anguish; the use of a doubled vision indicates more than simple simultaneity and fluctuates between the consciousnesses of these two characters. Accordingly, Marie's vision of John constitutes the psychological focus of the sequence, even while John's reaction to the news item remains the final represented narrative action. The oscillation between two states of mind depicted in this sequence of *'Twixt Love and Ambition* perfectly embodies the sense of suspension signaled by the title.

Selig's *The Devil, the Servant and the Man*, also from 1912, features an extended dream sequence in its second half wherein an errant husband imagines being led by the devil to witness his wife at various nightspots. (In reality, of course, his wife is the wronged one.) Just as he is about to

exact retribution, a corresponding
vision of her asleep appears to him,
which prevents him from killing
her. But finally he does shoot her
and attempts to do the same to himself after returning home. Christ
then appears to show him that his
wife is not dead at all, but still
sleeping. The husband awakes and
begs forgiveness. While sleeping,
the husband has found his dreams
interrupted by visions, themselves

Figure 3.14. A dream provides spatially
impossible simultaneity in *The Devil, the
Servant and the Man* (1912).

images drawn from reality. Understanding his dream world as the real one,
the husband perceives the images of his sleeping wife as idealized, although, ironically, they are the truth. (The dream scenarios she enacts,
meanwhile, are thinly veiled dramatizations of his own behavior.) Part
morality play, part psychological study, the film employs spatially impossible simultaneity (wherein the wife appears as a partygoer and faithful
spouse at the same time within the same shot) in order to embody the internal conflict the husband experiences (fig. 3.14). Another possibility,
however, would have the visions functioning differently for viewer and
husband. In other words, the images of the sleeping wife can operate both
as his dreaming notion of what she should be/has been and also as a re-
minder to us of what she is still doing as he dreams. Complex examples of
visions such as those found in *'Twixt Love and Ambition* and *The Devil,
the Servant and the Man* indicate that exploring character subjectivity in
depth can also entail ambiguity for the viewer.

"Unbeknownst to Her . . . ": Hierarchies of Knowledge and Articulated Views

Seeing what a character thinks can deepen the viewer's awareness of subjectively inflected story information; seeing what a character *sees* can offer
up other narrational possibilities. Exploited as a visual phenomenon, cinema had demonstrated a fascination with masked and magnified views and
other variations on point of view from its beginnings. But apart from liter-
alizing a character's actual perception, cinema also possessed the capacity to provide (and manipulate) viewpoints, which, in Ben Brewster's
words, would "make possible hierarchies of relative knowledge for characters and spectators" (1982, 7).

Examining Griffith's Biograph films from this period, Brewster cites numerous examples of narratives entirely constructed around the differences in character and viewer knowledge. Even without benefit of literal point-of-view shots, these films explore "point of view, in the sense of narrative perspective, the measurement of the relative perceptions and knowledge of the characters by the development of the narrative" (1982, 12). However, filmmakers other than Griffith also investigated the possible hierarchies of knowledge afforded by articulated views; indeed, such strategies constitute one of the salient narrational traits of the last few years of the transitional period.

If the vision renders the workings of the inner mind concrete, thereby potentially heightening the viewer's sense of characters' mental subjectivity, the articulated view negotiates the actual perceptual subjectivity of the diegetic onlooker, but with varying repercussions for spectatorial knowledge. One can imagine the options available to the articulated view, ranging from a situation where the diegetic viewer's ability to see is blocked (as is the corresponding access to information such a view would provide) while the spectator's is not, to one where both have equal knowledge, to one where the diegetic viewer's perspective is superior (in terms of access to information) to that of the spectator.

In the case of the first situation, which is by far the most common, films of the period vary in their approaches to setting up the articulated view. One that involves "true" point of view is the oft-cited example from *A Friendly Marriage* (Vitagraph 1911), where, after showing us the "full" view of the husband and the vicar's daughter (engaged as his secretary [fig. 3.15]), the film then sets up a three-shot sequence of viewer/viewed/viewer establishing that his wife has seen only a partial view of the working couple's interaction and misconstrued it as a romantic liaison (figs. 3.16 and 3.17).[46] As Kristin Thompson has pointed out, the horizontal nature of most camera angles at this time does not help to designate point-of-view shots as such, so in instances like the one in *A Friendly Marriage*, a framing window establishes the view as diegetically motivated (1985b, 207). However, other alternatives during the period resist the breakdown of point of view into discrete shots. In Edison's *A Test of Friendship* (1911), a single-shot composition features a man standing to the side of his dresser mirror, which reveals a reflection of his girlfriend and friend in a seemingly compromising embrace (fig. 3.18). Again, as in the previous example, the spectator has already learned of the innocence of this interchange in a previous shot (fig. 3.19). But this time, the character's view is full and accurate even if it

Figure 3.15. The "full" view only the spectator sees in *A Friendly Marriage* (1911) . . .

Figure 3.16. . . . before a character looks at the same situation . . .

Figure 3.17. . . . followed by her view.

Figure 3.18. Viewer/viewed in the same composition in *A Test of Friendship* (1911), compared to . . .

Figure 3.19. . . . the corresponding "full" view.

Figure 3.20. The deep-enfolded view in
Love Hath Wrought a Miracle (1912).

Figure 3.21. Looking in on a character in
the background in *A Baby's Shoe* (1912).

proves equally uninformed. Finally, a character may appear in the background of a shot, positioned to misinterpret the actions of characters interacting in the foreground, such as in Biograph's *The Failure* (1911).

Compositions involving the viewer and viewed parties simultaneously in the same frame necessarily set up discrepancies of knowledge among characters, if not between diegetic viewer and spectator. In what I call the deep-enfolded view, a character placed in either the foreground or the background looks upon characters within the opposite plane without their knowledge. In *Love Hath Wrought a Miracle* (Vitagraph 1912), an incapacitated man watches his neighbors from the privacy of his garden without their being aware (fig. 3.20). This deep-enfolded view can also operate as a variant on true point of view, involving a multiple-shot articulation. In *A Baby's Shoe* (Edison 1912), shots of a distressed father's attempt at theft alternate with those of the intended victim, his employer, who observes the man's actions while sequestered behind curtains (fig. 3.7, p. 71; fig. 3.21). In both examples, the articulated view provides the diegetic viewer and the spectator with equally valid story information. Note as well that the deep-enfolded view depends upon contiguous spaces. *A Romance of the Coast* (Lubin 1912) features an observed rescue at sea, the outcome of which the diegetic onlookers know (and react to) before the spectator is aware of it. Whether this is a deliberate narrational ploy or an unsuccessful rendering of point of view is unclear; nonetheless, the substantial distances between viewer and viewed in this film (shot entirely outside) prohibit reliance on the deep-enfolded view.

The arrangement of characters' looks can affect the ways that viewers acquire knowledge both inside and outside the diegesis and can also construct hierarchies within the film's fictional world. Failures of vision, wherein characters do not respond properly to a look (or don't notice it at

Figure 3.22. The first shot of a comic variation on the eyeline match in *A Comedy of Errors* (1912) . . .

Figure 3.23. . . . followed by the second half of this "mis-match."

Figure 3.24. A point-of-view shot in *A Comedy of Errors* (1912).

all), often put these characters at a disadvantage in subsequent narrative situations. In Selig's *Euchered* (1912), the lawman hero, despite looking off in the apparent direction of the characters depicted in the next shot, does not see them at all. As superior observers in this lopsided eyeline non-match, they *do* see him failing to notice them, however, which allows them to dupe him. In *Broncho Billy's Narrow Escape* (Essanay 1912), Billy and his girlfriend fail to notice a jealous rival spying upon them repeatedly, which results in the titular predicament. A comic variation, Solax's *A Comedy of Errors,* also from 1912, presents a successful eyeline match linking departing husband and waving wife which a third party then misinterprets; the third party only connects visually with the latter half of the first eyeline match, willfully "seeing" his own leering gaze reciprocated by the wife's loving kiss (figs. 3.22 and 3.23).

This last example, which goes on to compound the problems of vision by extending the joke through a series of cut-in point-of-view shots of incriminating objects (fig. 3.24), brings us as close as any film discussed to the narrational strategies of the classical film. By 1912–13, some films began introducing techniques for articulating diegetic visual relations, such as eyeline matches and shot/reverse shot, which would become commonplace after the mid-teens. But the transitional period's changing approaches to the challenges of narrative do not constitute an eventual manifestation of the classical system so much as a testing out of workable models, with filmmakers exploring different ways to increase narrative complexity, enhance viewer comprehension, and clarify character motivation.

The double causal plot structure, the valued object, the letter insert, and the deep-enfolded view all stand as experiments of the transitional period, designed to satisfy the need for a story that was "vital and unified in its action" (Ball 1913, 24). Filmmakers would retain and modify whatever proved valuable as a narrational device, incorporating it into progressively conventionalized storytelling procedures. The increased efficiency of production practices involved training filmmakers to employ proven systems of representation. However, during the transitional period, especially in the earlier years, companies could not be certain which approaches would prove workable, and often filmmakers gravitated toward easy solutions, such as excessive titling or extended takes dense with narrative action, before switching to alternatives. Hence, advice from self-proclaimed experts, within both the trade press and how-to manuals, coupled with the ability of filmmakers to assess the efforts of competitors working on similar problems, helped to shape narrative strategies. This could result in widespread imitation of seemingly successful approaches: witness the relatively rapid proliferation of such devices as inserts, valued objects, and vision scenes.

Transitional Narration: The Containment of Attractions

In chapter 1, I contrasted the differing approaches to preclassical narration advanced by Kristin Thompson and Tom Gunning; I would like to reintroduce that comparison to consider the issue of narrational self-consciousness. Because the shift in narrational norms evident during the transitional period resulted in a radical realignment of spectatorial address, we need to be clearer about what kind of changes we are describing. Specifically, how does one reconcile the apparent opposition of Thompson's model of early cinema's narration as relatively unselfconscious with Tom Gunning's concept of the cinema of attractions, the latter dependent on a sense of deliberate "display"? And what ramifications does such a discrepancy have for the model of narration I have outlined in relation to the transitional period?

I believe we must understand Gunning's concept to exist outside the model of narration constructed here. Flamboyant display presupposes an independence from any developed narrative context, to an extent that renders principles applicable to a coherent narrative all but irrelevant. As André Gaudreault has noted, filmmakers operating within the cinema of attractions context demonstrate "an alternative attitude toward story-telling, one less focused on the story qua story" (1987, 112). The concept of variably self-conscious narration only becomes analytically viable if one understands it to operate against a background of a range of obtrusiveness. The notion of address that the cinema of attractions depends upon, however, precludes any such range: defined by display, such a cinema is always obtrusive.[47] Conversely, those films from the primitive period that Thompson labels relatively unselfconscious typically do involve extended narratives but remain undernarrativized.[48]

More than ever before, filmmakers during the transitional era abandoned previously accepted notions of address and opted more consistently to focus on the narrative for its own sake. Because storytelling becomes uppermost in filmmakers' minds, the residual lure of the attraction finds itself more fully contained within a narrative context. At this point, questions of relative self-consciousness do gain relevance; while not eliminated altogether, the effect of the attraction does become progressively regulated, to the extent that one can assess its effect on films' narrational stance.[49]

This shift—from direct address, with an emphasis on attractions, to a distinctly different if fluctuating mode of narration—helps define the nature of transition. Eventually, the changes to narration that this period inaugurates would solidify into the system associated with classical filmmaking. But whatever degree of stability we can attribute to later films does not yet apply to those of the transitional period. Though the trade press urged filmmakers to develop characterization and provide unified plots in order to mount compelling narratives, many filmmakers remained uncertain how to achieve these goals. This uncertainty, as much as the one-reel format, may help to explain why particular devices often strike us with the prominence of their deployment in transitional films. While one could argue that this phenomenon operates as a variant of the attraction, I think we should understand the insistence on repeating techniques within individual films in a different way. Before their actual acceptance as dependable storytelling devices, newly devised strategies still had the appeal of novelty.[50] Repetition of such techniques allowed filmmakers to stress the novelty while testing out its usefulness in narrational terms. If other filmmakers noticed the device, and agreed upon its narrational potential, they would appropriate it—sometimes quickly, as with inserts, and sometimes after an appreciable delay, as we will see with crosscutting. Modifying the overt address of the pretransitional years while retaining the lure of selected exploitable techniques represents yet another way that filmmakers adapted to the demands of increased narrativization. The next two chapters will examine in more detail how filmmakers manipulated the constituent elements of the medium in response to those demands.

4

"An Immeasurably Greater Freedom":
Time and Space in Transitional Cinema

The main advantage of the moving-picture play over the traditional types of drama is that the author is granted an immeasurably greater freedom in handling the categories of place and time.

> CLAYTON HAMILTON, "The Art of the Moving Picture Play"
> (14 January 1911)

When Mr. Griffith suggested a scene showing Annie Lee waiting for her husband's return to be followed by a scene of Enoch cast away on a desert island [in *After Many Years*, 1909], it was altogether too distracting. "How can you tell a story jumping about like that? The people won't know what it's about."

"Well," said Mr. Griffith, "doesn't Dickens write that way?"

"Yes, but that's Dickens; that's novel writing; that's different."

"Oh, not so much, these are picture stories; not so different."

> LINDA ARVIDSON GRIFFITH, *When Movies Were Young*

The cinematograph has some advantages, not only over the cheap shows which it at first rivaled, but over any previous form of dramatic art. The most conspicuous of these is spaciousness, distance. . . . The moving picture has it in its power by alternating scenes to show us what is going on simultaneously in two different places . . . [and] can vary at will the distance of the stage, giving us a closer view at critical moments."

> editorial, *New York Independent* (15 October 1910)

The photoplay sacrifices not only the space values of the real theater; it disregards no less its order of time. . . . The pictorial reflection of the world is not bound by the rigid mechanism of time. Our mind is here and there, our mind turns to the present and then to the past: the photoplay can equal it in its freedom from the bondage of the material world.

> HUGO MÜNSTERBERG, *The Photoplay: A Psychological Study*

REGARDLESS OF THEIR ORIGIN — newspaper editorialist, faceless industry skeptic, or eminent Harvard psychologist—the epigraphs chosen to open this chapter hold in common that at its root, cinema is a medium defined by its spatial and temporal properties.[1] It became a trade and critical commonplace to compare the spatiotemporal characteristics of the cinema to those of other cultural forms, particularly the theater and the novel, both in order to differentiate the cinema from its forebears and to establish parameters for film's formal operations. If, however, commentators widely acknowledged that cinema possessed unique capacities as a medium of time and space, they expressed less consensus concerning how to marshal those capacities (as the range of positions embodied by the opening quotes indicates).

Cinema's status as a spatiotemporal medium owed as much to its historical context as to its technologically granted abilities. Debuting at the end of the nineteenth century, the moving picture stood as the culmination of a series of inventions that emphasized the capacities of technology to collapse conventional boundaries of time and space. The cinema operated as part of a continuum that stretched from the telegraph and the telephone (which had enabled communication to take place between two locations separated by considerable distance), through to the locomotive and automobile (which allowed their passengers to traverse substantial areas with previously unequalled speed, thereby collapsing travel time), and the phonograph and photograph (which had frozen time through the capturing of sound and image, respectively, from reality via a photoelectric process). Cinema was the latest of inventions expanding the traditional sense of how to represent and conceptualize space and time.[2]

Initial exploitation of cinema's technological base recognized the medium's fusion of photography and motion: advertisements for the first projections described film as "actual life movements" and "living moving pictures."[3] Some of the earliest genres of cinema played up the sensations of rapid movement through space that the medium afforded either in the form of panoramas or motion films. The latter, which emulate the passage of trolley cars or train engines through a variety of spaces by mounting the camera directly on the means of locomotion, adopt the perspective of the technology of transport itself, thereby explicitly equating cinema's spatiotemporal abilities with those of this new era of travel.[4] Similarly, from about 1903 onward, films highlight cinema's affinities with photography via narratives hinging on either of these media's ability to record a truth from the past and reproduce it in the present. *The Story the Biograph*

Told (1904), *Getting Evidence* (1906), *Bobby's Kodak* (1908), *Falsely Accused* (1908), and others build to a climax involving public display of the (often incriminating) moment from the past, either when the filmed activity is projected or the photographic record distributed.[5] Tellingly, we as viewers have already seen that "piece of the past" through the agency of the film itself. These reflexive scenarios point to the capacity of cinema (as a descendant of photography) to replay past moments of time and to duplicate portions of its own materiality. Inasmuch as cinema is an art form able to rearrange time for its own purposes, it is also a technology defined by its capacity for reproduction.

Even as early as *The Story the Biograph Told,* one can discern an impulse to integrate the display of the photographed or filmed action into an enveloping narrative of exposure or vindication.[6] In fact, cinema's indebtedness to the properties of time and space helped link it to other narrative art forms: as an image-based medium of movement devoted to "realistic" representation of the lived moment, cinema shared obvious affinities with the theater; conversely, film's ease in altering its defining space and time frame via the shot transition aligned it with the apparent freedom from physical bonds and temporal constraints enjoyed by the novel. But this "freedom" that Clayton Hamilton had stressed when describing the medium would demand harnessing as transitional filmmakers tied cinematic space and time to narrative prerogatives. Filmmakers would need to transform the unbounded domain of the panorama into the circumscribed and divisible narrative space of drama; similarly, what Tom Gunning has labeled the "sudden burst[s] of presence" (1993b, 6) characterizing time in the cinema of attractions required reshaping to attain a pattern of logical successivity. To identify the challenges filmmakers faced in rendering time and space intelligible within the context of a narrative, I will invoke categories of temporal organization (order, duration, and frequency) and spatial relations between and among shots (involving alterity, proximity, or overlap).[7] First, however, I must address the spatiotemporal logic prevalent in cinema prior to the transitional period.

Primitive Cinema: Space over Time

As André Gaudreault (1983) has demonstrated, spatial concerns overrode attention to temporality in the pre-1907 period. Even in multishot films, space preserves a priority, with minimal attention paid to the temporal relations among shots. Gaudreault's explanation of why space takes precedence over time suggests that cinema's spatiotemporal logic would require rethinking to allow for representational shifts inaugurated in 1907:

> Early filmmakers were more or less consciously considering each shot as an autonomous, self-reliant unit; the shot's objective is to present not a small temporal segment of the action but rather the totality of an action unfolding in an homogeneous space. Between unity of point of view and unity of temporal continuity, the former takes precedent. Before releasing the camera to a subsequent space, everything occurring in the first location is necessarily shown. Spatial anchorage prevails over temporal logic. Stability, persistence, and uniqueness of point of view remain so important that they supersede anachronism. (1983, 322)

Put another way, one could argue that the principles underlying the single-shot film (specifically, an overwhelming devotion to a unity of viewpoint which adherence to a single space—or framing of that space—entails) persevered even when films began to introduce multiple shots.[8] But the very act of multiplying shots (and thereby increasing spaces) precipitated the investigation of space that would allow for a more developed incorporation of time.

The advent of the chase film proved the crucial intervention. Tom Gunning (1984) has cited the chase film as the chief exemplar of what he calls the "genre of continuity," wherein a sustained and extended narrative action linking diverse spaces supersedes the status of the individual shot. Similarly, Noël Burch (1990b) credits the chase with helping implement the linear logic so essential to the Institutional Mode of Representation. Yet in terms of the actual conception of filmed movement within defined space, the chase film still reaffirms the autonomy of the shot, to the extent that only when every character has passed through a space (i.e., when a space is completely "used up") does the shot end.[9] Even so, by introducing the possibility of multiple spaces, the chase film initiates a disintegration of the principle of unity the single shot ensured. The "block of action" identified as essential to the primitive mode gets broken down during this phase, at least to the degree that the accumulation of spaces can intimate a coherent geography. Aggregate space comes to equal narrative space in this procedure; however, the lack of any temporal dimension beyond successivity in pre-1907 chase films probably prevents any further breakdown of the spaces depicted.

The refusal of spatial analysis, or purposeful fragmentation, separates the earlier chase film from its counterpart within the transitional cinema.

The version of the chase that culminates in the last-minute rescue typifies this form of spatial organization, one defined by alternation and guided by a sense of temporal urgency. The early chase film knows no temporal bounds except those provided by each shot's own actions. Variation and eventually repetition become the defining principles. But these principles significantly amend the previously dominant logic of spatial singularity: the sheer number of locales introduced by the chase invites a reconsideration of the utility of space, the possibility of transforming the anonymous setting for action into a specified narrative space. One can see this in transitional films from 1907–8, which return to previously viewed spaces, tacitly recognizing that a space can acquire renewed value over time. Even without explicitly evoking time, a return to familiar space holds forth the promise of narrative development. But whatever degree of alternation may accompany a central principle of repetition or return in these films, *spatial* articulation still prevails. Hence, a film like *The Boy, the Bust and the Bath* (Vitagraph 1907), which I will discuss in the next section, stresses contiguity over simultaneity, while in *The Elopement* (Biograph 1907), crosscutting, introduced only at the final stage of a car chase, conveys increased physical distance between the parties involved rather than suspense.

Transitional Cinema: Contiguous Comedy, Timely Reminders

Analyzing space could entail either the dissection of a singular space (through changed perspective or camera distance) or the relation of one space to another. As early as 1908, Rollin Summers approved the general idea of cutting between distinct spaces: "In the moving picture play . . . the principal characters, having been once well identified, may be separated and the scene [i.e., shot] shift from one to the other and back again" ("The Moving Picture Drama and the Acted Drama," *Moving Picture World* 3, no. 12, 19 September 1908, 213). While the chase film had spread its action across a diverse range of spaces, films shot in interior sets could encourage examination of spaces defined by their proximity and avoid confusion in the simplicity of their spatial relations.

Unlike the last-minute rescue, a later development in spatial analysis that favored suspense, the initial exploration of contiguity often occasioned humor, as two Vitagraph comedies of 1907–8 reveal. Little more than a series of visual gags based upon misrecognition, *The Boy, the Bust and the Bath* (1907) plays upon the contiguous spatial relationship between hall and bathroom by alternating between the two spaces quite rigorously throughout. The second shot maps out the film's insistence on spatial proximity: it introduces the interstitial space of the hallway, consisting of four doors, each of which the various characters will use to enter and exit for the remainder of the film. Alternation of a limited number of spaces predominates: of the film's twenty-two shots, all but four involve the repeated view of an already established space. As might be expected, the hall appears most often and serves as a pivot (as well as a point of origin) for all other spaces. The film's emphasis on voyeurism marks it as a descendant of earlier "keyhole" films (e.g., *A Search for Evidence* [Biograph 1903]), but the difference lies in the tying together of action and vision. The contiguity implied by the linked view of the earlier versions becomes manifest in the match-on-action cut employed here.[10]

In spatial terms, the exaggeratedly enclosed world of *The Boy, the Bust and the Bath* anticipates the emphatic contiguity one finds in many Griffith-era Biographs. This principle would become so ingrained that it could lead to near-parodic reliance on joined spaces, as a *Nickelodeon* review of the company's *How Hubby Got a Raise* indicates: "We wonder what kind of an apartment house that was, with such a queer cul-de-sac of a hall, doors leading in every direction. Of course, this arrangement centralized the wife's borrowing excursions, but it was too impossibly convenient" (4, no. 8, 15 October 1910, 226). Lasting thirty shots, *How Hubby* stringently reduces spatial choice: the film relies on only three sets introduced in the first three shots, alternating amongst these repeated spaces for the remainder of the film.

Vitagraph's *Get Me a Step Ladder* (1908), though just nine shots long, manages to emerge as a virtual primer on spatial relations. Because of the film's brevity, I can provide a shot breakdown in its entirety and thereby demonstrate the patterning of space:

Shot one: (parlor)
A husband and wife deliberate over a picture they wish to hang; the
     husband suddenly finds himself stranded precariously on the wall.

Shot two: (adjoining room)
The wife begins to move through the house looking for a stepladder.

Shot three: (as shot one)
The husband awaits the wife's return.

Shot four: (another room)
The wife continues searching for the ladder.

Shot five: (as shot three)
The husband is still waiting.

Shot six: (kitchen)
The wife finds the ladder and heads back.

Shot seven: (as shot four)
Destruction results as the wife carries the ladder through the room.

Shot eight: (as shot two)
Similar consequences result in her passage through this room.

Shot nine: (as shot five)
The wife returns to the parlor, having demolished everything in her
    wake.

The elaboration of space in this film, as in *The Boy, the Bust and the
Bath,* proves integral to the comic effect. Here, however, the far more systematic treatment of space, which incorporates both crosscutting and contiguity (and/or proximity), allows one to formulate it as a pattern:
A/B/A/C/A/D/C1/B1/A1. The film neatly divides at its midpoint (shot six,
or D, the only nonrepeated spatial element) and transforms itself from a
comedy based on mild suspense (will the wife find the ladder in time?;
shots one through six) to one that depends upon accumulated destruction
over joined spaces (shots six through nine). Elaboration of the space between the suspended husband (a literal case of a "dangling cause") and
discovery of the ladder prepares for the ensuing destruction; that is, revealing the space of shots two and four prolongs the husband's suffering
while also setting up these rooms for comic effect when the wife returns to
them in shots eight and seven. The film's dual focus means that space performs a double function: the structure of the comedy depends upon both
a demonstrated spatial progression (which gains new relevance in its repetition, as each of the rooms revealed will undergo a transformation once
destroyed) and alternation of spaces (crosscutting between the husband's
dilemma and the wife's search for a solution, causality motivating the latter action, and temporal pressure binding them together). Spatial relations

so clearly determine the comic effect that a cut does not return us to the husband's situation once the wife finds the ladder, so as not to dissipate the accrued sense of disaster wrought by the mishandling of the ladder in each subsequent room.

In instances such as these two Vitagraph films, the filmmakers likely found inspiration for their examinations of space from such contemporary models as comic strips.[11] The circumscribed nature of the comic strip, wherein panels typically dictate the parameters of the narrative space, allowed for systematic spatial analysis. Comics often used the confines of the panel format to emphasize notions of spatial contiguity or alternation. These principles could serve as the foundation for the comic's visual humor, as one sees in "A Chapter of Catastrophes" (fig. 4.1) (*Harper's Bazaar* 28, no. 2, 1895). As long as filmmakers restricted the spatial design of their films in similar ways, such models could prove quite helpful in solving localized problems of spatial articulation.

The underdeveloped nature of the narrative material in both the Vitagraph films probably permitted spatial analysis of considerable complexity (each involves little more than a comic situation). Developing a singular formal trait within the confines of a specific genre stands as the legacy of the primitive period, where whole genres would depend upon "their relation to the articulation between shots in terms of space and time" (Gunning 1984, 105). As the humor in the films derives from their spatial systems, one can conclude that the comic format proved an ideal pretext for exploring space at this time, or that thoroughgoing examination of space lent itself best to a comic context.[12] The eventual ascendancy of the more psychologically motivated "dramatic" comedy (such as Vitagraph provided with increasing regularity starting in late 1909) probably contributed to the contiguity comedy's decline (if not its demise).[13] However, as exercises in mastering spatial dissection, these comic films ultimately would prove as valuable as the chase to filmmakers crafting developed narratives within genres dependent on exterior action like the western.

The ongoing articulation of space precipitated by the chase film's development and extended within the comedy of contiguity found its temporal counterpart in a growing insistence on representing time around 1907.[14] At first novelty takes precedence over functionality: when filmmakers begin featuring clocks within the *mise-en-scène*, they often fail to provide them with moving hands; occasionally, the clocks are simply painted on the wall. In *The Energizer* (Biograph 1907), a clock figures prominently in the *mise-en-scène* of the first shot while a character draws attention to its presence (and, presumably, the significance of the time it

Figure 4.1. Spatial contiguity in a comic strip:
"A Chapter of Catastrophes" (1895).

Figure 4.2. Rearranged *mise-en-scène* elements signal temporal advancement in *A Daughter of Dixie* (1911) . . .

Figure 4.3. . . . as the clock advances, the characters' positions shift.

is telling). Unfortunately, the condition of the print makes it impossible to tell whether the clock's time has changed in the second shot (which seems to take place at a later time, though in the same locale). *Lost in the Alps* (Edison 1907) employs a clock to signal some missing children's lateness, but the time it reads remains unvaried from one shot to the next, undercutting its usefulness. Conversely, in *The Tired Tailor's Dream* (Biograph 1907), the clock that reads four o'clock prior to the patron's demand that his suit be completed has advanced an hour for the subsequent shot when the man returns. The one-shot format of Biograph's *Fussy Father Fooled* (1907) does not allow for a strategically positioned grandfather clock to reveal itself as functional, but the timepiece still proves an ideal narrative tool: not only does it help the viewer realize it is too late for the daughter to be up (by virtue of the father's angry gesturing at its face), but it also hides her intruding boyfriend at the crucial moment.[15]

In an effort to move away from the "undetermined temporality" of the pre-1908 era (Gunning 1991, 97), filmmakers would assert the primacy of time within the narrative by reinforcing its function through multiple (and even redundant) means. In *The Fatal Hour* (Biograph 1908), D. W. Griffith not only employs a working clock but also constructs his first sequence of extended (and temporally inflected) parallel editing tied to the movements of that clock. Even the title announces its insistence on temporality, a fitting designation for the first of the director's "last-minute rescues." Other films tried different approaches, often still tied to deadlines. *A Daughter of Dixie* (Champion 1911) combines a prominently featured working clock with pointed rearrangement of characters (who consistently gesture toward its face) from shot to shot to signal the advancement of time (figs. 4.2 and 4.3). *The Dynamiters* (IMP 1911) uses temporally specific intertitles to mark the progress of time upon which its story depends.

The trade press's endorsement of representing temporality fit within their broader mandate of encouraging improved narrative clarity. A 1909 review of Vitagraph's *The Belated Meal* (note again the temporally oriented title) remarked approvingly upon the employment of a clock to indicate a character's lateness (*Moving Picture World* 4, no. 18, 1 May 1909, 554), while another critic praised the same company for *A Friend in Need Is a Friend Indeed* because "they remembered one detail . . . which many forget. The office clock actually moved forward with the passage of the day" (*Moving Picture World* 4, no. 26, 26 June 1909, 873). The following year, the handling of time in Edison's *A Great Scoop* sufficiently impressed Lux Graphicus that he punctuated his observations with an exclamation mark: "There on the screen was the clock telling us irrefragably that it was a quarter to one; ten minutes to one; five minutes to one!" ("On the Screen," *Moving Picture World* 7, no. 9, 27 August 1910, 461). For the trade press of the day, registering temporality not only ensured viewer comprehension, it instilled a sense of verisimilitude (note how the second cited comment sees it as a "detail" easily forgotten). Nonetheless, the insistence on noting its proper observation as late as 1910 indicates that when filmmakers devoted seemingly excessive attention to time in a film like *A Daughter of Dixie*, they did so with justification.

"The Lapse of Years Must Be Great": Aspects of Temporal Duration

Prior to 1907, filmmakers rarely attempted to tell stories whose time span expanded much beyond that of the plot (i.e., the story's rendering via narration); as David Bordwell puts it, "at the level of the whole film, equivalence among syuzhet [plot], fabula [story], and screen duration can be found in very simple narratives, such as 'primitive' films" (1985b, 81). Development of more complex narratives sometimes introduced a distinct discrepancy between story duration and that of the plot. In such cases, filmmakers had to figure out ways to help the viewer decipher the resultant gaps.

Two representative reviews from the transitional period confirm how mishandling temporal gaps could lead to spectatorial confusion:

> There is nothing in the story of the film indicating how long a time has elapsed from the killing of the girl until she is discovered. . . . It is just these incongruities of time and plot that make so many moving pictures weak and untrue to life. (*Nickelodeon* 3, no. 7, 1 April 1910, 178)

> Then follows a series of complications, ending with an involved love
> story, rather difficult to understand. The lapse of years must be great,
> since later Jim's mining partner is made to fall in love with the baby girl,
> grown up. (*Moving Picture World* 8, no. 16, 23 April 1911, 898)

As the first review indicates, not only would improper signaling of a temporal gap prove a dramatic liability, it could also weaken a film's claim to verisimilitude, with the uncertain negotiation of time pointing to cinema's constructed nature. Miscommunication of larger temporal gaps, the second review suggests, could sabotage an entire film's structure. Even when filmmakers made reasonable attempts to convey the changes involved over many years of story time, the results could prove disorienting, as Epes Winthrop Sargent warns in his advice to aspiring screenwriters: "A story starting in the past and brought down to the present day is to be avoided. Lapse of time requires dual make-up and confuses the identity when the break comes. Do not start with your heroine a little child and stick to her until she lands in some Home for Old Ladies, as one author sought to do, all within twenty minutes" ("Technique of the Photoplay," *Moving Picture World* 9, no. 5, 19 August 1911, 451).

Temporal gaps, whether small or large, presented their own challenges. Viewers might overlook slight temporal gaps altogether, which explains why filmmakers resorted to clocks as a way of communicating small-scale gaps. In *A Daughter of Dixie*, cited earlier, the gaps in story duration marked by the shots of the advancing clocks involve mere half-hour intervals. In instances where minimal temporal progression occurred within the same setting, filmmakers could look to models established by static narrative forms, such as stereographic cards and lantern slides. In media such as these, the *mise-en-scène* can be consciously manipulated in order to underline the advancement of time that occurs in the gaps between images. Because most items within the *mise-en-scène* remain stable, the slight changes to specific elements (such as clocks) or the repositioning of characters becomes more noticeable. (An unnamed stereographic card set [figs. 4.4 and 4.5] and a lantern slide series named "Father, O Father" [figs. 4.6, 4.7, and 4.8] provide representative examples.) The deliberately staged poses struck in *A Daughter of Dixie* point to the film's reliance on strategies developed within these static visualized narratives.

However, not all temporal gaps lent themselves to this type of representation, as clocks could not convey the passage of either indistinct or substantial periods of time. Without the ability to communicate such temporal

Figure 4.4. Static visualized narratives model how to represent minimal temporal advancement such as this unnamed stereographic card set . . .

Figure 4.5. . . . which shows time's progression through changed figure positioning and a prominent timepiece.

Figure 4.6. The daughter's first attempt in the lantern slide series "Father, O Father" . . .

Figure 4.7. . . . one hour later . . .

Figure 4.8. . . . one hour more has passed.

gaps, filmmakers would find themselves restricted to stories whose duration did not exceed a few hours. Accordingly, when titles gained acceptance as a narrational device, filmmakers acquired the ability to mark the
passage of time through written text. The wide range of temporal applica-
tions for the expository title becomes evident as early as 1908: *At the
Crossroads of Life* (Biograph 1908) employs both "Five years later" and
"Some months later"; *The Last Cartridge* (Vitagraph 1908) uses a title
reading "Two days later"; and Biograph's *The Princess in the Vase,* also
from 1908, conveys an impressively large ellipsis via the title "3,000 Years
Later." By 1909, temporally oriented expository titles are commonplace,
their prevalence either a symptom of the increased popularity of stories
involving substantial temporal gaps or a factor in that growth.

Even so, critics of titles did not consider them ideal ways to mark
temporal gaps in all instances, regardless of how economical they proved.
Eustace Hale Ball voices a typical condemnation of the practice: "If possible, it is best to show perfect sequence without the aid of geographical
jumps or drops in time, such as 'Three Weeks Later,' 'Five Years
Afterward' and such subterfuge" (1913, 46). Critics feared the availability
of such titles might lead to an excessive reliance on them, as one finds in
Vitagraph's *An Alpine Echo* (1909): of this film's six titles, five indicate
temporal gaps, ranging from one month to ten years. An insistently advancing story line poses problems for the film's scenario, because the plot
must compress close to fifteen years of story action at fairly regular intervals; this demonstrates the narrational limits imposed by the standard one-
reeler's running time. Most scripts from the period attempt a much less
ambitious narrative in terms of story duration or make sure to limit the
number of temporal gaps necessary for its telling.[16]

However, even films incorporating story duration more manageable
than *An Alpine Echo*'s would want to avoid too many temporal expository
titles. One alternative involved substituting an insert containing similar
information for an intertitle; even dating a letter insert could provide an
indication of the temporal gap involved. In 1909, the first year in which inserts appear consistently, more than half of the letter inserts invoke temporality by imposing deadlines or setting up appointments. The text of an
insert from Lubin's *The Call of the Heart* (1909) reveals the multiple narrational tasks such inserts could perform: "Dear Robert, I must see you at
once. As soon as you receive this, please come to 'Lookout Point' where I
will await you. In haste, Anna." In typical fashion, the writer of the letter
refrains from establishing a specific time frame while still conveying tem-

Figure 4.9. Static visualized narratives model how to represent substantial temporal advancement in the lantern slide series "The Sickle and Sheaf" . . .

Figure 4.10. . . . as dramatic changes to the *mise-en-scène* convey time's passage.

poral urgency. And in the course of preparing the next stage of narrative action, the letter's message also supplies its location. Filmmakers employed inserts as their chief means to supply deadlines and appointments throughout this period, though the insert's formulation would become more complex by the later years.[17] Nonetheless, commentators encouraged adoption of other methods to signal temporal gaps that would satisfy the trade press's preference for visual communication.

When indicating large-scale temporal gaps, filmmakers could change the appearance of the actors or the décor to indicate time had passed. Again, these approaches recall strategies employed in preexistent models such as lantern slides. (Significant changes to *mise-en-scène* elements indicate substantial temporal ellipses in such lantern slide series as "The Sickle and Sheaf" [figs. 4.9 and 4.10] and "Where Is My Wandering Son?" [figs. 4.11, 4.12, and 4.13].) Often this procedure implied an interdependency of time and causality; the changes might signal that within the elapsed time the protagonist's actions had resulted in good or bad fortune, mirrored in the alterations to his clothing and surroundings. One such example occurs in *A Range Romance* (Bison 1911), a film that begins and ends in the same room but with a thirteen-year interval interceding between the events depicted in these bookend shots. In the final shot, the two central characters, Mary and Bob, have both been aged through makeup, while improved furnishings within their home indicate not only their superior financial standing but also the stability of their marriage (in

Figure 4.11. The stages of a son's life shown in "Where Is My Wandering Son?" . . .

Figure 4.12. . . . the boy grows older . . .

Figure 4.13. . . . the mother left alone.

doubt at the beginning of the film).[18] Even in this case, however, the film-maker inserts a title stating "Three Years Later" before the final shot, in-dicating a preference for possible redundancy over the chance of the au-dience failing to notice the temporal gap.

Thus, while critics might prefer filmmakers to convey temporal gaps in purely visual ways, these methods could produce unwanted ambigui-ties. With increasing frequency, filmmakers would elect to employ edit-ing as a way of absorbing inconsequential temporal gaps. Crosscutting provided a means of smoothly integrating small-scale ellipses by allowing time to elapse in one place while cutting away to depict action in another. Conversely, in order to accommodate an extensive amount of story time, one could abandon strict chronological ordering of narrative events and invoke the past through flashbacks.

The Flashback: Reordering Story Time

Flashbacks not only offered a novel method of reordering story information, they could also develop characterization by tying an invocation of the past to character memory. Yet filmmakers adopted this device quite tentatively: apart from *Fireside Reminiscences* (Edison 1908), *Napoleon, Man of Destiny* (Vitagraph 1909), and *The Yiddisher Boy* (Lubin 1909), no other examples of flashbacks occur in the films I have viewed until 1911, after which point they appear with some regularity.[19] Filmmakers probably delayed employing the flashback because of fears that the disturbance of story order would cause problems for viewer comprehension. Further, audiences might have difficulty distinguishing the flashback, or "memory scene," from the vision or dream. Establishing two preconditions for the flashback helped differentiate it from other subjectively motivated devices: first, the flashback must portray a portion of story time preceding the events leading to the introduction of the memory itself (unlike the vision); and second, the character from whose memory the flashback emerges must be conscious at the time the flashback occurs (as opposed to the dream). Initially, however, filmmakers experienced difficulty harnessing the flashback to the task of temporal reordering. Two of the three pre-1911 flashback films I have seen are constructed as a series of linked recollections, varying the structural ploy preferred by dream comedies. Both offer limited character development while being marked by distinct temporal irregularities.[20]

In the case of *Fireside Reminiscences*, the final memory image of the protagonist (which appears, like the others, as a superimposition within his fireplace) turns out not to be a flashback at all, but rather an actual simultaneous event. As Tom Gunning has noted, "these temporal ambiguities make the reading of the film's imagery through a character's psychology problematic" (1991, 117). In *Napoleon, Man of Destiny*, shots of the emperor reflecting on his achievements give way to depictions of those events; however, the final image in the series refers to a future occurrence, which disrupts the pattern of alternation between present and past.[21] Moreover, the use of a flashforward casts doubt on whether Napoleon's consciousness operates as the consistent source of the images provided. The film's episodic structure further weakens any collective utility the flashbacks might possess in deepening character subjectivity: each memory constitutes a detachable unit, emphasized by a single-shot tableau rendering. Maureen Turim has suggested that the film recalls "the popular 19th-century staged tableau and the history painting; that earlier aesthetic of spectacular vision in its theatrical presentation may not have needed a device to smooth the ellipses in the chronology. In film, the framing device of remembering from a vantage point in the present that implies causality or nostalgia serves to connect the tableaux and contextualize the ekphrasis of the posed images" (1989, 28). I think Turim overstates *Napoleon*'s reliance on the narrativizing power of remembrance; in fact, neither of these examples has sufficiently integrated the device of the flashback to render it an unselfconscious narrational tool. Each film presents its flashbacks as a series of visual events instead, not as a moment of character recall aimed at establishing causality or conveying prior story information economically.[22] From 1911 on, filmmakers would modify the flashback in order to tie its function more directly to character memory.

As flashbacks entailed not only temporal reordering but also access to a character's psychology, their development initially occurred in tandem with that of the vision. However, filmmakers learned to articulate each in a manner distinct from the other. Flashbacks were designated as separate shots probably because they represented a shift from one time frame to another; by the same token, movement between discrete spaces necessitated a shot transition. The coding of different techniques established itself fairly quickly: spatial articulation occurred via a straight cut, temporal reordering was usually marked by dissolves or fades, and visions were depicted as superimpositions.[23]

Possible narrative uses for flashbacks assumed recurrent patterns only by 1913, at about the same time as their coded representation. One such use explored the flashback's ability to develop character psychology through sustained recollection. Elaboration of the format employed for *Fireside Reminiscences* allows a character to recall past events from a present-day perspective (as in *The Fiddler's Requiem* [Kalem 1911], *Sweet Memories* [IMP 1911], *In a Garden* [Thanhouser 1912], and *Just a Shabby Doll* [Thanhouser 1913]). In these cases, the film's narrative assumes the structure of either an extended flashback—a story within a story—or a series of linked recollections. In the 1912–13 versions of the latter type, cues maintain a sense of the separate time frames (including dialogue titles that function as a form of voice-over narration and recurring shots of the taleteller/recalling figure in the present), while dissolves articulate the temporal transitions.

Other films feature circumscribed recollections that occupy a much briefer span of time within the plot (typically no more than several shots). In such instances (exemplified by *Her Bitter Lesson* [Selig 1912], *Now I Lay Me Down to Sleep* [IMP 1912], and *The Lieutenant's Last Fight* [Bison

1912]), when the flashback occurs
sufficiently early in the plot, it can
provide motivation for a character's subsequent actions as well.
For example, in *The Girl of the
Cabaret* (Thanhouser 1913), the former cabaret entertainer's recollection of her earlier days as a performer causes her to abandon her
boring life in the country with her
husband, which leads to the actions
constituting the film's second half. If

Figure 4.14. A revelation flashback—re-
counted, enacted and overheard—in *A
Special Messenger* (1911).

a flashback occurs late in the narrative, it can produce a resolution, as happens in Thanhouser's *The Cry of the Children* (1912), when the factory owner's
wife decides to improve working conditions for the poor after a guilt-inducing
flashback. A review of a Yankee film from 1911, *The Man Underneath*, suggests how the trigger of memory could effect a last-minute transformation:
"He determines on vengeance and would have carried out his intention, only
a little child entered to kiss her father good-night. The memory of his own
child was aroused and his reason restored" (*Moving Picture World* 9, no. 3,
29 July 1911, 212). Within the constraints of the one-reel format, the flashback could expedite a denouement dependent on character conversion.

A less common function, one I label "revelation," stresses communicating crucial narrative information over cultivating the psychology of the
recalling character. In films featuring revelation flashbacks, depictions of
past events provide story information left uncommunicated by gaps in the
plot. Kalem's *A Special Messenger* from 1911 offers an interesting example
of a character recounting a crime he has committed, while the crime is
also enacted visually via a superimposition in the upper-right-hand corner of the frame[24] (fig. 4.14). Though later convention in sound films would
have the character begin by recounting the events, leading into a transition to the flashback mode, this film presents both simultaneously. The
film's handling of the situation also has repercussions for hierarchies of
knowledge: the spectator grasps the contents of the criminal's conversation to his confidante, while also noticing that a character in the background—unseen by the discussants—overhears the same information.

Typically, revelation flashbacks answer questions posed when the plot
discloses insufficient story information. Thus, in *One Hundred Years After*
(Selig 1911), the descendant of a murder victim "recalls" the events leading

Figure 4.15. A single-shot revelation flashback in *The Lieutenant's Last Fight* (1912).

up to the death of a character who disappeared in the film's prologue. A less convoluted example (and one quite typical of classical practice) occurs in *Blazing the Trail* (Bison 1912): an informed observer provides additional story information about partially depicted events to fill in the spectator's incomplete knowledge. When Natives attack a wagon full of settlers, we see only the aftermath, as witnessed by a returning member of the party who had gone off for water. We only fully understand what transpired when one of the survivors recounts what occurred (via a single-shot flashback). Here, the flashback redresses a deliberately constructed lack of spectatorial knowledge that necessitated the revelation.

Given the narrational economy of the single-shot revelation flashback exemplified by *Blazing the Trail* or *The Lieutenant's Last Fight* (fig. 4.15), one might ask why the extended flashback format persisted in the transitional period's final years. The appeal of the innovative structure probably attracted filmmakers: so-called "story within a story" films like *Just a Shabby Doll* or *Bragg's New Suit* (Edison 1912) allowed them to create doubled story lines while pushing cinema's limits of temporal representation.[25] As a 1911 feature review of Thanhouser's *The Judge's Story* indicates, filmmakers could use the story within a story as a showcase for cinema's distinct ability to bend time to narrative demands:

> Whenever a film maker skillfully seizes and elaborates certain possibilities peculiar to the moving picture, as distinguished from the conventional stage, he is entitled to special credit. The story within a story is peculiarly within the province of the moving picture, and the makers of this film have shown themselves well capable of grasping and using this singular advantage. . . . The charm of the story lies in the quick change from drama to dramatic narrative and the display of a fine ability to sustain the character of both equally well. (*Moving Picture World* 9, no. 4, 5 August 1911, 274)

Still, the *World* writer's celebration of the story within a story acknowledges that narrative rules must govern the play with time. Unlike novelties from the era of attractions, medium-specific innovations during the transitional period had to fulfill aesthetic requirements of verisimilitude and unity. When early theorist Hugo Münsterberg, echoing the reviewer of *The Judge's Story,* proposed stressing the "peculiarities of the medium" in order to establish film's status as art, he also linked cinema's representation of time to unity.[26]

Münsterberg, Time, and Unity

Most scholars credit Hugo Münsterberg with writing one of the first theoretical works on film, *The Photoplay: A Psychological Study,* initially published in 1916. Though his writings postdate the time span of this study somewhat, his insights possess relevance, not the least because he "argues for serious intellectual study of how films treated temporality and memory at a time when few considered the theoretical implications of cinema from a scientific and philosophical perspective" (Turim 1989, 30). In particular, Münsterberg celebrated cinema's liberation from the "forms of the outer world, namely space, time, and causality . . . by adjusting the events [of its story] to the forms of the inner world, namely attention, memory, imagination, and emotion" (Münsterberg 1970, 74).

As a professor of psychology at Harvard, Münsterberg existed in a world apart from the moving picture industry. But if one strips away the intellectual aspirations of Münsterberg's theoretical investigation of cinema, one finds at its core a set of assumptions shared by the practical minds at work in the trade press. In particular, both Münsterberg and trade critics embraced the need for unity as a governing aesthetic principle. While Münsterberg ceded to cinema freedom from such laws as dictated theatrical practice, he compensated by advising strict adherence to others:

> Just as music is surrounded by more technical rules than literature, the photoplay must be held together by the esthetic demands still more firmly than is the drama. The arts which are subordinated to the conditions of space, time, and causality find a certain firmness of structure in these material forms which contain an element of outer connectedness. But where these forms are given up and where the freedom of mental play replaces their outer necessity, everything would fall asunder if the esthetic unity were disregarded. (1970, 80)

Münsterberg goes on to identify three laws of unity that film must obey— unity of action, character, and form. In each instance, he stresses the

importance of central organizing principles, as when he says of characterization that "the chief demand is that the characters remain consistent, that
the action be developed according to inner necessity and that the characters themselves be in harmony with the central idea of the plot" (1970, 81).

Many trade commentators during the transitional period shared
Münsterberg's concern that temporal and spatial freedom might invite narrative chaos. For that reason, the call for unity (as an implicit corrective)
becomes a recurring refrain. Witness the following examples:

> Whenever a thousand feet of film is taken, it is desirable to insure that it
> has plenty of action, and, moreover, that the dramatic interest is
> sustained and cumulative. Then a powerful motive should be visible all
> through the story. . . . ("A Note of Warning," *Moving Picture World* 5,
> no. 22, 27 November 1909, 751)

> The method of the untrained dramatist would produce a simple, artificial
> melodrama, such as are too many of our picture plays; that of the trained
> dramatist, a strong, purposeful play, every element of which is organic,
> taking its place as a part of the play's structural progress to the end.
> (George Rockhill Craw, "The Technique of the Picture Play—Structure,"
> *Moving Picture World* 8, no. 4, 28 January 1911, 180)

> The plot, if there is a plot, must be simple, and every move made by the
> actors must be concentrated upon the development of that plot. ("The
> Picture the Audience Likes," *Moving Picture World* 8, no. 6, 11 February
> 1911, 310)

> The fault with the plot [of Edison's *Ononko's Vow*] is that it attempts to
> cover too long a period of time, two generations of characters being
> involved; dramatic unity is thereby cleft in twain. (*Nickelodeon* 4, no. 8,
> 15 October 1910, 224)

This last-cited quote is particularly appropriate, as it signals the wariness
of the trade press toward films that exploited temporal (and spatial) freedom to the detriment of narrative comprehension.

If representing scenarios of excessive story duration could threaten
narrative unity, so too could scenarios incorporating an extensive variety
of settings. Apparently this did not bother Münsterberg: " . . . through our
division of interest our mind is drawn hither and thither. We think of
events which run parallel in different places. The photoplay can show in
intertwined scenes everything which our mind embraces. Events in three
or four or five regions of the world can be woven together into one com-

plex action" (1970, 74). However, here Münsterberg and the trade press part company aesthetically: contemporary critical reaction to crosscutting and related techniques betrayed a fear of their power to disrupt spatial unity that Münsterberg does not express.[27] The exploration of space initiated by the minimal narratives of 1907–8 developed considerably in the following years, and filmmakers would have to find ways to prevent the increased cutting from seeming overtly discontinuous. As Kristin Thompson has suggested, "unless the filmmaker finds cues for conveying the spatio-temporal relationship between shots, the effect of the cut is a perceptible break between bits of subject matter. . . . [T]he need which arose with the advent of the multiple-shot film . . . [was] to find a means of unifying an extensive series of disparate spatial and temporal elements in the plot in such a way that the spectator could grasp the story events" (1985b, 162, 175). The arrangement of space within a discernible temporal context stands as one of the key developments in transitional cinema from 1909 onwards.

Constructing Legibility: Placing Space

The malleable nature of cinematic space permits manipulation in two basic ways: one can mold the space before the camera, or one can articulate spatial relations between one shot and another.[28] The latter method, achieved through editing, requires further subdivision if one wishes to define the nature of possible spatial constructions. Measuring relative distance between the spaces of successive shots involves the application of one of three categories: overlap, proximity, and alterity. In overlap, the second shot contains some portion of the first, reproduces it in a changed context of scale, or presents it from a different angle; cut-ins function as a straightforward instance of overlap.[29] Proximity involves a relationship of relative closeness between two spaces; contiguity represents the most common kind of proximity. Because the two spaces are physically distinct, filmmakers usually must supply cues to suggest proximity, sometimes in combination, such as reciprocated gazes, matching of character movement across spaces, and continuity of décor in shared space. Finally, when the transition from one space to another involves a significant physical distance, alterity comes into play. Note that any type of spatial relationship can enter into an alternating series, though crosscutting typically involves alterity.

As the need for cues to establish proximity attests, any act of cutting from an established space can risk producing spectatorial confusion. The first multishot films courted such a risk, but attachment to a unity of point of view rendered logical relationships among shots less important than the spatial status of each individual shot. The advent of the chase film required spectators to adopt a more fluid sense of spatial relationships. Tom Gunning rightly ties this shift to the chase film's enhanced narrativity:

> [The chase's] fascination lay in the spatial continuity it rehearsed, the possibility of stitching together a larger spatial whole from separate shots. This spatial synthesis of separate shots depended on narrative structure. . . . No longer simply observing the action or directly addressed by an attraction, the spectator now knitted together the space and time of the film following the logic of the narrative. (1991, 67)

If the chase film rehearsed the construction of spatial continuity, subsequent dramatic films operated as equivalents of opening night. Filmmakers introduced a repertoire of space-defining strategies designed to help viewers negotiate the potential disruptions involved in increased spatial fragmentation. Some of the approaches that filmmakers devised developed into cornerstones of the continuity system, consistently refined into the classical era; others proved to be short-lived experiments doomed by their expense or limited applicability. As always, the trade press stood poised to issue reviews that would keep the show running or close it down before it could tour. By considering the shifting function of devices introduced to affect the perception of space and aid in the comprehension of spatial relationships, we can arrive at a clearer sense of how filmmakers achieved continuity.

Close Together but Still Apart: Articulating Proximity and Overlap

Editing allows for sustained analysis of space but must alter the integrity of the viewed scene to do so. Filmmakers relinquished their devotion to the principle of an integral and singular dramatic space out of necessity: representing proximate spaces separated by physical barriers seemingly demanded recourse to editing. (Filming both a home's exterior entryway and the adjoining interior room as a single space would pose difficulties, for example.) Yet initially, filmmakers attempted to retain a sense of spatial wholeness by marking out contiguous spaces within a single set, splitting the set down the middle and filming it so that the division appeared as a vertical bar running down the center. *Deaf-Mutes' Masquerade* (Biograph 1907), *At the French Ball* (Biograph 1908), and *Man in the Box*

Figure 4.16. Contiguous spaces within a split set in *At the French Ball* (1908).

Figure 4.17. Simultaneous action depicted via a split set in *Man in the Box* (1908).

(Biograph 1908) all rely on split sets of this kind (figs. 4.16 and 4.17).[30] In the last-named film in particular, the split set helps depict a series of complicated interrelated actions that the viewer must understand as spatially contiguous and simultaneous. To suggest the spatiotemporal relations without a split set would involve sustained cutting between the two rooms. Instead, the use of the split set at the end of this four-shot film means the final shot's running time nearly doubles that of the other three combined. However, use of the split set created problems of its own. Depending on the size of the set, such an approach could force the action even farther from the camera, rendering certain actions almost indecipherable. Moreover, representing two or more actions within a split set might prove more difficult for spectator comprehension than dividing the space through editing. Finally, a split set only works for certain narrative situations; filmmakers would find that other common cases of contiguity, such as interior/exterior, did not lend themselves to the split-set solution.[31]

Kalem's *Ben Hur* (1907) offers a spatially inventive variation on the vertically split set by employing an exaggeratedly "high" set which is then divided in two along a horizontal axis. The first shot of this space shows the set (a domestic interior set atop an arch) in its entirety, though only the top half features dramatic action; after a cut, shot scale adjusts to show just the bottom half. Because the first shot incorporates the unused bottom portion of the set, the shot seems top heavy: an inordinate amount of empty space occupies the bottom of the frame, inverting the principle of leaving excess space at the top of the frame that prevails in 1907. Aside from the strains this approach places on verisimilitude (why would Ben Hur's home be located on top of an archway?), its convoluted representation of adjacent spaces almost ensures that this variant remain an anomaly.

Figure 4.18. Linking spaces across an axis in *The Last Cartridge* (1908) . . .

Figure 4.19. . . . via a 180-degree cut to the other side.

Nonetheless, joining the top of one shot's space to the bottom of the next invariably provided strong cues for spatial connection, as demonstrated by Biograph's *The Black Viper* (1908). During a chase up a mountain ledge, the upward movement of the actors' climb implies contiguity from the first shot of the sequence to the next. The downward direction of the rocks they throw (in the second shot) further confirms this. Moreover, the directional cues prompt the viewer to relate the third shot as a portion of the mountain directly underneath (especially when the rocks fall into this lower space). The film provides a subsequent example of spaces joined in vertical contiguity in its final shots: the villains try to burn a man inside a building in the first of these shots, but then point upward prior to a cut to a second shot, which shows the man escaping through a trap door in the building's roof.

Just as joining vertically contiguous spaces could reduce spatial ambiguity across cuts, so too could linking spaces across an axis. A number of Vitagraph films from 1908–9, including *The Last Cartridge* (1908), *Oliver Twist* (1909), and *Romance of the Umbrella* (1909), as well as IMP's *Hiawatha* (1909), feature 180-degree cuts designed to show a space directly opposite that depicted in the prior shot. *The Last Cartridge* features a group of characters enclosed within a besieged building, its outer wall the barrier separating them from their attackers; the film's restricted space encourages reliance upon contiguity, with the 180-degree cut used twice to show both sides of the wall during the attack (figs. 4.18 and 4.19).[32]

The 180-degree cut also promotes alternation, supplying the viewer with both sides of a situation. When depicting adjacent spaces, filmmakers could incorporate alternation as well; when characters moved through contiguous spaces, alternation often occurred, though it tended to be of the "in and out" variety rather than the "back and forth" popularized by Griffith's treatment of alterity via crosscutting. Editing connected contiguous spaces with greater regularity from 1909 onward, and most of the cuts involving character movement from one space to the other built on the model typified by an early version of this variant, Edison's *The Rivals* (1907):

Shot five:
A man sees his rival asleep on a bench and puts a baby in his arms.

Shot six:
A woman (the baby's mother?) returns to a different bench and finds the
     carriage she left unattended now empty; a boy nearby points off
     frame right.

Shot seven: (as shot five)
The first man reenters with the object of the two men's affections and
     shows her his rival with the baby; the mother enters from bottom of
     frame and takes her baby back while the boy gestures accusingly.

Narrative situations did not always afford the circumscribed spatial relations possible in a setup involving adjoining rooms; in such cases, filmmakers would need to supply additional cues, such as the directional gesture toward the proximate space (and, more often than not, consistent directional movements out of the one shot/space and into the next). Though the edited linkage of closely related spaces, supported by directional cues when necessary, would emerge as the preferred method for handling proximity, it was no more common at the beginning of the transitional period than other options explored. The 180-degree cut and the split set, which now strike us as more self-conscious ways to represent contiguity, probably fell out of favor because they lacked the versatility provided by cutting between two laterally arranged spaces.[33]

Arranging spaces to suggest proximity through editing represented one challenge for transitional filmmakers; analyzing the same space from different vantage points, or articulating overlap, would prove another. Chase films had promoted accumulation of space, and soon films built on this model by returning to previously viewed spaces. The principle of repetition evidenced in films such as *Train Wreckers* (Edison 1905), *Life of a Cowboy* (Edison 1905), and *The Flat Dwellers* (Vitagraph 1906) demonstrates the narrative value of returning to a space: once time has passed, subsequent events can render the same space narratively significant for future action. Moreover, returning to an already established locale orients the viewer spatially and lessens the amount of change introduced by a cut. Actual analysis of repeated spaces, a function of overlap, occurs at the beginning of the transitional period, once filmmakers alter the camera position or shot scale used to shoot the same space.

Biograph's *Nurse Wanted,* from 1906, offers an early example by showing the same building from three different perspectives. In many initial cases of overlap, one remains uncertain whether such changed views of the same space deliberately offer an altered perspective or whether production circumstances prevented replicating the original set-up. By 1909, however, the practice of returning to a space in order to modify its representation has gained acceptance as an intentional strategy. One can see developed examples of this in such 1909 films as Lubin's *A True Patriot* (figs. 4.20 and 4.21) and Essanay's *A Ranchman's Rival* (figs. 4.22 and 4.23), where subsequent shots of repeated spaces provide substantially altered views of the depicted settings. Often, shifting the perspective on a space extends the boundaries of the frame, allowing a new character to exit or enter; at other times, extending the space assumes narrational significance through revelation of an additional door or previously unseen corner. In such cases, a changed camera position operates as an alternative to beginning with the original framing and converting to the modified version via a lateral camera movement. (In the same way, using a closer shot scale for the subsequent shot substitutes for a camera movement in toward the depicted space.) To discuss why filmmakers typically opted for the already altered view on a space over modifying it via camera movement would take me beyond the concerns of this chapter (and would also speak to the degree that technology can influence the choices available to filmmakers at any given time); suffice to say that the prevalence of altered views via cuts after 1909 indicates filmmakers progressively viewed cinematic space as malleable. Not unexpectedly, shooting outdoors encouraged this tendency. The increased flexibility in depicting spatial relations of proximity and even overlap coincides with the growth in popularity of certain genres (such as the western), which allowed extensive exterior shooting. Production companies sought out locales that offered photogenic vistas and in the process expanded editing's potential to analyze exteriors as parts comprising a whole. Adopting varied perspectives on an overall exterior space becomes progressively more common after 1910. The expansive sense of space such approaches provided pointed to a changed attitude toward

Figure 4.20. A version of overlap in *A True Patriot* (1909) . . .

Figure 4.21. . . . achieved by altering the view of the same space in its subsequent appearance.

Figure 4.22. The camera adopts one perspective on a space in *A Ranchman's Rival* (1909) . . .

Figure 4.23. . . . and shifts to another when the space reappears.

narrative as well. Dramatic action was no longer rooted to a single spot, nor did a unitary action command the viewer's attention. As spatial exploration persisted, developed narrative frameworks held together a more complicated set of actions represented by a disparate but systematically employed set of devices.

Capturing action in motion further spurred filmmakers to pursue an analytical approach to representing exterior spaces. IMP's *In a Sultan's Garden* (figs. 4.24 and 4.25) and Vitagraph's *Proving His Love* (figs. 4.26 and 4.27), both from 1911, reposition the camera in order to accommodate the movement of a boat and a car, respectively. In these examples, the profilmic action mobilizes the space, forcing a cut: the repositioning of the camera provides the viewer with an ideal view of the changing action. The increased reliance on exteriors and the depiction of more physically expansive dramatic action prove logically interdependent; for that reason,

Figure 4.24. As a boat moves through space in *In a Sultan's Garden* (1911) . . .

Figure 4.25. . . . the camera repositions itself to capture the boat's movement.

Figure 4.26. An automobile's progress in *Proving His Love* (1911) . . .

Figure 4.27. . . . . causes a shift in camera position.

the more intricately edited cases of overlap in the next few years typically involve large-scale action sequences.

Kalem, a Trust concern known for its location shooting and open-air studios, provides ample evidence of the increasing fluidity filmmakers demonstrated when stitching together spatial relationships of proximity and overlap. Two Kalem films of 1911 exemplify how proximate actions staged over several shots could employ a shared dramatic space. In *On the War Path*, following a title, "The settlers reach the shelter of the stockade," a three-shot sequence illustrates the action described. In the three shots, the stockade's gate serves as the locus of the action, but in each instance, a cut allows the camera to adopt a different perspective that best serves the action of the moment.

Shot eleven:
Oblique angle on a gate, positioned toward the left background, as
　　　settlers ride toward it.
(fig. 4.28)

Figure 4.28. Proximate actions occur over a series of three shots in *On the War Path* (1911): first, the settlers approach the gate . . .

Figure 4.29. . . . then, seen from within the gates, they enter . . .

Figure 4.30. . . . finally, outside the gates, Indians advance.

Shot twelve:

Camera repositioned on interior side of gate, with the gate centered as
    riders pass through.

(fig. 4.29)

Shot thirteen:

Camera now on exterior side of gate, showing the last of the settlers
    entering, as the attacking Indians press toward the gate, just as it
    closes.

(fig. 4.30)

The action of the pursued settlers, though directionally distinct in each shot, threads through the different vantage points each shot affords of the gate, binding the shots together. Such an approach to editing, while splintering a uniform space (the gate and its environs), draws the viewer into a more engaged relationship with that space, articulating spatial relations in order to draw out the imminent attack and engender suspense.

In the second example, *By a Woman's Wit,* breaking down space permits analysis of a complex action. The altering of shot scale and camera position over two shots maintains viewer orientation and establishes the necessary spatial relations to set up the subsequent two shots as contiguous.

Shot twenty-three: (as shot twenty-one, prison interior)
The prisoner is in the background at the door, with a note and the rope
      for rescue positioned on table in foreground.
(fig. 4.31)

Shot twenty-four: (shot scale and camera position altered to render
      upper portion of set above door visible)
The prisoner throws the rope up toward the window at the top of frame
      right.
(fig. 4.32)

Shot twenty-five: (in a space meant to be above that shown in shot
      twenty-four)
The prisoner has climbed through to the rafters, and begins punching
      through to . . .
(fig. 4.33)

Shot twenty-six: (exterior of roof)
The prisoner emerges.
(fig. 4.34)

Here, a cut can even reformulate interior space, and editing in conjunction with figure movement and directional cues ties together distinct spaces into a supposedly integrated diegetic space.

One film that does not depend on exterior shooting at all to offer distinct perspectives on the same space is Edison's 1911 *A Stage Romance.* The film's distinctive setting—a theatrical stage—leads to a more intricate handling of interior space than is typical at this time. Awareness of the obvious limits of the diegetic audience's vision forces the filmmaker to place action behind and beside the confines of the stage. Adopting different perspectives on the stage permits visual access to the areas flanking it while also keeping some portion of the central stage in view as well, for the purposes of spatial orientation (figs. 4.35, 4.36, 4.37, and 4.38).

Figure 4.31. A complex action depicted over four shots in *By a Woman's Wit* (1911): first, the prisoner at the door . . .

Figure 4.32. . . . next, the space above which will provide his escape is shown . . .

Figure 4.33. . . . then, the prisoner is about to break through the rafters . . .

Figure 4.34. . . . finally, he emerges on the roof outside.

Ironically, the filmmaker never elects to adopt the diegetic audience's vantage point on the stage, reinforcing a conception of space tied to narrational ends.

Few films must observe the spatial strictures imposed upon *A Stage Romance,* but the representation of space becomes increasingly intricate in the final years of this period. By 1912, the practice of analyzing space often incorporates multiple shots, depicting everything from complex action (the attack on a stagecoach in *The Lieutenant's Last Fight* [Bison 1912] [figs. 4.39 and 4.40]) to straightforward activities (a woman walking from an exterior staircase to a nearby gate, executed over four shots, in *Man's Calling* [American 1912] [figs. 4.41 and 4.42]). The representation of a gun battle staged around a cabin, central to *In the Service of the State* (Lubin 1912) indicates the trend developing by the end of the period: editing alternates between long views of the cabin and closer-scaled shots, drawing the viewer back and forth between relevant sectors of the space (figs. 4.43, 4.44, and 4.45). When necessary, an even closer segment of the

Figure 4.35. One of four different perspectives on the stage and surrounding areas in *A Stage Romance* (1911) . . .

Figure 4.36. . . . another perspective on the stage . . .

Figure 4.37. . . . only a small portion of the stage is included in this view . . .

Figure 4.38. . . . while the diegetic audience's perspective is never adopted.

Figure 4.39. Analyzing space to depict an attack on a stagecoach in *The Lieutenant's Last Fight* (1912) . . .

Figure 4.40. . . . shifting shot scale to depict action in exterior settings.

Figure 4.41. Multiple shots employed to depict a simple activity in *Man's Calling* (1912) . . .

Figure 4.42. . . . as the walk continues over several shots and spaces.

Figure 4.43. Alternation among a variety of shot scales in *In the Service of the State* (1912) . . .

Figure 4.44. . . . provides an instance of both crosscutting . . .

Figure 4.45. . . . and an example of spatial overlap.

space will be shown to offer an improved view of a crucial action. Unlike cutting that shifts from one distinct space to another (in cases of alterity), the editing of the cabin sequences in this film alternates between aspects of the same space, emphasizing the potential for spatial analysis available by 1912. Moreover, the atomized treatment of space in this film, which involves a tripartite instance of overlap, coincides with a reliance on a version of crosscutting. *In the Service of the State* culminates with a protracted gunfight/rescue, involving four different agents and lines of action. At times, only the scale of shot employed separates the lines of action represented. By the tail-end of the period, most action films employ crosscutting, analyzing space within the context of alternation. Crosscutting merits closer attention, because it offers a specialized instance of spatial relations, often informed by a temporal urgency.

"Rapidly Alternating Scenes": Temporal and Spatial Dimensions of Crosscutting

Of the many items of received wisdom passed down concerning early cinema, those crediting D. W. Griffith with the development of crosscutting may well possess the most validity. While certainly not the "inventor" of crosscutting, or even the first to use it for dramatic purposes, Griffith does appear to have been in the vanguard of employing this device, relying on it more often and more extensively in his first years at Biograph than any other filmmaker during the same period. *The Guerilla* (1908), which alternates among three related actions, provides a particularly well-developed early example (figs. 4.46, 4.47, and 4.48).[34] As Tom Gunning has noted, "with Griffith . . . parallel editing . . . becomes a narrative structure, a way of shaping the relations of space and time that can be used in a variety of situations and with a range of effects" (1991, 204). Eventually, the employment of crosscutting would become the norm (though not until 1914, according to Kristin Thompson [1985b, 212]), signaling the widespread popularity of rescue scenes by the end of the transitional period. Though crosscutting need not be limited to rendering "last-minute rescues," most filmmakers mimicked Griffith's use of it to create suspense through rapid alternation.

An examination of one of Griffith's "typical" versions of the rescue scenario during his first year at Biograph will indicate how he used the device to shape a narrative's progression. *The Cord of Life* (1909) involves a simple (if improbable) revenge plot: an unpaid moneylender decides to penalize a family in arrears by hanging their baby out of the window in a

Figure 4.46. An early example of Griffith's vaunted crosscutting in *The Guerilla* (1908) . . .

Figure 4.47. . . . demonstrates how editing can alternate spaces . . .

Figure 4.48. . . . to generate suspense.

basket, with the cord suspending the basket secured only by a closed window. Once the moneylender informs the father of his baby's predicament, the man races back to his apartment to prevent his wife from opening the window and accidentally killing their child. Tom Gunning argues that by 1909 Griffith had refined his crosscutting technique so that suspense operated through both the attenuation of the potentially (and often inadvertently) menacing act—in this case the mother opening the window—and the steady progress of the rescuer. Gunning further notes that Meir Sternberg labels the principle of delay that generates suspense a "retardatory structure"; as such, it can occur either at the level of diegetic events or through structuring devices (such as crosscutting).[35] Griffith relies on both in *The Cord of Life*, as a shot-by-shot analysis of the rescue portion of the film reveals:

Shot twenty: (exterior/rock face)
The father descends and runs forward.

Shot twenty-one: (as shot fourteen, interior/apartment)
The mother returns and goes toward the window, but a neighbor
    interrupts; after helping her, the mother goes over toward the
    window again, at which point there is a cut to . . .

Shot twenty-two: (ext/path)
The father runs toward the camera.

Shot twenty-three: (ext/park)
The father rushes past two policemen, who attempt to stop him; he
    resists their efforts and continues.

Shot twenty-four: (as shot eight, ext/apartment entrance)
The father rushes in, followed by the police.

Shot twenty-five: (as shot twenty-one)
The mother gets food from the oven and discovers it is ruined; she turns
    toward the window, holding the food. [At this point, there is a
    splice, suggesting the insertion of a title explaining why she does
    not open the window.]

Shot twenty-six: (as shot twenty-five)
The mother is back away from the window, but then heads toward it
    again; at that moment, the father enters and stops her; the police
    come in and help the father go out via the top of the window so as
    not to disturb the cord.

At only seven shots, this is a relatively truncated version of the last-minute rescue, given the lengths to which such sequences would run in the near future. Even so, Griffith employs both editing (the interrupting cut at the end of shot twenty-one, which leaves the mother poised at the window) and various delays planted within the diegesis (needy neighbor, interfering police) as retardatory devices. As Griffith developed crosscutting within the rescue format, he would extend principles of delay so that the number of shots increased, with each line of action constantly interrupting the other. Unlike this example, where the actions of the mother interrupt the father's return only twice, later versions would alternate events much more systematically and would likely feature shots of the imperiled party as well, thereby creating a three-way parallel situation. Such procedures demonstrate how

Figure 4.49. Humorous juxtaposition through crosscutting in *How Brown Got Married* (1909): the groom's predicament . . .

Figure 4.50. . . . contrasted to the bride's preparations.

editing can break down space to encourage spectatorial involvement, the viewer left dangling much like the baby at the end of the suspended cord.[36]

By 1912, extended sequences of crosscutting for rescues exist not only in canonical examples like the Griffith Biographs *The Lonedale Operator* (1911) and *The Girl and Her Trust* (1912) but also in films from other companies, such as Bison's *An Apache Father's Vengeance* (1912). Each agent assumes a pertinent narrative function in preparation for the ensuing rescue: fort under siege/imperiled agent (A), marauding Natives/agent of destruction (B), an Apache daughter/agent of knowledge (C), and the cavalry/agents of rescue (D). Moreover, spatial distribution situates each function, with A and B in proximity from the beginning of the sequence and C separating itself in order to communicate to D. Resolution occurs when C and D arrive in time to prevent B from reaching A. An ever-decreasing spatial divide between relevant agents, framed by increasing temporal pressure, locks time and space into an effective inverted relationship that informs all last-minute rescues.

Griffith also employed crosscutting to construct parallel narratives of social criticism, such as *A Corner in Wheat* (1909) and its quasi-remake, *The Usurer* (1910). The editing in these films promotes irony by deliberately juxtaposing shots of rich characters' revels with shots depicting the suffering of those whom the wealthy have exploited to amass their fortunes. Other filmmakers found crosscutting could produce ironic humor, as in the juxtaposition of the bound groom being forcibly—and grotesquely—outfitted by hooded figures and the bride readying herself in appropriate finery surrounded by attendants in *How Brown Got Married* (Lubin 1909 [figs. 4.49 and 4.50]). But parallel editing could also emphasize the discrepancy between audience knowledge and character knowledge. In Vitagraph's 1912 *The Loyalty of Sylvia,* the cutting alternates shots of an ailing doctor imagining his ward in thrall to her fiancé with those of the woman returning her ring to the fiancé for his lack of moral fiber. Kalem's 1911 *The Mexican "Joan of Arc"* shifts between shots of a woman pleading with an officer for her male relatives' lives and those showing the execution of the same family members.

The Usurer also highlights how the technique of crosscutting can substitute a simultaneous action for a potentially offensive one, as when a cut to the usurer enjoying a meal occurs at the moment one of his debtors shoots himself. In effect, such a substitution works on two levels: it operates as a graceful means of displacement while also reinforcing the causal logic that binds the two actions. Epes Winthrop Sargent provided a less morbid example of how crosscutting could eliminate distasteful visual material:

> It may be that the scene is an actress's dressing-room. She enters in street clothes and prepares to assume her stage wardrobe. Nothing can happen to advance the plot until she has changed, yet it is impossible to keep the scene going. . . . Suppose that in the dressing-room scene you broke to the stage, and showed the hero waiting for the overture to be called. He and the villain pass and exchange glances. ("Technique of the Photoplay," *Moving Picture World* 9, no. 5, 12 August 1911, 363)

In the same article, Sargent notes that crosscutting can compress time, the inverse of its retardatory function:

> The burglar digs a hole in which to hide his booty. To complete the task will require a greater space of time than is allotted to the entire reel. . . . Your burglar starts to dig. Perhaps there is a posse looking for him. Flash ten feet of the posse and come back to the burglar. (*Moving Picture World* 9, no. 5, 12 August 1911, 363)

Again, Griffith demonstrated skill in developing this aspect of crosscutting, as evidenced by *Over Silent Paths* (1910). In this film, a "desert wanderer" accidentally kills a miner while the latter's daughter is off getting water. (Here, too, the editing reinforces cause and effect—were the daughter not absent, the father might have lived. However, it also serves to connect the characters of daughter and wanderer early on, a narrational ploy of some importance, as the next portion of the film will show the two meeting again, without knowledge of this past act which links them.) Griffith uses crosscutting to compress how long it takes the daughter to return to the campsite (and her father's dead body) by inserting a shot of the wanderer running off into the desert.

Kristin Thompson has noted that in the early teens, "short film lengths led to highly condensed presentations of action. At that point, summary titles, telegraphic pantomime gestures, and other devices had combined to pack a great deal of action into a short span. Now crosscutting could create a similar effect, but in a less obtrusive way" (1985b, 212). This suggests that crosscutting functioned alongside other techniques that performed parallel narrative functions. By the same token, devices like crosscutting could prove instrumental in shaping trends in narrative structure. For example, the repeated alternation crosscutting provides suited the parallel or two-pronged plot that became popular around 1912 in such films as *The Empty Water Keg* (Bison), *The Jealous Wife* (Powers), and *The Thief's Wife* (American).

As a distinct formal system emerged during the transitional era, the changes in story structure and narrational methods that filmmakers devised found a complement in increased control over cinematic time and space. Filmmakers had to abandon the spatiotemporal principles animating cinema's first decade in order to extend story duration, manipulate temporal order, and clarify spatial relations within the confines of the single-reel format. The strategies that emerged indicate that filmmakers had no set master plan, but they improvised within a context of externally imposed checks and balances. Accordingly, only some of the approaches they devised persisted beyond a few years: to depict proximate spatial relations, contiguity editing and matches on action gained favor over split sets; the flashback structure condensed extensive story duration more expediently than the ellipses conveyed via expositional title cards. Critical reaction in the trade press and audience acceptance helped signal to producers which options worked most effectively, while the constraints imposed by production practices and technology shaped emergent norms.

Near the end of the transitional period, increased reliance on editing accelerated trends in filmmakers' approaches to articulating spatiotemporal relations. Filmmakers carved exterior spaces into separate shots while reinforcing connections among those spaces; changed narrative structures incorporated temporal gaps or crosscutting elided them. The changes to configuring time and space would continue beyond 1913: crosscutting had not yet assumed dominance, while scene dissection and other features of classical editing practice had scarcely been initiated. But what of the other features of style, primarily *mise-en-scène* and cinematographic properties? How did their development affect filmmaking from 1907 to 1913? In tandem with the shifting narrational norms and spatiotemporal articulation already examined, this distinctive set of stylistic features collectively defines the formal achievement of the transitional period. It is to the analysis of transitional style that we now turn.

5

"The Modern Technique of the Art": The Style of Transitional Cinema

ON 3 DECEMBER 1913, an advertisement placed in the *New York Dramatic Mirror* trumpeted the achievements of D. W. Griffith, the hitherto anonymous "producer of all great Biograph successes." As a way of establishing Griffith's prominence within the industry, the ad listed an extensive selection of the films he had directed during his tenure at Biograph, while also laying claim to a number of "innovations," including: "The large or close-up figures, distant views . . . , the 'switchback,' sustained suspense, the 'fade-out,' and restraint in expression, raising motion picture acting to the higher plane which has won for it recognition as a genuine art" (*New York Dramatic Mirror* 70, no. 1824, 3 December 1913, 36). As an act of self-promotion, the advertisement rivals the best efforts of Carl Laemmle, but as a reliable historical document for assessment of Griffith's actual achievements, its status is suspect.[1] My primary interest lies less in the ad's accuracy in reflecting Griffith's contributions than in its function as an index of what the industry considered significant features of film style, circa 1913. Because the ad copy stresses that such "innovations [as Griffith introduced] . . . are now generally followed by the most advanced producers," it provides us with one way of gauging which devices the industry viewed as essential to "the modern technique of the art" (as the ad proclaims).

It seems fitting that promotion of a director should have motivated this early guidepost to distinctive stylistic practice: typically, film study has formulated its concepts of style in authorially defined terms. Even studies of national cinemas inevitably locate the central stylistic features of a film movement in selected auteurs (e.g., neorealism equals the style of Rossellini and De Sica; the French New Wave is defined by Truffaut and Godard). The appeal of an author-centered analysis of film style is not surprising, given a pervasive tendency since the Romantic-era to link distinctive artists with notable stylistic innovations. Within such a schema, certain styles emerge because of an artist's desire for self-expression via an expansive sense of the medium's potential. Accordingly, the *Mirror* ad stakes an argument for Griffith's greatness in terms of artistry manifesting itself through style. By promoting the notion of the expressive artist, the film industry attempted to gain cultural status and override its association with cheap entertainment. Prominent transitional period directors could even encourage stylistic trends (e.g., Griffith and crosscutting) while enhancing cinema's reputation.

However, these arguments have not convinced me to adopt an authorially driven approach in this chapter's analysis of transitional style. Given that my goal is to establish the norms and the range of stylistic options in a specific national cinema within a defined historical period, I believe the best evidence involves a broad survey of works rather than a focus on the efforts of a small number of auteurs.[2] Thus, I choose to apply the concept of group style to a study of this period. However, can an era defined as transitional possess a set of sufficiently stable norms to justify the group-style label? What factors help determine this emerging group style? To answer these questions, we must reintroduce the figure of the filmmaker, not as an exceptionally gifted auteur, but rather as a problem-solving agent functioning within a system of checks and balances. Filmmakers made active decisions throughout the transitional period, devising methods to address the challenges of crafting comprehensible narrative films in a context defined by industrial pressures, trade press expectations, and medium-defined constraints.[3]

Three factors seem particularly salient in shaping the group style of the transitional period: the role of genre, the perceived value of different stylistic features, and the differences in production practices and competencies of manufacturers (recall the *Mirror* ad's reference to the "most advanced producers"). To take the last first, companies might make films using roughly similar methods, but these would still allow for considerable differentiation of finished product. The preeminent production companies tended to develop distinctive stylistic trademarks to distinguish themselves from the competition: Vitagraph positioned the camera differently from other companies around 1909; Biograph adopted crosscutting in late 1908 and prided itself on an acclaimed performance style. Less-accomplished manufacturers might advise their filmmakers to emulate the more easily copied techniques proven by production leaders; conversely, a new company hoping to make its mark might encourage its directors to be adventurous. Trade press acceptance of specific features could spur production companies to follow the critics, especially if developing stylistic tendencies favored by the press enhanced a manufacturer's reputation.[4] (In the case of those aspects of style that critics resisted, such as quicker cutting rates, being an "advanced producer" might actually prove a liability.) Finally, generic conventions sometimes translated into stylistic norms. Comedies from 1907–8 often feature more extensive editing than dramas of the same period, even when produced by the same company; westerns shot in exteriors devise staging techniques for action sequences scarcely suited to intimate domestic dramas.

Each of these factors affected the stylistic choices made by filmmakers but did not alter the film industry's collective pursuit of identifiable goals, such as achieving verisimilitude, maintaining narrative legibility, and clarifying spatial and temporal relations. I have already addressed some of the strategies that filmmakers devised to solve problems of viewer comprehension and narrational fluidity, but other problems remain, related directly to the domain of style: What mode of performance would best convey the emotional shifts demanded by character-centered scenarios? How could changes to set décor meet standards of realism without becoming visually distracting? Would closer shot-scales direct audiences to notice important narrative developments without rendering the playing space unnaturally cramped? What would heighten dramatic tension the most, increased cutting or playing out a scene on a multiplanar set? The solutions devised by directors in response to such problems established the contours of the transitional period's group style. When one examines the individual devices employed within this style, one finds the same ones in place as in earlier years but now employed for different purposes. As Ben Brewster has explained, various figures, such as the point-of-view shot or the cut-in, shed their status as attractions and reappear more fully narrativized: "It is, however, typical that, although primitive cinema is characterized by the flourishing of specifically cinematic devices, such devices often constituting the promoted attractions, the dramas and comedy-dramas of the teens tend to subordinate such devices; indeed, in the 1905–10 period there is in these genres a kind of tabula rasa of devices, which are gradually reintroduced, but only insofar as their narrative motivation is so strong as to draw attention from their character as devices" (1991a, 11).[5] Promoting film's increased narrativity, then, became the signal objective of the group style developed during the transitional period.

In the sections which follow, I will treat this group style as a system, but for purposes of clarity I will separate out the contributing strands into three broad categories: *mise-en-scène,* cinematographic properties, and editing. In certain instances, the seeming arbitrariness of such categorical distinctions may cause the reader to question my choices: why, for example, should a cut-in be considered a function of editing rather than of cinematographic properties, when it typically involves a change of shot-scale? I will attempt to address such issues as they arise, but my primary aim is to analyze each stylistic device as an element contributing to an emergent system of style, a system sufficiently developed by 1913 that Griffith would lay claim to his part in establishing it.

Mise-en-scène: Creating a Believable World

> Now . . . the technical ne plus ultra of picture drama — of all drama, in fact — is to form an illusion, to make the audience believe that the thing really has happened as a matter of life, or is happening as such. Otherwise, why do producers go to such pains to have costumes and scenery and characters conform to the manners and customs of the time and environment of the play? It is to prevent jarring incongruities that may divert the mind of the audience from its interest in the thematic progress of the play. That is the vital reason for artistic perfection in the drama, a perfection that will create the illusion of actual life.
>
> GEORGE ROCKHILL CRAW, *Moving Picture World* (4 February 1911)

Mise-en-scène, which involves all those elements placed before the camera, afforded filmmakers a wide range of opportunities for guiding viewers' attention and enhancing their comprehension while also strengthening the medium's claim to verisimilitude. The term *mise-en-scène* comes from the theater, and the influence of principles derived from that art form, as well as from photography and painting, colored filmmakers' approaches to décor, composition, and performance.[6] Moreover, as any first-time viewer of early film will attest, changes to the *mise-en-scène* during the transitional period dramatically affected the actual appearance of films, as the transformations in sets, props, and acting styles all cultivated "the illusion of actual life" prized by Craw and other like-minded trade-press critics.

Décor

Rising rates of production, reformed means of distribution, and a growing exhibition sector signified that the film industry was increasingly gaining strength after 1907, and this vigor translated into expanded production values for filmmakers. Improved production circumstances created new approaches to set construction and decoration, especially a tendency to fashion sets with greater attention to detail than had been customary during the primitive period. However, stylistic innovations derived from more than just increased funds; there were other factors involved. First, more elaborate sets would indicate the seriousness of film as an enterprise and would impress spectators with the effort made to provide a visual spectacle; second, sets would achieve increased verisimilitude if filmmakers replaced painted backdrops with convincingly decorated volumetric playing spaces. One can find evidence of the first approach—the use of spectacle—in films before 1907, particularly in the work of Georges Méliès, whose visually lush fantasies depended for a good deal of their effect on fanciful and detailed sets. But as American filmmaking came to feature more "quality" productions (such as Kalem's *Ben Hur* [1907] and Vitagraph's *Francesca di Rimini* [1908]), producers made concerted attempts to foreground period costuming and well-appointed sets, spurred by the prestige accorded the *film d'art* productions from France.[7]

The trend toward increasingly lavish set and costume design in certain specialized productions encouraged the trade press to monitor the appropriateness of choices in décor, both in historical and contemporary films. Trade critics, particularly attentive to how films might achieve verisimilitude, discouraged any flagrant violation of period accuracy and advocated using research methods that assured meticulous reproduction. *Moving Picture World* applauded Kalem's approach to ensuring such accuracy in *The Cave Dwellers:* "It is too often the case nowadays that in Western pictures and also in historical pictures, inaccuracies and anachronisms occur. The Kalem Company have prevented this by preparing the costumes and scenes of the pictures from plates and drawings in the possession of the American Museum of Natural History" (6, no. 20, 21 May 1910, 830). Similarly, Vitagraph raided the arsenal of historical painting to produce impressively detailed settings for historical dramas based on the lives of Napoleon and Washington.[8]

Shoddy sets would immediately mark producers of films like Lubin's *A Broken Heart* as inferior: "Painted accessories no longer can replace the real article, now that keen competition on quality exists among the manufacturers" (*Moving Picture World* 6, no. 9, 27 February 1909, 238). The trade press expected manufacturers to provide more detailed sets as a sign of their commitment to creating a visually convincing (and hence involving) film world; as C. H. Claudy complained in *Photo Era*, "cheap scenery and poor acting carry no conviction in a moving picture." Claudy also tied proper lighting to the creation of a believable set:

> So to make a film real, and so artistic and beautiful, it is essential to get rid of all that is ugly and cheap and common and untrue in the necessary surroundings. If a drama must start with an interior, why in the name of all that is prodigal in the American showman who spares neither expense nor time, should he not have a real interior, and, if it is necessary, yank off the roof and put his light above—take out a wall and make them shine from the side, but have the background and what is recognizable, actual, familiarly genuine, not what is evidently "make believe" of so coarse a kind that none of us who see can forget it? (Quoted in *Nickelodeon* 1, no. 5, May 1909, 122)

The protests of commentators like Claudy no doubt encouraged many companies lacking sufficient resources to film their narratives entirely out-doors, thereby ensuring a depiction of reality. Such tactics could result in appreciative reviews, as *Moving Picture World*'s reaction to Kalem's *A Child of the Sea* attests: "Here are no painted cloths or made-up build-ings, but just the scenes of pretty actuality" (4, no. 23, 5 June 1909, 753).[9]

Nonetheless, interiors often proved essential, particularly for domes-tic dramas; the task facing filmmakers involved how to fashion studio sets so that they lacked any obvious intimations of "make-believe." In part, this meant dressing the sets so that they assumed the features of actual homes, offices, and the like by replacing painted-on renderings of props (such as vases, clocks, fireplaces, and so on) with three-dimensional ver-sions of the same objects. As *Nickelodeon* advised, "If we are to elevate the pictures, let's begin by ridding them of their incongruous and impos-sible . . . properties" (3, no. 4, 15 February 1910, 95). But to place these real objects in sets lacking volume and depth would only point up a dis-crepancy in verisimilitude. Filmmakers tackled this problem in different ways: first, they added texture to sets by adding three-dimensional deco-rative features, such as curtains, paneling, and doors; second, they re-jected a purely frontal perspective when filming or constructing sets, by having one corner angled obliquely within the set; third, especially near the end of the period, they employed sets with increased depth, often of-fering a glimpse of a room behind the main interior.[10] These strategies, coupled with greater attention to details of set decoration, so that rooms possessed something approximating a "lived-in look," attained the desired degree of verisimilitude advocated by the trade press.[11]

Not surprisingly, producers developed realism in décor with varying degrees of speed and consistency.[12] Vitagraph's sets attained a high degree of verisimilitude by 1910 in such films as *Brother Man* (fig. 5.1), *The Love of Chrysanthemum* (fig. 5.2), *Ransomed, or a Prisoner of War,* and *Renunciation.* Even so, Vitagraph produced other films the same year in which the décor harkened back to earlier approaches: in *A Life for a Life,* the set for a hospital ward relies on painted-in perspective (fig. 5.3), while in *Victims of Fate,* action which supposedly takes place outdoors occurs within constructed sets (fig. 5.4). In fact, in 1910, one can still note sets within a single film demonstrating a range of verisimilitude, as is the case in Edison's *Pardners* and Thanhouser's *Young Lord Stanley.*

The substitution of sets for exterior shots in *Victims of Fate* indicates that filmmakers still had reasons to avoid shooting outdoors even when a loss of realism resulted. However, by 1910, the Eastern-based companies routinely began traveling to distant locales. The landscapes of California, followed by those of the United Kingdom, Canada, and Cuba, among others, functioned as exotica but also as marks of authenticity. Once location shooting emerged as an accepted practice and marketable production value, employing unrealistic sets became even more problematic, especially when meant to represent the outdoors. The principal drawback derived from the discrepancy between the appearance of exteriors and interiors. If a filmmaker chose to use both sets and location shooting in combination, the apparent authenticity of the latter would expose the counterfeit nature of the former. Any open window or door within a set would necessarily feature a portion of a fabricated landscape, subsequently shown in its actual form via outdoor shots; in these areas, the evident discrepancies would cancel any effect of realism. As mentioned already, filmmakers could refrain from filming interior scenes altogether, and numerous companies (such as Selig, Essanay, and Bison) had a penchant for employing extensive exterior shooting in action-oriented genres such as the western.[13] A related strategy involved constructing sets outdoors, so that a window or door literally did open onto the surrounding countryside. (Such an approach would eventually lend itself to certain pictorial effects, such as the open-door shot, which I will discuss later in this chapter.) Sometimes, however, the elements visibly intruded, rendering these ostensibly indoor sets more rustic than intended: wind whistling through the placid parlor of a well-to-do family posed a further challenge to sustaining believability.

The discrepancies caused by matching interiors to exteriors remain in evidence throughout 1910. Essanay's *Pals of the Range* features a cabin

Figure 5.1. A verisimilar set from Vitagraph in *Brother Man* (1910).

Figure 5.2. Detailed décor marks a set in *The Love of Chrysanthemum* (1910).

Figure 5.3. Painted-in perspective employed for a hospital set in *A Life for a Life* (1910).

Figure 5.4. Constructed sets stand in for exteriors in *Victims of Fate* (1910).

set with a painted back wall and door, even though it opens directly onto the actual landscape. In Bison's *A Cowboy for Love,* the open doorway of a kitchen interior provides the view of a drawn facsimile of an exterior, but that drawing in no way matches the topography of the subsequent exterior shot. In addition, Powers's *The Newspaper Error* uses an extensively detailed painted backdrop for a scene purportedly set in Mexico (which *Moving Picture World* praised as "eminently satisfactory" [6, no. 18, 7 May 1910, 738]), but the film still relies on painted-on props for simple cabin interiors (fig. 5.5).

Though one can find such inconsistencies after 1910 as well, a trend toward increased verisimilitude becomes more apparent from this point onward.[14] And while the trade press obviously supported aggregating details to create a believable diegetic world, they imposed limits on how far filmmakers should go to attain believability. As early as 1909, *Moving Picture World* conceded that one need only pursue realism to the extent necessary to preserve the *illusion* of reality: "Apparent, if not real accuracy, is all that we ask for" (5, no. 2, 10 July 1909, 57).[15] Details should never call attention to themselves as details, for that would detract from the overall power of illusionism created to sustain the dramatic effect of the narrative.[16] Moreover, details in settings should ideally function as a unified system of sub-

Figure 5.5. Painted-on props appear in a cabin set from *The Newspaper Error* (1910).

ordinated elements. When they did not, spectatorial distraction might result, as a review of Thanhouser's *Pocahontas* notes: "[One] scene seemed to lack the element of grandeur, which in many cases, is obtained by simplicity of line rather than ornate detail. In this scene, the background is cut up with a number of queer shaped windows that have a tendency to draw the eye to them and away from the actors. . . . The windows being odd in shape, start one speculating unconsciously on their form" (*Moving Picture World* 7, no. 15, 8 October 1910, 818). In such reviews, trade press critics defined the terms of appropriate verisimilitude: consistency in settings and props and avoidance of excesses that might dislodge the primacy of character and narrative action.

By 1911, trade press expectations meant companies that could afford to should aspire to the level attained by films like Edison's *The Black-Bordered Letter*, cited by *Nickelodeon* for "settings [which] are commendable for their richness and depth" (5, no. 5, 4 February 1911, 139).[17] Depth emerged as a key factor in conveying a sense of believable space within interior sets, as a negative assessment of IMP's version of *The Scarlet Letter* makes clear: "The scene of the public street showing the stocks seemed rather flat and shallow. A street scene, above all others, should convey the idea of depth or distance, which this scene did not. It is very obviously a painted drop upon which shadows fall, and it was also very easy to see the line of connection it made with the stage" (*Moving Picture World* 8, no. 16, 22 April 1911, 882).

Though altering the appearance of the set could promote a sense of depth, filmmakers also experimented by arranging items within those sets, particularly actors, to maximize depth. Filmmakers attempted to enhance whatever depth the set might possess by marking off the outer limits of the

Figure 5.6. Enhancing a set's depth in *A Cure for Pokeritis* (1912).

set with furniture or objects in the foreground, sometimes even extending beyond the camera's view; and actors were encouraged to move from foreground to background as well. (See Vitagraph's *A Cure for Pokeritis* [1912] for a representative example; fig. 5.6.) Just as infusing settings with detail might result in increased verisimilitude, so too would emphasizing depth. Writing in *Moving Picture World*, George Rockhill Craw added further incentive by claiming "the better the illusion, the better the box-office receipts." For that reason, he argued for increased depth whenever possible: "Producers should try to relieve the cramped appearance of indoor scenes. Instead of the single room, wherever it is comfortable with the requirements of the play, vistas should be shown beyond, either through doors or windows at the rear, opening into other rooms or upon out-of-door prospects" ("The Technique of the Picture-Play—III," 8, no. 5, 4 February 1911, 229).

One can note greater depth in the films of most companies by 1912, attributable not only to the advantage taken of exteriors' deep spaces, but also to the extension of the space depicted within interiors. Most strikingly, near the end of the period various films feature sets deepened by making an extra room visible in the background. The presence of this "space behind" facilitated the staging of action on more than one plane.[18] Promoting depth became one motivation among many guiding the staging and compositional strategies that filmmakers developed during this period.

Staging and Composition

Trade press critics had their own notion of what constituted proper staging, attributable in part to their understanding of how the camera's frame imposed spatial limits on the depicted action.[19] Critics advised against "crowded groupings" for numerous reasons: first, if a massing of characters seemed unnaturally pressed together, it would expose the limits of the shooting conditions and destroy the illusionism that cinema was meant to sustain; second, such unnatural staging would violate the standards of composition derived primarily from photography, which stressed balance and order;[20] and third, overly compressed staging might obscure the central narrative action and create problems of comprehension for the viewer.

The trade press strongly advocated "natural groupings" (much as they would also push for a natural acting style), implicitly—and sometimes explicitly—rejecting arrangements of characters before the camera that borrowed from theatrical methods:

> We were immensely pleased with the natural groupings of the characters around the family table and the very natural way in which they comported themselves. (*Moving Picture World* 5, no. 23, 4 December 1909, 798)

> The tendency to crowding is not so apparent here as it is in some instances, and yet there is an impression of number sufficiently to make the scene look real. (*Moving Picture World* 8, no. 18, 6 May 1911, 1021)[21]

> The action is restrained and free from that bane of many a picture, theatrical grouping and posture-taking. (*Moving Picture World* 8, no. 19, 13 May 1911, 1081)

Critiques of poor staging practices derived from knowledge concerning the dimensions of the playing area before the camera, an area limited by the distance of the camera from the filmed action, the configuration of the depicted screen space, and the properties of the lens employed.

To understand why critics believed that theatrically influenced modes of staging might not have worked, one need only compare how film renders space versus its existence on the dramatic stage. As Ben Brewster and Lea Jacobs have pointed out, stage space operates as a trapezium, with the back of the space narrower, while film playing space widens at the back, thereby funneling visual information which appears closer to the front.[22] Accordingly, filmed characters placed within the nearer reaches of the provided performing space could appear to be squeezed together by virtue of the inverted relationship between stage and film space. Eustace Hale Ball summarized the problems this posed for filmmakers: "The director is compelled to rehearse, again and again, the movements of the actors in order to keep them within the field of vision, and at the same time to utilize each movement without showing unnatural closeness" (1913, 19).

Establishing the actual parameters of the playing space helps render the limitations imposed more concrete. Epes Winthrop Sargent provided a detailed account of relevant dimensions in 1911:

> The photographic stage differs from the actual setting in that the
> important action is planned to occur at a distance of from ten to twenty
> feet from the camera according to the lenses used. The stage is six or
> eight feet wide by six deep, and though the horizon may form the actual
> limitation of the setting or be laid within an interior ten feet by twenty,
> the photographic stage remains the same. ("Technique of the Photoplay,"
> *Moving Picture World* 9, no. 2, 22 July 1911, 108)[23]

Sargent found it advisable to "bring the active characters to the fore," and
filmmakers made concerted efforts to have actors work the depth of the
film stage rather than its width. Even so, bringing characters "to the fore"
involved the risk of crowding. The following review aptly demonstrates
how attempts at narrative clarity could undermine the maintenance of narrative believability: "Another fault lies in the narrowness and circum-
scription of the pictures; this was done intentionally, no doubt, to bring
the actors nearer to the audience, but it has the negative feature of ne-
cessitating such a close grouping of the eavesdroppers that the effect is
absolutely lacking in plausibility" (*Nickelodeon* 4, no. 10, 15 November
1910, 280).

Though the trade press developed an aversion to a closer shot scale for
other reasons as well, the strain "closer views" placed on uncramped
groupings of large numbers of characters remained a central concern. The
majority of quality productions (such as literary adaptations and historical
dramas) probably retained longer shot scales and reduced cutting rates on
similar grounds: such stylistic decisions aided in preserving a maximal visible width for a substantial duration which, in turn, facilitated the legible
mounting of group arrangements.[24] (Thanhouser's 1910 adaptation of *The
Winter's Tale* offers one such example of staging in a quality production
[fig. 5.7].) Commentators apparently set aside the negative connotation of
theatricality often associated with certain staging strategies when considering these quality productions, as in *Moving Picture World*'s assessment
of the Vitagraph version of *A Midsummer Night's Dream:* "Something of the
atmosphere of the play as we saw it acted on the regular stage some years
ago was imparted to this beautiful film, a marvel of decorative richness,
with well drilled crowds of actors and actresses . . . we seemed to be looking upon [scenes] from the very play itself as we remembered it when seen
on the ordinary stage" (6, no. 1, 8 January 1910, 10–11).

Indeed, William Uricchio and Roberta Pearson have suggested that
"a process of iconographic standardization" occurred in certain Vitagraph

quality films, which involved the
emulation of previously established
theatrical staging techniques and
popularized settings. This ensured
the proper cultural connotations for
the company's adaptations of material with a developed history of
theatrical presentation (1993, 100).
Similarly, many high-end productions, or those with cultural preten-
sions, would deliberately copy the
compositional features of a famous

Figure 5.7. Staging in a quality production: a group arrangement in *The Winter's
Tale* (1910).

source painting or the general strategies of particular artists: Uricchio and
Pearson (1993) have demonstrated by way of illustrative example how respected sources like David, Gérôme, and Vernet served as inspiration for
the staging and composition of individual scenes in various Vitagraph
quality films; in scrupulous detail, Herbert Reynolds has examined
Kalem's *From the Manger to the Cross* (1912) and determined that over 75
percent of the scenes are patterned directly on images from James Tissot's
illustrations for his turn-of-the-century picture Bible; critics widely acknowledged Griffith's citation of Millet's *The Sowers* for the opening of *A
Corner in Wheat* (Biograph, 1909) upon the film's initial release.[25]

Yet, such studied borrowing from visual sources within the other arts
proved relatively uncommon during the period, even as absorption and
modification of their general staging and compositional practices occurred. Insofar as such absorption promoted depth, it also contributed to
the dynamization of screen space, especially before intrascene cutting became the preferred means of achieving the same end. Accordingly, in extended scenes of dramatic action unbroken by cuts, one sees evidence of
filmmakers working through problems of how to arrange actors' movements to punctuate important plot points and maintain legibility.

Orchestrating how actors moved throughout a scene became more
complicated as a greater number of performers appeared in a scene at
once. Directors need not employ a principle of depth when arranging actors in such scenes. In *His Lost Love* (Biograph 1909), Griffith relies primarily on a single plane of playing space to move as many as four actors
through a series of actions designed to chart the transfer of a woman's affections from one brother to another. A table in the middle of the set helps
to divide the laterally arranged space while providing a crucial prop as

Mary telegraphs her decision to drop Luke in favor of James. Griffith prepares for the staging of Mary's change of heart, conveyed primarily in two successive shots, with an introductory shot employing the same set as the subsequent developments. In this first shot, Mary and Luke initially occupy opposite sides of the frame, with Mary's father all but obscured while sitting behind her. When Mary and Luke announce their betrothal, the father emerges from his chair, giving them his blessing. Griffith selectively employs this method of bringing forward momentarily significant characters from a position behind foreground material that has virtually obscured them: most of the pertinent staging in *His Lost Love* will involve the centrally located table instead.[26]

For the arrival of James, Griffith has Luke come around from behind the table and bring Mary over to meet the newly returning brother, positioning himself in the middle. Called out by Mary's father, Luke leaves the two behind, and James eventually sits against the table, with Mary about to join him before Luke comes back to the room. This staging recalls the earlier intimate pairing of Mary and Luke, suggesting that James could well supplant Luke as Mary's love. The shot ends with Luke repositioning himself beside Mary, though they remain standing, and she discreetly brushes his kiss from her lips.

In the next shot, James comes upon Mary in the same room and they eventually embrace, only to be discovered by Luke, who slowly moves into the space left by their now separated bodies and crumples onto the same table he had sat upon with such casual happiness in the film's first shot. Realizing the couple's love for each other, Luke relinquishes his claim to Mary, remaining resolutely behind the table while he acts out his decision via a number of coded arm gestures and then leaves. The father, who has also reentered the room, stands at the center of the set between Mary and James before moving off to his initial position in shot one and finally exiting (neatly reversing the pattern of his actions from the first shot). The shot ends with Mary and James turning back toward each other; each then each lays a hand on the table before they clasp hands and ultimately embrace. Griffith's practice of rhyming compositions and using furniture to separate the actors at key moments helps communicate the narrative information economically while preventing any "crowded groupings."

Other directors preferred deeper staging than that used by Griffith, especially those directors not predisposed to analytical editing.[27] Deep-staging techniques could vary the visual presentation of information and separate out spheres of relevant narrative material. As late as 1911, Epes

Winthrop Sargent would counsel prospective screenwriters on how to provide "stage" directions for such situations as simultaneous action, thereby assuming that crosscutting would not be employed automatically:

> Because of the narrowness of the stage it is not always easy to handle the action when two sets of characters occupy the photographic stage alternately, but it can be done. There are exceptions to this as to all other rules, but keep your active characters down front as much as possible. By active characters is understood those who are advancing the story at the moment. ("Technique of the Photoplay," *Moving Picture World* 9, no. 2, 22 July 1911, 108)

Filmmakers had to balance the demands of both verisimilitude and narrative clarity. For that reason, deep staging usually maintained a principle of centering, or alternatively, emphasizing (for spectatorial attention) the central causal agent at the required moment.[28] Poor staging was not only aesthetically improper but also inadvisable for purposes of narrative comprehension. Moreover, too much narrative information presented at once could create spectatorial overload. Deep staging remained permissible as long as it did not result in an overly busy or potentially confusing presentation of information, as pointed out in a review of an Edison comedy, *Uncle's Birthday Gift:*

> The one telling scene—the climax, where the uncle at last opens up the rubber plant—loses force because the interest is divided between the uncle, the messenger boy behind the screen, and the two distracted women, anyone of whom may "do" something, and consequently must be watched. It is a three-ring circus effect, where in trying to watch all rings at once, one really sees none of them. (*Nickelodeon* 5, no. 4, 28 January 1911, 110)

For this reason, when employing deep staging, filmmakers tended to exercise care in clarifying which actions possessed the greatest causal salience when characters appeared in both foreground and background. Filmmakers could maintain a well-established center of interest by using different types of framing devices, usually intradiegetic and therefore fully naturalized, to direct viewers to pertinent background action. Thus, in Vitagraph's *Love Hath Wrought a Miracle* (1912), garden foliage perfectly frames the female characters centered in the shot's background; by turning toward them, the viewing character in the foreground also guides our

Figure 5.8. Framing the background action renders it more noticeable in *On the
War Path* (1911).

Figure 5.9. A deep set permits multiplanar action in *The Girl in the Arm-Chair*
(1912).

attention deeper into the frame (fig. 3.20, p. 78). In Kalem's *On the War
Path* (1911), the only opening in a structure occupying the mid-ground of
the shot provides a view of secondary action in the background, which
helps the viewer focus on it much more easily (fig. 5.8). And Solax's *The
Girl in the Arm-Chair* (1912), which features a particularly deep set, stages
action on three different planes while still drawing the eye inward toward
the presence of the female character in the far background (fig. 5.9). Of
these three examples, only the Vitagraph film supplements the deep staging with a subsequent closer framing, and even in that instance, the employment of a closer shot scale occurs a number of shots after the composition's original appearance.

In single-shot compositions, deeper spaces allowed filmmakers to
move characters from background to foreground as an alternative (or supplement) to the kind of lateral staging found in films such as *His Lost
Love*.[29] In the final shot of Vitagraph's *An Official Appointment* (1912), the
seated (and initially sleeping) figure of the colonel anchors the composition, his chair positioned at the left of the frame's foreground. Other characters enter from the space behind the chair, two moving to a spot beside
it, one remaining at the doorway. When the characters beside the colonel
determine that he has died, the sole figure in the background moves in
from the doorway, until she comes to rest behind one of the shocked foreground figures. This clears the area behind the chair, allowing the viewer
to refocus attention on the colonel in the foreground. When reaction to his
death takes precedence, the other two figures turn away to allow emphasis to shift to the grieving party's response. In this way, developments in
staging not only guide viewers' attention, but also help showcase parallel
changes to performance style.

Performance

Scholars have generally conceded that performance style underwent a substantial transformation during the transitional period. Virtually all actors in the first years of the period relied on a codified system of distinct and presumably easily identified gestures. Because narrational norms (the absence of intertitles, long shot scale) imposed limits on spectatorial comprehension, actors responded by reducing their performances to a set series of gestures and poses designed to signify discrete emotional states. By 1913, on the other hand, the majority of actors (except, perhaps, in the more physical versions of comedy, such as slapstick) have abandoned the previous performance style for one based on accretion of detail, derived from smaller-scale gestures, a greater reliance on facial reactions, and the incorporation of various props. Following the lead of Roberta Pearson, who has traced the shift from the one performance style to the other in Griffith's Biograph films, I will label the earlier form "histrionic" and the latter "verisimilar."

Though she restricts herself almost entirely to one company's output, Pearson's book-length study of early film acting remains the most thorough account available. She traces both performance styles to their genesis within the theater: the histrionic approach derives from such coded systems of theatrical performance as the Delsarte method, while the verisimilar is indebted to the late-nineteenth-century trend toward realism on the dramatic stage (1992, 18–37).[30] More recently, Ben Brewster and Lea Jacobs have criticized aspects of Pearson's approach, particularly her notion that realism precludes "an emphasis on attitudes and posing" (1997, 101). Brewster and Jacobs dispute the validity of categories based on purported distinctions in theatrical practice, but they agree that the transitional period witnesses a marked change in performance style. I see no reason to abandon the descriptively useful terms Pearson has devised, but I concede that the noticeable "theatricality" of early performances often resulted from inexpert application of stage-honed technique to film, exacerbated by the constraints filmmaking imposed on the actor's power to communicate.[31]

We can attribute the slow and gradual transformation in acting style to both the uneven adoption of techniques that could alter performances and the uncertainty of filmmakers, trained in the histrionic mode, as to whether audiences would understand the verisimilar approach. The position of the trade press did not hasten change either: most critics did advocate the employment of a performance style that stressed "naturalism"

Figure 5.10. A mixture of performance styles in *Man's Calling* (1912).

as early as 1909 (which is to say, some time before even the most "advanced" American companies used the verisimilar approach with any consistency); yet these critics maintained an equally entrenched resistance to adopting a closer shot scale. They upheld their opposition even though moving the camera closer would have helped audiences to notice easily overlooked aspects of the verisimilar performance style (e.g., an eye movement or hand gesture). Once manufacturers started employing closer shot scale, a shift to the verisimilar style typically followed.[32] At a company like Vitagraph, where filmmakers began moving the camera in with some regularity in 1909, one sees a concomitant adoption of the verisimilar mode. Other companies (such as Rex) that retained long-shot framings until a relatively late stage continued to depend upon the histrionic (as in *Leaves in the Storm,* 1912 [fig. 3.9, p. 72]). Even so, as Pearson points out, adoption of the verisimilar style within a single studio could prove halting and inconsistent: one can see intimations of the verisimilar in Biograph films as early as 1908, while vestiges of the histrionic linger in 1912 (1992, 50–51).

Similarly, a mixture of performance styles often occurs within a single film, especially in the period's middle years, but still apparent as late as 1913. In *Man's Calling* (American 1912), J. Warren Kerrigan, the lead actor, alternates between doleful glances characteristic of the verisimilar style and a recurrent declamatory rubbing of the chest which harkens back to histrionic methods (fig. 5.10). As Pearson has also indicated, even the individual performance styles themselves allow for a fair degree of latitude: she differentiates between the more extreme or unchecked version of the histrionic method, wherein "gestures are quickly performed, heavily stressed, and fully extended," and the checked version, with "slower, less stressed, and less extended gestures" (1992, 27). By the same token, the verisimilar could gravitate toward a degree of restraint in performance which virtually negated the signifiers of "performing" altogether, as when the actors turned their backs to the camera or temporarily withdrew from the camera's view into an off-screen region.

Various factors could lead to the mixture of performance styles within individual films. Generic norms helped shape the styles employed. For ex-

ample, in Vitagraph's *A Friendly Marriage* (1911), the histrionically inflected mugging of the supporting actor playing the butler contrasts with
the lead performances enacted in the verisimilar style.[33] Expectations
concerning how "ethnics" should behave led actors to stick with the histrionic when cast as Native Americans, Italians, or Mexicans (such as the
actress in Powers's *The Newspaper Error* [1910] [fig. 5.5, p. 133]) while at
the same time, actors portraying white Americans employed the verisimilar. Even in instances where the histrionic approach was allowed, excesses could draw fire, as C. H. Claudy's comments in "Too Much Acting"
prove: "No other kind of Indians that the popular mind conceives, ever
gesticulated so violently, so rapidly, so much. They lose all dignity, all realism, when they spend most of their time with their arms in the air!"
(*Moving Picture World* 8, no. 6, 11 February 1911, 288). One can find justification for Claudy's complaints in a film like Selig's *The Totem Mark*
(1911): the actors who play the Natives represent ethnicity by repeatedly
raising their arms over their heads, thereby distilling the signifying powers of the histrionic code to the point of *reductio ad absurdum.*

The trade press's growing acceptance of the verisimilar style helps
confirm the aesthetic values which come to predominate during this period. In the first years of the transitional era, writers acknowledged that
action drove motion-picture plots more so than detailed characterization;
moreover, the single-reel length required actors to perform at quicker tem-
pos.[34] An interview with a stage director who switched to motion pictures
indicates the prevailing industry practice circa 1909:

> "Do you find this work much different than staging a regular piece?" was
> asked.
> "I should say I do," he replied. "I found I had to unlearn a great many
> things when I started in this work, and so do all the actors who take part in
> it. In the first place, to get an effect with moving pictures there has to be
> plenty of action. With the average actor, repose is one of the strongest
> methods of obtaining an effect, but it is exactly the opposite here. The
> gestures have to be quick, and the expression of the features has to change
> rapidly to convey the idea we wish to." (W. W. Winters, "Moving Pictures
> in the Making," *Nickelodeon* 1, no. 1, January 1909, 25)

While trade press critics conceded the necessity for action, they increasingly expressed a desire for the "natural" depictions of behavior favored
by the verisimilar style.[35] In a 1909 article titled "Motion ad Nauseam,"

a *Nickelodeon* critic suggests that action and excessive movement equated with audience acceptance, while repose and emulation of "real life" were more akin to art: "There is enough motion in any acted moving picture play to satisfy the popular demand for activity without requiring unnatural and ridiculous movement. If the action of the story allows its characters any rest whatever, for art's sake, let them sit still occasionally" (*Nickelodeon* 2, no. 2, August 1909, 38). The *Nickelodeon* writer may not have intended a wholesale rejection of the histrionic mode when he advocated an artistic performance style (at one point in the same article he speaks approvingly of "every motion [having] its meaning"). In general, though, as the trade press stepped up its promotion of acting as a reflection of real life, the precepts of the histrionic style fell into increasing disfavor.[36]

A clear indication of why the trade press began to find the histrionic approach untenable emerges in a *Nickelodeon* review of Edison's *Frankenstein,* which complains of an actor using "practically only four gestures, repeating them with very little variation" (3, no. 7, 1 April 1910, 177). The codified nature of the histrionic mode undermined its claims to believability; repetitive and formulaic gestures revealed themselves as part of a preexistent system rather than casually discovered tics of unique behavior. The vaunted naturalness of the verisimilar approach appealed to a trade press pushing to have the industry eliminate all vestiges of artificiality. In earlier films, performers exploited an awareness of the camera, expressing self-consciousness through direct address of the camera (and, by extension, of the spectator); however, these intimations of anti-illusionism now struck critics as tokens of amateurishness.[37] The diegetic world of the film should insist on its self-sufficiency, reinforcing believability by dispelling all marks of fictionality and pulling the viewer along in the process. The evolving rules of performance articulated within the trade press provided ample motivation for this shift.

"The best moving picture acting is that which is the most natural" declared *Nickelodeon* in 1910 (3, no. 9, 1 May 1910, 236), and reviews consistently singled out the productions of Biograph and Vitagraph for acting prized as "subtle," "restrained," and "discriminatingly subdued."[38] The verisimilar style of acting benefited from connotations of culture and refinement assigned to it by the trade press.[39] By mid-1909, advocates of the verisimilar approach denigrated the stylized motions which defined the histrionic method:

The day of extravagant gesturing has passed—that of quiet, tense action and meaning conveyed by facial expression has come. ("The March of Progress," quoted from *Edison Kinetogram, Moving Picture World* 5, no. 9, 9 August 1909, 276)

The acting is so natural that it appears on screen as though the operator had made his exposures unknown to the group who were chiefly interested. (*Moving Picture World* 5, no. 12, 18 September 1909, 377)

The acting seem[s] like the work of real people, rather than the pictorial reproduction of what actors have performed. (*Moving Picture World* 6, no. 7, 19 February 1910, 258)

Indeed, the player who can only express his emotions by contortions of the face is no real picture player at all, and he should get out of the profession. ("Spectator's Comments," *New York Dramatic Mirror* 48, no. 1638, 14 May 1910, 18)

There is no need to introduce motions as if explaining the cause of their next move. If the plot is intelligent it can be understood, and, if so be that it cannot be readily grasped, let it create a demand for the use of a little verbal explanation rather than spoil a good piece and good acting by dumb motion. ("The Art of Acting before the Camera," *Moving Picture World* 7, no. 8, 20 August 1910, 405)

As the last-cited article makes clear, by 1910 commentators understood praiseworthy acting in direct opposition to "dumb motion." Restraint in performance involved limiting bodily activity to a minimum, and at least some of the studios actively pursued such an approach at this time, as Selig's "Pointers on Picture Acting" from 1910 indicates: "Do not use unnecessary gestures. Repose in your acting is of more value. A gesture well directed can convey a great deal, while too many may detract from the realism of your work."[40] Many reviews made a point of stressing the appropriateness of the less physically oriented verisimilar mode for conveying a character's mental states, as when *Moving Picture World* praised a director for being "an ardent exponent of the subtle and suggestive style of acting, as opposed to the use of shoulders, arms, legs, etc. to express what is in the mind" (7, no. 22, 26 November 1910, 1240). Moreover, the more nuanced method of the verisimilar approach could create the illusion of an actor unaware of the camera, enabling the viewer to feel as if she were coming across a life lived rather than being confronted with a performance crafted for effect.[41]

Figure 5.11. Introducing the stars of *'Twixt Love and Ambition* (1912).

While the trade press valorized a naturalist aesthetic within performance style, manufacturers began to concede the benefits of identifying the actors who performed in films. Some companies actively began to promote their stars through personal appearances, trade press profiles, and the listing of their names in advertisements and within the films themselves. One could argue that such measures might have dispelled the illusion of reality the verisimilar style worked to establish.[42] Instead, it appears that the industry used the disjunction to its advantage, as production companies accentuated the discrepancy between the image of the actor as trained performer and the quality of naturalness that the verisimilar style cultivated. *Moving Picture World* noted that "at the close of [*The Last Straw*] the two chief characters 'appear before the curtain' in real life fashion, to receive the applause of the audience" (7, no. 22, 26 November 1910, 1223) and confirmed in response to a letter of 1911 that Edison, Vitagraph, and Selig, among others, introduced actors by such a method at "the beginning of important reels" (9, no. 3, 29 July 1911, 236).[43] (The introduction of Edwin August and Ormi Hawley in *'Twixt Love and Ambition* from 1912 verifies Lubin engaged in this practice as well [fig. 5.11].) Though doubtless an extension of theatrical practice and yet another way of associating cinema with high-class drama, this device also underlines the skill involved in acting as though one is not acting. Rather than undercutting the illusionism involved in the verisimilar approach, these introductory shots served notice that manufacturers were ushering in a new era of performance. Inviting applause from viewers, such shots asserted that the seemingly effortless emulations of reality provided by the industry's emerging stars warranted the same approval that celebrated dramatic performers received.

One can find an even more canny and intriguing examination of the connotations of "performance" in several Vitagraph films that rather self-consciously construct narratives around the art of acting. Vitagraph was not alone in making films with plotlines that revolve around actors, nor was it the only company to foreground the craft of acting at this time. As Kristin Thompson has pointed out, "there may have been a small genre of character-sketch films, exemplified by . . . some of Griffith's early teens work," though the diegesis of such films need not involve professional actors (1985b, 190). Unlike similar efforts, however, the Vitagraph films of this type establish acting itself as a subject for examination *through the performance of the lead actress,* who usually plays the part of a performer herself.

Among the various films that explore the theme of performance in this manner, one can point to *Proving His Love* (1911) and *The Clown and His Best Performance* (1911), although the earlier *Renunciation,* from 1910, stands as the most fully elaborated. The film's plot revolves around Violet Leslie, an aspiring actress, and begins with her unsuccessful audition for playwright Robert Delaney. Later, when Violet's fiancé announces their engagement to his father, Delaney is present and identifies the photograph of Violet, informing the young man's father of her profession. Outraged at the inappropriateness of his son's choice, the father approaches Violet and persuades her to pretend that she is drunk when in the presence of his son, which will convince the young man to terminate the engagement. She succeeds in the ruse, and as recompense (or perhaps in recognition of her acting talent in this situation) Delaney offers her a part in his play. When Delaney is devising the offer, the fiancé overhears, and follows the playwright and his father to Violet's apartment. Distraught over the dissolution of her engagement and her role in it, Violet refuses both Delaney's offer and the entreaties of her fiancé, but finally relents when the father retracts his initial assessment of her character.

Centered on the acting of Florence Turner (who employs a verisimilar style to play Violet), *Renunciation* functions as a commentary on the levels and effects of performance. In her audition scene, Florence as Violet demonstrates that there is a discernible difference between (stage) acting and normal behavior; by extension, since Turner's acting of normal behavior occurs within a screen performance, the audition scene also confirms the differences between screen acting and stage performance. Later, Violet must function as an actress again in order to convince her fiancé of her unworthiness, though in this instance, the believability of her performance will confirm both her devotion to him and her ability as an actress. The film demonstrates implicitly that conveying the subtleties of these distinctions depends entirely upon the abilities of Florence Turner as an actress to portray the various "performances" of Violet Leslie. And for our purposes, without recourse to the methods of the verisimilar style, a narrative which hinges on such distinctions would be inconceivable.

The performance-centered Vitagraph films, much like their counter-parts at Biograph, show how indispensable the verisimilar mode proved in establishing more involved characterizations. Nonetheless, they may not provide the most accurate indication of representative verisimilar acting because of their self-conscious foregrounding of the idea of performance. Quite likely, companies designed films like these to showcase exceptional performances, such as one also finds in Biograph's 1912 *The Painted Lady* or its *The House of Darkness* and *The Mothering Heart,* both from 1913.[44] As a way of briefly summarizing some facets of typical verisimilar technique, I will refer to an apparently far more ordinary Vitagraph film, *Mr. Bolter's Infatuation.* A mild comedy from 1912, *Mr. Bolter's Infatuation* still indi-cates the care exercised in the crafting of performances, even by bit play-ers. Nuance enters into fairly minor moments: the showgirl's offhandedly impatient request for a pen to write a note helps establish characterization in a naturalized fashion; the delivery boy's rapport with Mr. Bolter's friend when the latter inadvertently keeps the boy's pencil contributes to a sense of mood. Moreover, such examples demonstrate how thoroughly props have been integrated into the performance style. The gradual accretion of seem-ingly insignificant gestures equally defines the verisimilar approach. In a shot near the end of the film, the title character's friend (played by Charles Eldridge) receives a telegram informing him of Mr. Bolter's humorous but embarrassing predicament. In the course of taking in the telegram's con-tents, Eldridge builds up a series of barely noticeable gestures—a back-ward settling into his sofa, manipulation of his glasses, a random motion across his brow—which collectively define both his character and his re-sponse to the news. One could argue that to adequately establish relevant narrative action scarcely requires inclusion of such behavioral tics. Instead, they work toward maintaining verisimilitude: each of Eldridge's gestures, intimate and seemingly inward-directed, bespeaks sustenance of a diegetic world populated by characters eminently familiar with it. Within classical narration, an unobtrusive guidance of the viewer's attention becomes a principal objective; refined versions of the verisimilar style evident in films like *Mr. Bolter's Infatuation* demonstrate one facet of transitional style which would contribute to such an objective.

Lighting

Odd man out among the *mise-en-scène* elements I will examine, lighting typically does not appear directly in the front of the camera. However, its effects registered in the "look" of transitional films, while it operated in concert with lens choice and film stock to improve the visual quality of the images. Technological developments during the period, primarily the widespread adoption of Cooper-Hewitt mercury vapor lamps as the standard source of diffused interior studio illumination and the increased use of arc lamps for isolated effects, offered a specific range of possibilities upon which filmmakers could draw to devise lighting innovations.[45] Generally, changes in lighting procedures work in tandem with related elements of the *mise-en-scène;* for example, as sets become more detailed, filmmakers increase their efforts to vary the directions of the light sources so as to feature the décor to its best advantage while also promoting a separation of figures from background. As Louis Reeves Harrison commented in previewing Rex's *Five Hours,* "[the light] comes from where it should come from. This is a most desirable feature in moving pictures; the high lights and shadows are so carefully adjusted as to perfectly mold the figures, bringing them out in clear relief from the background" (*Moving Picture World* 8, no. 13, 1 April 1911, 699).

Increased reliance on diverse sources of artificial lighting allowed filmmakers to manipulate studio-based illumination to create different lighting effects. For example, the strong shadowing associated with low-key lighting, with background illumination reduced, is created in Vitagraph's *Conscience* (1912) via judiciously employed arc lights. Filmmakers' attitudes toward lighting's potential uses range from perceiving it as a special effect, which could draw attention to itself as such, to seeing it as another device designed to increase verisimilitude, to understanding it as a tool for conveying mood, and by extension, character psychology. Apparently, these different attitudes coexisted, though only near the end of the period does one see numerous instances of atmospheric lighting, wherein illumination effects usually support characterization.

Initial trade concern for clear photography eventually gave way to a stated desire for "distinctive qualities of pictoriality." In an editorial comparing the "clearness and uniformity of picture" of Biograph films to the pictorial qualities of Gaumont's, *Moving Picture World* pointed out the virtues of "the French school of picture making":

A Gaumont picture . . . has certain distinctive qualities which impress themselves upon the mind of the careful observer. To begin with: the lights and shades, which are called in artistic parlance, the chiaroscuro, are always true to nature and well-balanced. The picture is always illuminated

> from the proper point, that is, in most cases, from the side or the back of
> the camera, and the result is naturalness of effect. ("The Qualitative
> Picture," 6, no. 25, 25 June 1910, 1089)

Clearly, the writer sees the pictorial qualities of Gaumont's approach as
instrumental in ensuring verisimilitude; increased care in lighting can actually promote a greater sense of the "natural." For that reason perhaps,
even the most striking lighting effects of the period tended to be those
which filmmakers could attribute to diegetic conditions, such as silhouettes at dusk or fireside illumination. If the scenario called for these lighting conditions, the press would demand their proper representation, or
cite the film as lacking believability.

By 1911, critics apparently expected filmmakers to modify lighting to
suit the needs of the production, as these two reviews attest:

> When you intrude the mechanism of production, Mr. Producer, you spoil
> the illusion. Much better no lantern when you have a moonlight bright
> enough to see by—but if you must have a lantern, then put a light in it
> and juggle the film, even if it is troublesome, so that the lantern appears
> to give light. (C. H. Claudy, "Half-Baked Picture Plays," *Moving Picture
> World* 8, no. 21, 27 May 1911, 1178)

> There is too much diffused illumination in the moonlit scenes. They would
> have appealed more strongly to the imagination if given in semidarkness
> so as to intensify the moonlight streaming through the windows. The
> nearest approach to the ideal condition is seen in the near view of the
> mother and child where the lighting was more in accordance with the
> spirit of the play with a corresponding gain in power. (*Moving Picture
> World* 8, no. 17, 29 April 1911, 940)

The latter review covers a Rex release; the *World* had already singled out
that company earlier in the year for "[a] series of admirably photographed
interiors [which] supply the background . . . [and show] the very perfec-
tion of photography in respect of light and shade and adequate contrast."
The article went on to indicate that the Rex studio had been outfitted with
"shaded arc lamps instead of Cooper Hewitt tubes" ("The Rex First
Release," *Moving Picture World* 8, no. 9, 4 March 1911, 464).

As was the case with set design, more inventive and detailed lighting
effects helped establish a company's concern with quality, and marked it
as competitive. In 1911, reviewers commended the Rex and Reliance pro-

duction concerns, both relatively recent Independent companies, for their employment of more developed lighting techniques, in particular silhouettes.[46] After praising Reliance's *In the Teepee's Light* for the "play of silhouette and bottom light," the writer went on to say that he found it especially "pleasing after so many minutes of plain white lighting in this and other films, and it makes one stop and wonder

Figure 5.12. A silhouette from *A Tale of the Sea* (1910).

whether the moving picture of the future will not depend upon more lighting effects and beauty . . ." ("Seen on the Curtain," *Moving Picture World* 8, no. 20, 20 May 1911, 1120).

Increasingly, producers took advantage of the pictorial effects they could derive from lighting techniques, whether shooting indoors or out. In 1909, *Moving Picture World* praised Edison for the "numerous lighting effects which assist materially in the story [of *His Masterpiece*], adding to the picture's effect" (5, no. 22, 27 November 1909, 751), while Biograph's *Pippa Passes* garnered acclaim for its depiction of dawn and nightfall within an interior set.[47] Sporadic attempts at depicting sudden illumination of a room (*Brother Man*, Vitagraph) and creating silhouettes (*A Tale of the Sea*, Selig [fig. 5.12]) distinguish 1910 films. The adoption of the open-door shot, in particular, signals the rise of pictorialism; *Moving Picture World* identified this technique's roots in still photography while discussing its appearance in Essanay's *A Bandit's Wife*: "Years ago, in stationary photography, quite a vogue arose . . . for what is known as the "open door" subject; that is to say, the picture would be photographed from inside a house or room, through a door, the landscape and the figures being shown beyond, thus creating a very marked effect of looking out of doors on a picture" ("The Open Door in Moving Picture Work," 6, no. 25, 25 June 1910, 1102). Though not employed extensively, the very existence of the open-door shot indicates cinema's willingness to appropriate any "high art" attributes of photographic practice it could emulate; moreover, the open-door shot permitted a means of incorporating landscape within a composition set indoors (thereby underscoring verisimilitude) while also playing with contrasts of light level and tonality. As the examples (from Vitagraph's *The Love of Chrysanthemum* [1910] [fig. 5.13] and American's *The Thief's Wife* [1912] [fig. 5.14]) demonstrate,

Figure 5.13. The open-door shot sets the mood in *The Love of Chrysanthemum* (1910).

Figure 5.14. Dramatic emphasis through the open-door shot in *The Thief's Wife* (1912).

the open-door subject proved an effective way of conveying the dramatic tone of a scene and/or a character's emotional state.[48]

Even with the lighting developments of the two previous years taken into account, 1911 marks the emergence of more concerted attempts throughout the industry to exploit lighting for increased verisimilitude and visual effect. In particular, filmmakers tested the potential of a reduced overall light level for dramatic purposes, producing atmospheric shots lit in a deliberately uneven fashion (as in Vitagraph's *The Voiceless Message* [fig. 5.15], *Proving His Love* [figs. 5.16 and 5.17], and Selig's *Cinderella*[49]). Other trends involved evocative silhouetting, sometimes within interiors (Kalem's *Rory O'Moore* and *Slim Jim's Last Chance;* Rex's *The Colonel's Daughter*) and films built around lighting effects (IMP's *The Lighthouse Keeper*). By 1912, extensive use of a diverse range of lighting effects indicates that this aspect of *mise-en-scène* had become a dependable element within cinema's visual and narrational repertoire, to the extent that even a minor comedy like Vitagraph's *Stenographer Wanted* would exercise care in the lighting of an office shot, to produce a play of light and shadow. Vitagraph's continued refinement of lighting techniques in this and other 1912 films, such as the aforementioned *Conscience* with its atmospheric low key lighting, *Love Hath Wrought a Miracle* (fig. 5.18), and *Out of the Shadows,* among others, lends credence to Barry Salt's claim that this company was at the forefront of studio lighting developments throughout the period (1983, 98). A shot in Kay-Bee's *The Army Surgeon* indicates the state of film lighting by 1912: at a pivotal narrative moment, when the title character elects to choose duty over love, he pauses to look longingly at his fiancée through an exterior window, the light from the party within bathing his face and chest (fig. 5.19). Here, lighting serves as one of numerous stylistic elements (shot scale, character

Figure 5.15. Reducing the light level in *The Voiceless Message* (1911).

Figure 5.16. Dramatically uneven lighting in *Proving His Love* (1911).

Figure 5.17. Atmospheric lighting in *Proving His Love* (1911).

Figure 5.18. Vitagraph's sophisticated use of lighting in *Love Hath Wrought a Miracle* (1912).

Figure 5.19. Lighting abets character development in *The Army Surgeon* (1912).

positioning, performance style) whose interlacing operates to crystallize and foreground a crucial narrative event based in character.

Cinematographic Properties: Adjusting the Viewer's Eye

> The motion picture is the audience, and the audience, therefore, may
> be taken by the artist into any viewpoint, at any distance from cities or
> civilization, to gain the setting of suitable scenery, either wholly natural
> or skillfully prepared. The selection of the exact viewpoint for the camera
> lens, and the selection of the angle to be included by the lens, determining
> the size of the setting to be placed upon the picture film, all are within
> control of the artist and each is a means to be used skillfully for the
> attainment of the desired end.
>
>   DAVID S. HULFISH, "Art in Moving Pictures" (May 1909)

Hulfish's utopian image of a cinema liberated from limits on its view notwithstanding, filmmaking during the transitional era rarely took advantage of the full range of possibilities afforded by properties of the camera and lens. Why did filmmakers not avail themselves more fully of the visual and narrational potentialities of camera placement (be it distance or angle), camera movement, and depth of field during this time? Technological constraints and cultural and aesthetic prohibitions operated in concert to restrict filmmakers' options. The cameras in use during this period did not allow viewfinding through the lens, which impeded shifting focus as well as executing pans of significant duration.[50] Filmmakers may have associated extensive camera movements (either via pans or mounted moving camera shots) with travel and motion films from another era, discouraging them from using such techniques in fictional works. The influence of the theatrical tradition caused some filmmakers to retain stable framing within individual shots.[51] Aesthetic norms derived from photography probably influenced notions of proper framing and focus. Collectively, these constraints prevented filmmakers from exploring the narrational capacities of cinematographic properties to the same extent they did those of *mise-en-scène* or editing.

Depth of Field and Focus

Filmmakers tended to maintain uniform focus for all visible planes of action; this proved a fairly simple proposition at the beginning of the period, given the restrictions placed on the nearness of subjects to the camera and the relative shallowness of playing space within interiors. Had conditions of filming not permitted filmmakers to achieve substantial depth of field, prevailing aesthetic norms probably would have dictated they do so. When shooting in exteriors, filmmakers employed a modified version of deep focus and commentators consistently praised cinematography that achieved even clarity of image. A *Moving Picture World* review of Selig's *Captain Kate* spells out the virtues of maintaining extensive depth of field:

> These pictures . . . with the detail so clearcut all over the picture that faces can be seen not merely in the near foreground but also in the middle and even in the distance, are worthy of the very highest praise—they are marvels of camera work. This art permits the acting, which in almost the whole cast is very praiseworthy, to carry the story to the audience very effectively. (9, no. 3, 29 July 1911, 211)

Commentators appreciated depth of field primarily because it provided maximal visibility; as this review intimates, visual clarity could also translate into ease of narrative comprehension.

Critics also valued depth for its own sake, in much the same way they had prized sets and staging techniques which deepened the playing space. Louis Reeves Harrison commended Reliance on its first release despite a deficient scenario because "the photography will make every producer in the Independent Camp sit up and take notice. In the many deep scenes there is that delightful quality not attained by four other houses in the world; the visibleness of every salient detail" ("Praiseworthy Production by a New Producer," *Moving Picture World* 7, no. 15, 8 October 1910, 801).[52] The critics' adherence to an aesthetic of clarity, depth, and "natural" appearance explains in part their resistance to closer shot scales (or characters placed too close to the camera). When characters walked toward the camera, it could result in blurring if they moved into the range outstripping the lens's depth of field; similarly, too short a lens might produce a distortion of figures in the foreground.[53] Either way, "proper" visual reproduction was violated, and commentators signaled their displeasure. For the trade press, depth ceased to be desirable if actors no longer stayed in full figure.

In other words, critical consensus held that pushing the viewer's vision back away from the camera—extending depth outward—remained commendable so long as everyone agreed where the foreground would commence. For this reason, the trade press expressed few reservations about capturing action in the far reaches of a shot in clear focus. The modified deep staging practices realized within late period films find their functional equivalent in various exterior shots that utilize an extensive depth of field to stress foreground/background oppositions. Westerns gained popularity in part because the staging of shootouts and Indian attacks often employed substantial depth of field within extreme long shots designed to incorporate large vistas of landscape.

In those rare instances when characters occupy the zone considered too close to the camera, filmmakers present it as an almost knowingly transgressive effect, with the figure moving quite deliberately toward the camera. Ironically, such attempts necessarily compromised the retention of uniformly sharp focus, compounding their transgressiveness: in these moments, filmmakers maintained neither the actor's proper distance from the camera nor maximal visibility.[54] The rarity of these violations during the transitional period underscores the relative conservatism of prevailing attitudes toward aspects of focusing and composition that flouted aesthetic norms.

Camera Position and Framing

If the trade press proved restrictive in determining acceptable distances between camera and performer, it remained all but mute on the subject of camera angles. This probably derived from the belief that proper camera placement should maintain a horizontal lens axis, another indication of the legacy of still photography.[55] Nonetheless, camera positioning did undergo change during this period, though the press registered its resistance to closer shot scale far more vociferously than to changes in camera height and angle.

Because variations in camera angle tended to be fairly slight and sporadic throughout the period, critics predictably paid them little heed. For the most part, filmmakers devised novel angles out of necessity, as when they used overhead shots for action set in the water, or positioned the camera to accommodate a character's placement on a roof or other unusual setting. (Frames from Thanhouser's 1910 *Not Guilty* illustrate representative examples [figs. 5.20 and 5.21].) When the incidence of markedly angled shots (nearly always some form of high angle) accelerates from 1911 onward, it coincides with the increased exploration of spatial opportunities provided by location shooting. Just as the expanses of West Coast exteriors probably prompted filmmakers to attend to how editing could log-

Figure 5.20. Certain settings required distinctive camera placement, such as the fire escape descent in *Not Guilty* (1910) . . .

Figure 5.21. . . . where a novel low angle accommodates the depicted action.

ically connect and dissect spaces, so too the terrain's vastness may have conditioned filmmakers to rely on overhead shots for ideal vantage points.

What began as a functional necessity for exterior shooting shows signs of becoming a narrational option for interiors by 1912. *The Massacre of the Fourth Cavalry* (Bison 1912) heightens tension by employing a striking high angle view of a mother loading a gun in preparation for an Indian attack. Lubin's *The Samaritan of Coogan's Tenement* (1912) establishes an unusual vantage point on a courtroom by setting the camera behind and above the judge; by rendering the court's presiding officer faceless, the film passes its own judgment on the justice meted out in the scene. The increased flexibility accorded the camera could extend to an emulation of the viewpoints of characters within the diegesis, as in the angled inserts of various personal belongings in Solax's *A Comedy of Errors* (1912 [fig. 3.24, p. 79]). Similarly, an angled shot linked to a character's glance could suggest an eyeline match, like the high angle shot used to show a male audience member watching a female musician perform in *The Girl of the Cabaret* (Thanhouser 1913).[56] If nothing else, the expanded role of camera angles at the end of the period demonstrates how filmmakers began to understand the camera itself differently. Haltingly, filmmakers incorporated the camera into the dynamization of space which pulled the viewer into the action; in the classical era, Hulfish's equation of the camera and the audience, with the latter "taken . . . into any viewpoint," would be realized.

While filmmakers varied camera angles only occasionally during the period, they instituted adjustments in camera height more systematically. In particular, Vitagraph made a switch from shooting with the camera at eye level to lowering it to chest (or even waist) level. This shift, in conjunction with Vitagraph's adoption of a closer shot scale, contributed to a particular "look" within their films, which angling of the camera exaggerated even further. (For a representative example of the effect of the "Vitagraph angle," see fig. 5.6, p. 134.) Typically, such tactics reduced the amount of "dead space" between the top of the actors' heads and the upper frame edge when the actors positioned themselves at the agreed-upon outer limit of the foreground. While the trade press did not target Vitagraph's innovation for criticism, reviewers lodged random complaints concerning "the heroic size" of actors, which suggests that the camera's position contributed to the problem as much as the distance between actor and camera.[57]

Reviewers seemed far more open to the potentialities of the stable frame, particularly in its capacity to create zones of off-screen space. Perhaps because such compositional effects were available to still photographers as well, the trade press expressed interest in certain types of off-screen space. Of course, cinema can mobilize off-screen space in a variety of ways, from camera movement to editing. The trade press acknowledged two methods for creating off-screen space: a character's glance off-frame signaling an undepicted occurrence, or a frame edge or barrier within the frame cutting off full view of an action.[58] Admittedly, neither of these methods is particularly innovative—one could imagine them modified for the theater, though the effect might differ—and this probably accounts for the trade press's approval of them. Nonetheless, critical acceptance of dramatic action occurring outside the view of both camera and spectator suggests a more open-minded conception of the film frame than the trade press's standard aesthetic precepts might lead us to expect.

A *Moving Picture World* article previewing *A Discarded Favorite* (a Vitagraph film released as *Jealousy* for which no prints survive) describes a film constructed entirely around the effects of off-screen space. In his account, Louis Reeves Harrison indicates that the filmmaker constantly redirects the attention of the viewer (and of the only character who is fully visible, played by Florence Turner) back to a set of curtains in the left foreground "behind which there is something transpiring unseen by the audience." What Turner understands to be happening behind the curtains dictates her responses throughout the film; we only glimpse synecdochic evidence of the obscured figures' actions when their hands protrude at pivotal moments ("Superior Plays," *Moving Picture World* 9, no. 5, 12 August 1911, 361–62).

We could label *Jealousy* an extreme case of foregrounding a device, but self-conscious employment of off-screen space occurs in other films as well. Biograph's *The Proposal* (1910), directed by Frank Powell, and Essanay's *A Child of the West* (1911) both feature hands reaching into the frame from an off-screen region, bearing objects crucial to the development of the narrative (a letter and a gun, respectively). Kalem's *Reconciled by Burglars* (1912) develops this use of off-screen space even further, effecting the reconciliation of the title via a number of actions performed by the female protagonist's arm, which reaches out into the frame from her doorway; in a visual *coup de grâce,* her hand wiggles its fingers in anticipation of receiving an engagement ring.[59] Even explorations of the most distinctive off-screen region—the space behind the camera—occur within this period. IMP's *Fruits and Flowers* (1910) features a shot where off-screen combatants hurl vegetables into the frame, while at one point in Lubin's *The Missing Finger* (1912) a criminal points off screen toward the camera, acknowledging the approach of pursuing detectives. As with uses of camera angling late in the transitional period, the development of off-screen space conveys filmmakers' mounting appreciation of how to expand narrative space, but also how to extend the principle of depth and complement the articulation of contiguity.

Camera Movement

Though camera movement could invoke off-screen space as well, the trade press did not cite this method as a preferred option. The narrational self-consciousness of employing any moving camera shots independent of character movement to reveal previously concealed action kept such uses of the mobile camera outside the purview of the trade press. Typical deployment of camera movement followed these unstated restrictions, meaning conventional usage restricted itself to keeping pertinent narrative action in frame. But how often did filmmakers rely on mobile framing during the transitional period, and how does its use from 1907 to 1913 compare to its function in previous years?

Looking first at instances of a camera moving through space, either by being mounted on a moving vehicle or a specialized dolly, one finds no more than a few examples of such shots each year between 1907 and 1911. By 1912, the number increases somewhat, but remains insubstantial. Despite the rarity of the device, some uses of these camera movements emerge as distinctive. The only example I noted of a camera moving in on a fully stationary subject occurs in Edison's *The House of Cards* (1909), when the camera dollies in on a violinist playing; once the camera movement stops, the altered framing has centered the protagonist seated next to the musician.[60] Kalem made a series of train films in 1911, most notably *The Railroad Raiders of '62*, featuring numerous shots with the camera mounted on a train. Lubin's *The Missing Finger* (1912) cuts together four moving shots which function as eyeline matches between two characters. Finally, in *The Trail of Cards* (American 1913), repeated tracking shots depict an abduction on horseback, while the playing cards of the title are dropped as clues. The self-consciously inventive nature of most of the examples indicates filmmakers still viewed this type of camera movement as a novelty of sorts.

Appropriately, then, historians studying camera movement have paid more attention to the comparatively common employment of panning; even so, they underestimate its frequency of use for the period. Eileen Bowser simply says that after 1907 "the camera rarely moved" (1990, 249). Barry Salt states that "the majority of American films were shot with a totally static camera" before specifying that approximately 10 percent of films from the period employ camera movement to reframe (1983, 86). My own research reveals a much higher rate of use: pans occur in an average of one out of every four films during the transitional period. This rate never falls below 15 percent for a given year and reaches as high as fifty; moreover, the rates show a steady rise from 1911 onward.[61]

Beyond the issue of frequency of use, we must also address typicality of function, especially as it compares to the years directly preceding the transitional period. If we refer to Jon Gartenberg's account of how camera movement developed prior to 1907, we learn that after "taking tenuous steps" from 1900–1902, filmmakers "integrated [it] into the narrative" by 1906 (1982, 179). Gartenberg cites numerous examples from 1906 Biograph and Edison films that demonstrate the extensive and varied use of pans in that year.[62] How can we explain this apparent shift in the value of the pan as a stylistic device? If reframing became the primary function of the pan, why do filmmakers abandon other possible uses?

Historians addressing this issue have provided three possible reasons to explain why the pan fell from favor during the transitional period:

1. Limitations of existing technology (particularly the inverted image provided by the camera's viewfinder) "provided some pressure

against the free use of panning shots in this period" (Salt 1983, 86; see also Bowser 1990, 249).

2. Editing usurped the role of the pan, which "would have seemed old-fashioned to the new generation of filmmakers" (Bowser 1990, 249).

3. Aesthetic norms of the time opposed the employment of extensive pans or tracks both because they might result in spectatorial distraction and because they "would call attention to the frame itself, rather than the action within it" (Thompson 1985b, 228; see also Bowser 1990, 251).

Let me address each of these arguments in turn. The first explanation regarding the limitations of technology seems logical, except that it fails to account for how panning reached a high level of use by 1906 but fell in popularity for the next several years. Without proof of a dramatic change in camera technology that further restricted panning, this argument fails to address the drop in frequency of use asserted by Salt. Why would filmmakers have expressed greater willingness to persist in the face of technological constraints *before* 1907 and not after? The second explanation, regarding editing usurping the pan, attempts to address that question, but assumes industry-wide conditions that may not have prevailed. Can one propose with assurance that the majority of filmmakers were predisposed to embrace editing's possibilities to the exclusion of previously established methods, especially given the erratic development of stylistic innovation? Also, does this argument possess applicability to any company other than Biograph, where a new director, Griffith, quickly became enamored of using editing for a variety of purposes, far in excess of the industry norm?[63] The last argument above—regarding aesthetic norms—emerges as most persuasive, and shares assumptions that guide my introductory comments to this section. Given critical resistance to other frame-modifying techniques, such as cutting in for a closer shot, I think it likely that reviewers would have opposed overt uses of panning. Moreover, the trade press began to exert an influence precisely at the time of the purported decline in use of panning beyond basic reframing. Even so, I have not come across any articles arguing against the pan (compared to numerous diatribes aimed at closer shot scale). This argument also takes for granted that industry practice necessarily would follow trade press prohibitions.

If none of these explanations is entirely persuasive, perhaps historians have attempted to explain a phenomenon that did not actually occur (at least not to the extent proposed). A more cautious approach to charting the fate of the pan's narrational value would acknowledge a tempering of its wide use after 1906 as part of a gradual shift toward finding different ways to employ isolated devices for storytelling purposes. (We can now recast the second explanation and see editing as a coexisting substitute, as long as we recognize that editing's growing acceptance involved a process more protracted and tentative than the current formulation of the argument implies.) However, an evaluation of the functions of post-1906 panning also requires a careful study of those instances when filmmakers enlisted camera movement for more than simple reframing.

Examples from films of the period show that filmmakers occasionally used pans to reveal deliberately withheld narrative information. In *An Irish Hero* (Vitagraph 1909), after the protagonists have fled to the shore to await an incoming ship, a pan extends the view beyond the shoreline to reveal an impressive shot of an expanse of water and the ship's arrival; within the same shot, the camera then pans back in the opposite direction to reveal that guards in pursuit of the protagonists have caught up with them. Apart from requiring a fair degree of planning, this double pan also brings together within the same shot the two forces currently defining the protagonists' predicament.

The Two Sons (IMP 1909) features a shot with an elaborately orchestrated series of linked pans, beginning with the camera focused on a sentry standing guard and then panning left to show the hero, Victor, coming through the bush. The camera follows Victor to the right until he pauses, at which point the pan continues, leaving him where he has stopped in order to reveal more guards emerging from the right background. A new sentry takes over, and then the camera pans back to Victor at the left; as he prepares to leave via the left side of the frame, the camera pans right one more time as the guard shoots. The extended pan in *The Two Sons* causes the shot to run over sixty feet; here, camera movement substitutes for editing, maintaining an unbroken spatial bond between the related actions, where editing would establish contiguity through cuts and sightlines. Eventually, the editing option would prevail, but that did not eliminate the use of the narrationally self-conscious pan, as its recurrence throughout the period attests.[64] By 1912, a single film might incorporate both extensive, space-expanding pans *and* crosscutting, as in IMP's *The Long Strike*. In this film, during a shot lasting close to 150 feet, four distinct pans mark off two separate areas of space without virtue of a cut, though a later sequence opts for extensive editing.

A few other misconceptions concerning camera movements on a fixed axis must be addressed. First, though less common than panning shots, tilts occur with some regularity throughout the period, especially in the last years, when their use often parallels the narrational function of pans. Examples include the tilt from cause (Natives) to effect (the aftermath of an attack) in *At Old Fort Dearborn* (Bison 1912)[65] and the tilt in *The Unwritten Law of the West* (American 1913) that reveals the dead body the hero has tripped over. Second, though pans and tilts occur more frequently in exteriors than interiors, one can find them used with sets as well, sometimes in particularly inventive ways. In Essanay's *[The Deputy's Duty]* (1910), the camera pans right once a female robber has entered a cabin to reveal a split set with a door opening onto an adjoining room. As the woman walks through to the next room (frame right), the camera pans to follow her. The filmmaker repeats this procedure several times, with the pan highlighting the split set's novel depiction of the narrative's spatial divisions.[66] In Selig's *The Devil, the Servant and the Man* (1912), a remarkable panning shot, used with a partitioned set, shows a dreaming man leaving his home with the devil, then continues to pan right in order to show his sleeping figure still in the house. Finally, some transitional films employ such types of camera movements repeatedly; Kalem's *Captured by Bedouins* (1912), for example, features four separate instances of panning, including a bravura extended shipboard pan in a shot running close to eighty feet.[67]

Lubin stands out as the one company employing pans more extensively than any other during the transitional period. In 1909, the first year I could obtain a sufficiently large sample for assessment, Lubin employs pans and/or tilts in nearly half of its films, a much larger percentage than the industry norm at this time. Again, in 1912, the next year with an adequate sample, 80 percent of the Lubin films rely on pans and/or tilts. Though many Lubin films simply employ pans to reframe, a significant number find other uses. Two pans perform a revelatory function in *The Hebrew Fugitive* (1908); a pan picks the protagonists out of a large crowd at a race track in *Sporting Blood* (1909); extensive pans follow complex character movement in *The Two Cousins* (1909); *Satin and Gingham* (1912) combines pans and tilts in several shots; and in *'Twixt Love and Ambition* (1912), a pan follows a child away from his maid until he reaches the road below, at which point he crosses in the direction opposite from her, with the pan reversing direction as well. By 1913, Lubin's *The Guiding Light*, a two-reeler, will feature no fewer than eighteen separate panning and tilting movements.

Like most companies during this period, but even more so, Lubin demonstrated increased dexterity in integrating pans and tilts into its storytelling and compositional methods. The fairly high incidence of pans by 1913 indicates filmmakers' developing comfort in employing them for myriad functions: pans could effect slight reframings or explore extensive portions of picturesque locales; follow one or several characters' actions or reveal an undisclosed piece of information. Perhaps to a greater degree than other devices, the use of pans represents a continuation and deepening of stylistic practice already established prior to 1907.

Shot Scale

Before 1909, the selected standard shot scale varied dramatically from one film to another.[68] Though both Vitagraph's *The Boy, the Bust and the Bath* and Kalem's *Ben Hur* (both from 1907) use a version of the long shot, with full figures of the characters visible, the performers in the latter film are much farther from the camera. Scholars concur that Vitagraph was in the vanguard of changes to shot scale, particularly in its institution of the so-called "nine foot line." Barry Salt has described this practice in exacting detail:

> This was a line, or in the case of studio scenes, a plank, laid down nine feet in front of the camera lens, and at right angles to the lens axis, and it represented the closest the actors were allowed to come forwards towards the camera. With the usual studio lens aperture setting of f5.6 to f8 a standard 50 mm. lens would give sharp focus from nine feet to about 50 feet if the focus was set at 15 feet. . . . The exact height included within the frame for the silent aperture when a standard 50 mm. lens is used is 3 foot 9 inches at 10 feet, since of course the actors would not stand right on the nine-foot line, particularly when it was a plank of wood. . . . (1987, 182–83)

Salt believes Vitagraph applied this policy inconsistently beginning in 1909, and one can see its effects in such films as *Romance of an Umbrella*. Vitagraph's adoption of the nine-foot line signals an attempt to expand the acceptable range of shot scales to include significantly closer framings. As companies began emulating this attempt with greater frequency after 1910, the trade press stepped in to challenge the change directly.

Ironically, prior to the actual practice of moving the camera closer, Rollin Summers had registered approval of such an approach: "Where shades of emotion are to be expressed the pictures as a rule should be at close range. The moving picture may present figures greater than life size without loss of illusion" ("The Moving Picture Drama and the Acted Drama," *Moving Picture World* 3, no. 12, 19 September 1908, 213). Though voicing a minority opinion, Summers does touch upon the central issue in the debate. Opposition to "close shots" (as the trade labeled those framings which failed to show the full figure of the actor) primarily hinged on their supposed anti-illusory effect. Two representative critiques clarify the aesthetic rationale behind this position:

> Of course the fundamental rule to be observed in this matter is that no figure should appear larger than life-size to the eye. ("Too Near the Camera," *Moving Picture World* 8, no. 12, 25 March 1911, 633)

> Aggravating and emphasizing the deficiencies of the actors . . . is the style of "close-up" photography which now prevails. This practice of stationing the camera almost within reaching distance of the performers is like putting everything under the magnifying glass. All the crass details obtrude with hard angularity. . . . Wherever there is anything false or flimsy we spot it at once, because things are viewed at such close range. . . . Under such circumstances there is no chance for illusion. Nowhere does the well-known adage, "Distance leads enchantment to the view," apply with such force as to dramatic performances. Distance is an absolute requisite to any kind of idealistic illusion. ("On Filming a Classic," *Nickelodeon* 5, no. 1, 7 January 1911, 4)

Commentators such as these believed that characters shown "larger than life" represented a direct affront to cinema's realization of verisimilitude. A prevailing tendency to literalize space as projected on the screen prompted reviewers to describe actors rendered in full figure as "life size"; critics also labeled closer views "grotesque" out of a conviction that an actor filmed too closely would appear as a literal giant to the audience in the theatre.[69]

Beyond concerns of distortion, commentators expressed fear that close shots would block backgrounds, causing reduced depth, while others claimed that the actors' makeup became too noticeable.[70] The common belief that a closer view destroyed the illusion of "the natural" so prized by the trade press at this time links all these complaints. This belief put opponents of closer shot scales in the decidedly rearguard position of championing filmmakers who resisted the trend toward closer shooting, such as Edwin S. Porter at Rex, or the director of the Powers film *Tip to*

Husbands, praised by *Nickelodeon* almost by default: "We like the 'distant' photography for a change. It relieves the monotony of the 'close-up' style, and has the positive advantage of adding breadth to the pictures" (5, no. 6, 11 February 1911, 169).

Those who encouraged the use of closer views did so out of a belief that it would improve narrative clarity and increase the spectator's emotional involvement:

> [The director of the motion picture] can vary at will the distance of the stage, giving us a closer view at critical moments. When we would see more clearly what emotions the features of the heroine express or what is in the locket she takes from her bosom we have no need to pick up our opera glasses. The artist has foreseen our desire and suddenly the detail is enlarged for us until it fills the canvas. ("The Drama of the People," *New York Independent;* repr. in *Moving Picture World* 7, no. 16, 15 October 1910, 865)

Conversely, trade press proponents of the longer view advocated principles of verisimilitude over those of narrational expediency. Commentators evidently allowed adherence to a revered aesthetic to override concerns about viewer comprehension.[71] When confronted with the position of the trade press, filmmakers had to decide for themselves which option best suited their narrational preferences. Tellingly, most would opt for a closer shot scale before the trade press sanctioned such a decision; by 1913, standard shot scale in some films occasionally approximated the medium shot, though framing the actors just below the knees remained the norm. The conflict surrounding proper shot scale during the transitional period indicates how stylistic choices were often forged without clear consensus within the industry.

Editing: Cutting Up a Storm

> A twenty scene drama is run up to fifty or sixty scenes, with an average time length of from fifteen to eighteen seconds each. Acting is not possible. Clarity of story is not possible. Unfolding of plot is not possible. There is a succession of eye-pleasing scenes, but no stories.
>
> EPES WINTHROP SARGENT, *Moving Picture World* (10 August 1912)

Sargent's opposition to increased cutting rates emphasizes editing's disruptive influence on narrative flow (conversely, in chapter 4, I argued for the centrality of editing to the transitional cinema's developing narrativization). Commentators like Sargent doubtless possessed a distinct sense of how to convey stories on film, one predicated on the duration of scenes dependent on acting. Sargent sees increased cutting rates as a threat to the coherence of this approach; I would revise his portrayal of editing's influence to suggest that editing reshaped virtually every aspect of cinematic style. One does not have to subscribe to the myth of editing giving birth to the movies in order to see that the concept of editing facilitated many of the changes that define the transitional period. Even so, arguing for editing's primacy over aspects of *mise-en-scène* (particularly staging and performance) would probably lead to a stalemate; this argument also counters the idea of style as a system. Editing's stylistic domination within certain genres, like comedy and the western, has a counterpart in the greater emphasis given to *mise-en-scène* elements in most domestic dramas. Rather than assigning any kind of comparative weight to editing's cumulative role in establishing the period's narrational norms, I would like to supplement the consideration given to cutting elsewhere in the book by discussing a few remaining salient aspects.

Cut-Ins

A distinct form of editing whose function and execution undergo substantial transformation during the period, the cut-in began as an obvious holdover from the primitive years. During that era, filmmakers devised two methods to provide closer views distinct from the shots surrounding them. The first, the emblematic close-up, usually features characters or elements associated with the diegesis but lacks any specified spatial context. Used as punctuation (and often appearing at the beginning and/or end of films), the emblematic close-up has been likened to the introductory panel of the comic strip—a detachable element divorced from the main narrative (Gunning 1982, 228). The second method, the detail cut-in, magnifies an action and functions as a form of overlap by presenting a closer-scaled portion of a previously viewed scene.[72]

Many emblematic close-ups featured actors gesticulating for the camera, the direct address to the camera reinforcing their function as attractions. [73] Retaining these shots proved increasingly problematic during the transitional period, because they potentially disrupted the enveloping fictionality of the rest of the film. Such unmoored close-ups of faces continue to appear in 1907–8, but by 1909, the approach to showing closer views of performers changes markedly.[74] The close shot still marks the end of the

Figure 5.22. A close shot of the title character in *She Would Be an Actress* (1909) . . .

Figure 5.23. . . . gives way to a longer shot which reveals the same décor . . .

Figure 5.24. . . . while an emblematic close-up occurs before a neutral backdrop.

film, but filmmakers reinforce connections to the diegesis by curbing direct address, encouraging the performers to "stay in character" and sustaining narrative action from the previous shot.[75] Equally important, such shots become literal cut-ins as the camera moves in slightly, typically preserving total replication of *mise-en-scène* if not exact continuity of action. One film from 1909, Lubin's *She Would Be an Actress*, still uses an emblematic close-up while also providing an example of its successor: the first shot features a close view of a woman reading a book entitled *How to Become an Actress*, with the surrounding décor of the following shot fully visible in the background (figs. 5.22 and 5.23); the last shot, which succeeds the narrative's resolution in the prior shot, is a closer view of the same woman and her husband smiling at the camera in front of a neutral background (fig. 5.24). Whereas the first instance of the closer shot provides visual information that a longer scale would not and also contributes to the subsequent unfolding story, the latter is purely emblematic and an

Figure 5.25. When a character tampers with a letter in *Pardners* (1910) . . .

Figure 5.26. . . . it requires increased contextualization of the affected insert.

auxiliary to the narrative. Not long after this, filmmakers would find it untenable that both options for the close shot could coexist.

Did the parallel development of increased reliance on the insert spur filmmakers to treat closer views of performers differently? Initial versions of inserts typically involve a visually nonintegrated text serving as a letter or other specified means of communication, but filmmakers soon tried rendering inserts as part of the diegesis, often by framing letters with hands. Even more significantly, instances of characters tampering with the textual material allow opportunities to match character action initiated in a long shot with the closer-scaled insert (as in Lubin's *The Unexpected Guest* [1909], or Edison's *Pardners* [1910] [figs. 5.25 and 5.26]). The increased diegetic contextualization of inserts permitted and possibly promoted bringing characters (as characters) into closer view.

Examples of cut-ins other than inserts occurring within the body of the film tend to focus on smaller significant objects (the clue on a suspect's jacket in Yankee's *An Italian Sherlock Holmes* [1911]) or complex processes requiring closer examination to be intelligible (the transfer of a stolen wallet in Thanhouser's *Not Guilty* [1910] [figs. 5.27 and 5.28]).[76] This type of cut-in is consonant with the developing narrational logic of the period, and one finds it in use from 1907 onward, though less so in the first two years. Cut-ins (and the full-action insert) may have helped lessen trade press resistance to closer views by demonstrating how narrationally useful close-ups could be. Epes Winthrop Sargent, generally not a defender of closer shot scale, allowed that some close-ups (or "bust pictures") could serve as an expedient to viewer comprehension:

> Bust pictures, which are enlarged views of limited areas, are useful in determining action that might be obscure in the large scene. It not only

Figure 5.27. Revealing the details of a small-scale action in *Not Guilty* (1910) . . .

Figure 5.28. . . . necessitates the use of a cut-in.

magnifies the objects but it draws particular attention to them. . . . Many points may be cleared in a five-foot bust picture which would require twenty to thirty feet of leader to explain, and the bust picture always interests. ("Technique of the Photoplay," *Moving Picture World* 10, no. 4, 5 August 1911, 282)

Eventually, integrated cut-ins incorporated facial close-ups as well; these shots often performed dual functions, with the closer shot scale registering both important details *and* character reactions (as in Edison's *The Test of Friendship* [1911] and Selig's *One Hundred Years After* [1911] [figs. 5.29 and 5.30]). By 1912, and with some regularity, filmmakers accorded characters closer views designed to heighten an emotional response to the figure depicted (as in Rex's *An Ill Wind* [figs. 5.31 and 5.32]). At this point, cut-ins quickly become part of the developing system of varied shot scale which worked to dissect space for narrative purposes, including the delineation of character psychology (evidenced by the perfectly matched cut-in in Essanay's *The Voice of Conscience* [1912] [figs. 5.33 and 5.34]). By 1913, closer views can introduce characters (as in IMP's *In Peril of the Sea*), indicating how flexibly filmmakers incorporated closer shot scale into editing patterns designed to facilitate viewer identification of characters and build intimacy. Viewer investment in character then prompts increased reliance on such shots for emotional emphasis: the recurring shot of the heroine in *In Peril of the Sea* serves to counterpoint a disaster at sea, foregrounding the overt narrational capacities of juxtaposing facial close-shots and causally crucial action sequences. The incorporation of cut-ins by 1913 suggests the growing interdependency of editing as a system.

Figure 5.29. Cutting in could reveal the details of a small object, as in *One Hundred Years After* (1911) . . .

Figure 5.30. . . . where facial reactions receive greater attention as well.

Figure 5.31. Providing a closer view of a character, as in *An Ill Wind* (1912) . . .

Figure 5.32. . . . heightens the emotional value of the shot.

Figure 5.33. Moving from a longer shot in *The Voice of Conscience* (1912) . . .

Figure 5.34. . . . to a closer view through an expertly matched cut-in.

Cutting Rates

The single-reel format remained the standard length for most films during the transitional period, particularly after 1908. This relatively consistent film running time provides a stable ground against which to measure an increase in shot numbers. As might be expected, cutting rates mount steadily from 1909 until 1913, with the most dramatic increase occurring at the tail end of the period. The trade press paid little attention to editing until 1912, when finally *Moving Picture World* conducted an informal survey and determined that virtually every company had been "bitten by the lightning bug."[77] The *World* held Biograph and D. W. Griffith responsible, protesting that "now that three times the proper number of scenes are used to cover up the thinness of Director Griffith's on-the-flap-of-an-envelope stories, everybody's doing it, and strong, vital, gripping plots are shelved in favor of the short story with numerous shifts" (Epes Winthrop Sargent, "The Photoplaywright: Scenes and Leaders," *Moving Picture World* 3, no. 6, 10 August 1912, 542).

The article goes on to stipulate that a single-reel subject should require only twenty to thirty "scenes" (which is to say, shots), a total consistent with other assessments by commentators from the period.[78] If one looks at the figures Tom Gunning has supplied for D. W. Griffith's films at Biograph during these years, one can see that Griffith employed an average number of shots per thousand-foot reel far in excess of suggested industry norms; for some instructive comparisons, I have compiled my own data for the years 1909–13 (table 5.1).[79] The gap between Griffith at Biograph and the other companies is not so striking at first, but it widens substantially until 1913, when Griffith's rate stabilizes and the industry norm begins to catch up. If one compares the Griffith titles that Gunning has identified as containing the largest number of shots for each year with those from other companies, the contrasting numbers confirm the trend indicated by average shot number per reel (table 5.2).

In all likelihood, one can attribute the increase in cutting rates at Biograph to the sustained reliance on and development of crosscutting. Certainly, the industry's belated adoption of crosscutting contributes to the upward trend in shots per reel at other companies by the period's end. However, other uses of editing develop in concert with crosscutting: a greater number of cut-ins, more instances of point-of-view editing, and variation of shot scale to effect rudimentary attempts at scene dissection. One cannot lay all these editing trends at the feet of Griffith, as he did not explore each of them with the same consistency as he did crosscutting.

Table 5.1. Yearly comparison of average number of shots per 1,000-foot reel

YEAR	GRIFFITH BIOGRAPHS	OTHER COMPANIES
1908	16.6	—ᵃ
1909	24.8	22.2
1910	44.4	21.9
1911	71.4	24.1
1912	82	37.7
1913	87.8	52

ᵃ Insufficient data exist to permit a reliable calculation.

Table 5.2. Yearly comparison of highest number of shots per 1,000-foot reel

	GRIFFITH BIOGRAPHS		FILMS FROM OTHER COMPANIES	
YEAR	FILM	NO. OF SHOTS	FILM	NO. OF SHOTS
1908	*The Guerilla*	45	*The Cattle Rustlers* (Selig)	29
1909	*The Lonely Villa*	52	*A Ranchman's Rival* (Essanay)	33
1910	*When a Man Loves*	85	*The Telephone* (Vitagraph)	37
1911	*A Terrible Discovery*	122	*A Special Messenger* (Kalem)	61
1912	*The Girl and Her Trust*	126	*With the Mounted Police* (Thanhouser)	76
1913	*The Lady and the Mouse*	118	*In Peril of the Sea* (IMP)	106

I would also stress that not all manufacturers increased cutting rates noticeably, and when increases did occur, they sometimes emerged inconsistently within individual studios. As late as 1912, one can point to a company using only sixteen shots over a thousand feet (Solax's *The Girl in the Arm-Chair*), while several never dip below thirty shots. Certain companies maintain a fairly consistent rate of cutting, while others, like Essanay, produce films with shots per thousand feet ranging from a high of forty-nine to a low of eighteen. The shot average of a few companies rises well above 1912's yearly norm of 37.7 (IMP at 50) while that of others falls considerably below (Rex at 23.8). Such variations do not argue against broad-based trends but rather demonstrate the inconsistency of change at levels of closer observation.

Altered cutting rates confirm the nature of stylistic change during the transitional period as distinct but halting, gradual and varied; other innovations to the developing editing system in the period's final years point to the increasingly interconnected character of film style. Filmmakers introduced both the eyeline match and shot/reverse-shot procedures, using characters' glances to tie together spaces separated by a cut.[80] (An eyeline match features a shot of a character looking off-frame, followed by a shot of the viewed scene; in shot/reverse-shot, a second character returns the gaze of the first.) These procedures cement connections between discrete spaces, employing cues supplied by actors' sightlines, body positions, and gestures and consistent décor elements across the spatial divide (in certain cases of proximity). As different editing devices coalesce into a system, filmmakers enlist a battery of stylistic features to consolidate and reinforce the narrational possibilities this system affords.

Moreover, the introduction of different devices allowed filmmakers to explore the merits of divergent approaches, oftentimes within the same film. *Broncho Billy's Capture* (Essanay 1913) features two instances of point-of-view editing, including a repeated eyeline match sequence, a directionally correct match-on-action, and four different perspectives on a single space; after relying on a varied range of editing options for the first three-quarters of the film's running time, the filmmaker then shifts to an unbroken take lasting more than one hundred feet in the film's final shot. Similarly, *Playing with Fire* (Vitagraph 1913) balances an eighty-foot shot dependent on staging in depth at the beginning with a rapidly edited final section, employing extended intrascene cutting. Here, an average shot length of thirty-five feet (for the film's first two-thirds) dwindles to ten feet in the final nineteen shots as intricate character repositioning gives way to alternating cuts (which occasionally incorporate shot/reverse-shot).

An overview of stylistic development such as I have supplied in this chapter can only hint at the range of narrational choices employed within individual films. Moreover, a sense of style as system gets slighted when categorical separations force the different elements apart, but I retained these distinctions for the purposes of descriptive clarity. In the next chapter, I effect reintegration through analysis, providing a study of transitional style via extended examination of sample films. In this way, I can chart narrational shifts across the transitional period, with the nature of change emerging as much between descriptions of films as within them.

6

Analyzing Transition: Six Sample Films

IN THE INTRODUCTION, I outlined some broad defining formal characteristics of the transitional period by analyzing the differences between two hypothetical films, *A Lady's Luck* and *Lila's Lucky Charm*. Now that we have examined the ways narrative and narration, spatiotemporal articulation, and style function in some detail during these years, we can return to the observations produced by that initial analysis and expand upon them. Rather than merely emphasizing that change does occur, as I did in my analysis of the two ideal films, I now want to demonstrate the *range* of stylistic usage and narrational strategies evident within the period.

No set of films can reflect fully the diversity of approaches filmmakers adopted to engage audiences while promoting viewer understanding of more complex narratives after 1907. Accordingly, my selection of films for analysis does not aim for comprehensiveness; instead, I was guided by two main objectives when making my choices. First, I tried to pick films representative of the various companies producing films during this period, including industry leaders Biograph and Vitagraph, Trust mainstay Selig, and more recent additions to the Independent camp, such as Rex. (In only one instance have I chosen to analyze two films from the same company, Biograph, in part to show the significant changes that occur within a two-year period.) These choices cut across genre lines and include comedies, period dramas, and action-filled suspense films. Second, I wanted to use films that would embody the nature of change in the manner it occurs, as a series of experiments and refinements. Had I wished to argue implicitly for a direct line of achievements leading to the ultimate goal of classicism, I could have stacked the deck, choosing the most accomplished films from each year of production. Instead, I have opted for a mixture of titles, which balance moments of inventiveness with scenes that recycle already-established methods. Nonetheless, I am certain the reader will notice an incremental development in narrational method that the cumulative weight of the chronologically advancing set of analyses provides.

Whatever correspondences or overt contrasts my analyses reveal among these films arise independently of the selection process I used. I did not choose the films because I hoped their comparison might reveal clever parallels or exemplify dramatic improvements. Such analytical felicities, while they can prove momentarily satisfying, ultimately betray the nature of transition. Instead, I settle for the more useful goal of reproducing the problem-solving procedures filmmakers engaged in throughout the transitional period, as an illustration of the diachronic dimension of a crucial narrational shift in American cinema.[1]

The Boy Detective (Biograph, March 1908)

A boy determines that two men have devised a villainous plot involving a young woman. He arranges to impersonate the woman and trick the men into exposing themselves before he halts their plan by the use of a toy gun.

While the narrative of *The Boy Detective* unfolds over twelve shots, involving a significant diversity in spaces, the film remains indebted to a model of narrative exposition derived chiefly from the chase format. In other words, action remains the film's primary focal point, with any explication of the narrative's main motivating cause (the plot against the woman) left underdeveloped. (Titles in the original print may have provided more detail, but in the absence of those, the filmmaker employs few other methods to clarify potentially confusing plot points within the story.[2])

While the filmmaker expends minimal effort in explaining the narrative, he does provide some visual cues to direct viewer attention. In the first shot, the framing sets the boy detective and his friend in the left foreground of the shot, so that when the two villainous men and their potential victim come into view, the adults occupy the center of the frame. Moreover, placing the boy detective at the frame's edge (and establishing his presence prior to any conflicting visual information) allows us to note his interest in the subsequent centered action. By having us watch the boy detective watch the characters in frame center, the filmmaker establishes hierarchies of knowledge at the same time he reinforces the importance of the villainous activity. Thus, even though we may not understand why the men are following the woman in the next shot, we at least know enough to view them suspiciously, which justifies the boy detective's pursuit of them. Finally, an attentive viewer will note that the toy gun that figures prominently in the film's resolution first appears here; however, the filmmaker does not deploy any narrational tools to point up its presence or hint at its future importance to the narrative's outcome.

With the component elements of a standard narrative situation in place (imperiled woman, pursuing villains, and rescuer), dynamic physical movement dominates the next seven shots, constituting almost a third of the film's running time. The filmmaker employs the structure of the chase initially, with all three sets of agents passing through distinct spaces in the next two shots. By shot three, however, the woman has exited to her apartment, and the villains cease their pursuit of her as of shot four. Shots five through eight involve the boy detective running alone through a variety of spaces, eventually returning to the woman's apartment. Once the original pursuit breaks down, the configuration of space becomes progressively more confusing, and any rationale for the boy's subsequent journey remains undisclosed. Spatial uncertainty commences at the end of shot three, once the woman has left: a cut to a closer framing of the two men seemingly functions as a cut-in on their progress as they proceed down the street, especially since their direction remains consistent from shot three. Unfortunately, the men have receded so far into the background of shot three by the time the cut comes that relating the space of shot four to the previously established locale proves impossible. This in turn renders the trajectory of the boy's run in shots five through seven geographically incomprehensible to the audience, even when he finally ends up back in the space of shot three by shot eight. One has to assume that shot four's space does not exist in proximity to that of shot three, or the boy's route makes little sense.

Just as shot one fails to provide informative details about the men's plot, so does shot four lack sufficient emphasis to indicate why the boy runs back with such urgency to the woman's apartment. (The boy does read a note possibly detailing the plot, but without an insert, the viewer remains ignorant.) Thus, a large burden of narrative explication falls upon shot nine, when the boy finally meets the woman. He communicates his warning to her primarily through several waves of his hands, but beyond expressing a general sense of endangerment, these gestures do little to provide any further information. Nonetheless, the woman seems to understand and helps the boy into an outfit that will allow him to impersonate her. As viewers, we must make sense of this turn of events as it unfolds: we are not apprised of the boy's plan, nor do we know how the use of the outfit will aid him in carrying it out. Given the amount of time devoted to the boy parading about in these clothes, one has to assume displaying the spectacle of transvestism (a gimmick of considerable appeal throughout early cinema) takes precedence over explaining its motivation.

Near the end of shot nine, characters look out the apartment window, which seems to signal the setup for an eyeline match; this provides the only cue linking the view from the interior to the subsequent shot, which replicates the frontal perspective of the space's previous rendering in shot eight. Shot ten does show the boy mounting a carriage and driving away, but without a return to the apartment window, this functions less as a viewed action than one in a series of successive events. The final shot in this loosely linked chain of actions, shot eleven, portrays the boy intercepting the villains; when he offers the police a cigarette from the gun he has used to detain the men, his action helps to identify the weapon as the fake that appeared in shot one.

The film ends with a medium shot of the laughing boy detective revealing the gun to be a cigarette holder; this coda to the film functions as a redundant joke. By clarifying a point of information crucial to the viewer's understanding of the narrative, the shot operates like a detail cut-in, but it stands divorced from the shot preceding it. The closer shot scale, in conjunction with a lack of contextualization, both temporal (the boy is now dressed in his regular garb) and spatial (he appears in front of a neutral backdrop), confirms its status as an emblematic closing shot.

Overall, the filmmaker presents virtually the entire narrative as blocks of action, played out in long shot. While events of narrative importance remain centered, either through staging or reframing with pans, the viewer receives few other aids to comprehension: even the coded gestures of the histrionic style of performance occur but rarely, and cues from the *mise-en-scène* do not combine effectively with editing to construct spatial relationships among shots. Only because of the slightness of the narrative situation in *The Boy Detective* can one make much sense of it at all.

The Forgotten Watch (Vitagraph, December 1909)

A judge forgets his watch at home and then wrongfully accuses a man of stealing it on the trolley car. When the judge returns home, he calls the police to explain his mistake and invites the man to come to his house so that he can apologize. While accepting the judge's apology, the accused man surreptitiously steals his watch.

The plot of Vitagraph's *The Forgotten Watch* revolves around a narrative situation scarcely more developed than *The Boy Detective*'s. However, the film's very title, a strategically employed single intertitle, and closer camera positioning clear up possible points of viewer confusion much more readily; spatial connections construct a coherent diegetic geography; and modifications to *mise-en-scène* elements, such as décor, performance, and staging, achieve greater verisimilitude while establishing a production company identity.

In functional terms, the opening shots of both *The Boy Detective* and *The Forgotten Watch* share common aims: to establish the basic narrative situation and to help characterize the central protagonist. But the Vitagraph film provides a surfeit of incidental details that sustain the sense of a believable fictional world. Moreover, the employment of a closer shot scale allows the actors to fill the frame while being cut off just above the ankles; this, in turn, renders the actors' expressions easier to discern. Furniture extends past the frame edge, and the set's depth permits incidental activity (such as a maid cleaning) to occur in the background while the judge prepares to leave. Not only does this provide the opportunity for more characters to occupy the shot than narrative necessity dictates, but it also facilitates the arrangement of those characters in an uncluttered and visually balanced fashion. Why does the filmmaker choose to surround the judge with three female figures (wife, daughter, and maid) when narrative advancement requires only one? First, it creates a fuller, more believable domestic backdrop, which confirms the judge's bourgeois background; second, and perhaps most pertinently, it lends credibility to the forgetfulness that prompts the main narrative incident. The opening shot implies that the judge depends upon the ministrations of the various women in the household. This strategy of enveloping the judge in a cocoon of female attentiveness quickly sketches a portrait of the protagonist as a coddled, somewhat distracted, "absent-minded" professional.

The first important narrative incident, the judge's departure without his watch, occupies three shots. Rather than simply extending the action of the first shot after the judge leaves the room so that a remaining character registers discovery of the forgotten watch, the filmmaker elects to break the action down into three separate shots. The judge exits the house in shot two, which then leads to a closer-framed shot of his wife discovering the forgotten watch (shot three); shot four shows her in the space of shot two, looking for the judge in order to alert him. The breakdown of this simple narrative event into several shots results in more economic storytelling despite the increased number of shots. First, by beginning with a shot of the departing judge and then returning to the wife discovering the watch, the filmmaker splits the site of narrative action in two; if he had sustained shot one until the discovery, introducing a relation of simultaneity would have proven more difficult. Shot two also provides an ellipsis between shots one and three, allowing the wife to move from the space of shot one to the place where the husband misplaced the watch. (Besides, having the wife find the watch in another room seems more "believable": discovery of the watch in the same room from which the judge had just departed might strike us as too coincidental.) Second, by switching back to the wife, who, after finding the watch, exits the house in a manner identical to the husband, the filmmaker can imply the time and distance separating the judge and her. Viewers can deduce that the judge has gone sufficiently far from home that his wife cannot return the watch to him. Such small-scale temporal gaps and spatial relationships of limited alterity do not lend themselves to expression through intertitles. How would one compose an intertitle to convey this situation? A possible solution, like "The judge has forgotten his watch, and by the time his wife discovers his mistake he is already on his way to the trolley," would prove far too wordy and awkward. Editing accomplishes the same objective; in conjunction with the title *The Forgotten Watch*, the cutting minimizes the possibility of viewer confusion.

Aside from the treatment of the forgotten watch's discovery, the only other editing pattern in the film that alternates between two distinct spaces involves shots eleven through thirteen, wherein the judge, having learned the truth, calls the police station. Shot twelve returns to the police station, with a closer framing of a portion of the space shown in shot ten. Why should shot twelve involve the closest framing in the film, when it relays information of relatively little narrative importance, depicting a decidedly minor character? In this instance, spatial concerns probably motivate the close view; because the phone call involves only one character, the filmmaker eliminates the rest of the space of the police station in the interest of clarity.

Much like the central portion of *The Boy Detective*, the middle section of *The Forgotten Watch* incorporates a form of chase. Here, however, the script motivates the chase more clearly: a title reading "The Judge thinks a pickpocket has stolen his watch" precedes a depiction of the judge checking his pockets before he sets off after a man seen dashing off-frame. The chase itself is quite brief, covering only two shots. Arguably, the shortened status of the chase here indicates that emphasis has shifted from the spectacle of movement, still evident in *The Boy Detective*, to the irony of the situation, a by-product of the narrational decisions made in the first few shots. Because we saw the wife discover the judge's forgotten watch, we now know it cannot be stolen; in this case, the viewer's superior knowledge fuels the humor of the chase more so than any action actually depicted.

This discrepancy between viewer and character knowledge will be sustained until the judge learns of his mistake in shot eleven. The film's final joke requires the setup provided by the interceding shots nine and ten, where the judge demands that the accused give back the watch he thinks the man has stolen. In the last shot, when the judge apologizes, the joke's punch line reestablishes the viewer's superior knowledge, as we see the accused steal the judge's real watch while he fails to notice.

The filmmaker does not break down the story into brief segments of action throughout: for example, shots one, ten, and fourteen, all in separate spaces, have the longest running times and depict the most involved narrative moments. Nonetheless, the compositional strategies used (variations on depth staging inform character movement in the judge's parlor and at the police station) aid in specifying causally significant actions, while the closer shot scale facilitates comprehension of the performances. For that reason perhaps, even though *The Forgotten Watch* is a rather simple comedy, the acting rarely relies on expressly gestural pantomime. Developing narrational expedients and deploying style to increase verisimilitude mark *The Forgotten Watch* as a typical Vitagraph film of late 1909. At the same time, elements aligned with the primitive period (the chase, the underdeveloped narrative situation) still coincide with more recent innovations (closer framing, modified crosscutting).

Rose O'Salem-Town (Biograph, September 1910)

A Puritan accuses a young woman and her mother of witchcraft after the young woman resists his advances. The true object of the woman's affections, a trapper, enlists the aid of some Natives with whom he has traded in order to prevent the young woman from being burned.

Both *The Boy Detective* and *The Forgotten Watch* are split-reelers, so the full reel *Rose O'Salem-Town* possessing a higher shot count should not surprise us. But *Rose*'s shot total of forty-three substantially exceeds the combined total (twelve plus fourteen) of the two split-reelers, resulting in a noticeably quicker cutting rate, especially for a drama. Indeed, dramas are often cut more slowly than comedies, especially those containing chases, but as we shall see, *Rose O'Salem-Town* contains a variation on the chase as well. For a Griffith Biograph of 1910, however, the number of shots per thousand feet approaches the average, and the film relies on the crosscutting, contiguous spatial relations, and frontal, relatively shallow interior staging typical of the director's work for the company at this time.

Compared to *The Forgotten Watch, Rose O'Salem-Town* features relatively "advanced" storytelling strategies, particularly a deft handling of space. Even so, one can cite aspects of the film that appear less developed than the Vitagraph example of a year earlier. For example, no interior shot in *Rose* possesses the kind of compositional depth one finds in the opening of *The Forgotten Watch;* moreover, those shots featuring considerable numbers of characters look cramped, with the majority of actors massed in the mid-background, arranged laterally. Still, in his communication of story events, Griffith carefully promotes comprehension throughout. In order to expedite this process, the director relies extensively on titles which function as both overt commentary and redundant exposition; he also clarifies spatial relations through a variety of related cues (off-screen glances, matches on action for contiguous spaces, and consistent directionality).

Rose O'Salem-Town begins with two atmospheric shots that establish the film's setting while stressing its scenic splendors. The unusual overhead angle employed in shot two privileges scenery over the character, who enters the composition seven seconds into the shot. As the first title ("The Sea Child") indicates, these shots also function to establish the main character's innocence and affinity with nature. While the openings of the earlier two films made some effort to establish basic characteristics of the protagonists, they restricted this to only one shot while initiating the narrative action at the same time. *Rose O'Salem-Town,* on the other hand, provides nothing of narrative relevance beyond character evocation within the first two shots.

Before bringing the woman and the trapper together, Griffith introduces the second character separately, in part so editing can connect the two before they meet (a common Griffith strategy); however, this delay also allows him to associate the trapper with the Natives, who will play a significant role later in the story. In fact, the trapper and the woman will not meet until shot five, which permits the shots of the woman near the water to enfold our first view of the trapper before he in turn comes to the shore and hears her. Having established a mutual attraction in shot six, Griffith quickly shifts to the complicating factor within the narrative, signaled by the title, "The Puritan hypocrite attracted by the girl." By so describing the character even before depicting him, Griffith predisposes the viewer to assess the Puritan negatively. To cement the causal connection between the Puritan and the young woman's mother, Griffith introduces the latter character directly after the heroine has rebuffed the Puritan; the mother's actions will provide the villain with the opportunity to accuse her and her daughter of witchcraft. This section of the film closes with a shot of the Puritan looking in at the two women in their cottage and shaking his fist menacingly before pantomiming that he has an idea. The next title reiterates the information just conveyed—"Next Day. The Puritan's advances repulsed by the girl, he vows revenge."—risking redundancy to ensure clarity.

The subsequent shots alternate different strands of narrative action, which will converge in the arrest of the two women. Immediately after the Puritan's threat (communicated by the repeated use of a two-fingered gesture), and another anticipatory title of explanation, he convinces a group of town officials that the women are witches. Griffith reintroduces the interweaving between the romance narrative and the threat from the thwarted Puritan that he intimated in shots six and seven, following the shot of the accusation with one of the trapper bestowing a token of love (a necklace) upon the woman. The trapper will rescue the heroine from death in the film's climax, and the necklace will remind us of their bond even while they remain separated physically (from this point until shot forty-two).

In the next two shots, the Puritan establishes the grounds for accusing the women of witchcraft by spying on the mother and presenting her actions to the town officers as proof. Here the overtly commentative nature of the titles conditions our knowledge. After we have seen the mother advise a woman with a sick child and go out to collect plants to help her, a title reads: "The old mother's kindness purposely construed to be witchcraft." Without such guidance, we might wonder if the Puritan's charge has some merit, even if the mother seems benign. (For example, she does warn the ailing child's mother to keep their meeting secret.) The title intervenes to ensure that we realize the injustice of the charge. The following five shots involve the men's return to the cottage and their subsequent apprehension of the women. Several of the actors rely on selected histrionic postures while the young woman touches her necklace repeatedly throughout.

More redundancy occurs with the trapper's discovery of the heroine's predicament, conveyed first by a title and then its depiction in the following shot. Rather than have the trapper learn of the woman's arrest secondhand, Griffith places him—perhaps too conveniently—at the scene. To

lessen the obvious coincidence of this occurrence, Griffith tries to stage
the event casually, with the trapper in the mid-background asking questions of two men before Puritans bring the women in across the fore-
ground.³ Once the trapper's level of knowledge equals that of the audience, the film shifts into a fully realized crosscutting structure, with
increasingly rapid and systematic alternation between the trapper and the
woman.

The crosscutting must convey two different stages of the last-minute
rescue—the trapper's attempt to secure help for his rescue mission and
the rush of the rescuers back to the village. These alternate with scenes
of the women's trial, imprisonment, and (eventually interrupted) punish-
ment. The last-minute rescue unfolds in a manner quite typical of
Griffith's treatment of the device at this time, but several features bear
examination. First, Griffith carefully particularizes the features of the
space the trapper exits through in shot twenty-three. The distinctive composition, with dark barriers marking off the borders of the frame, helps
the viewer remember the space when it reappears in shot thirty-seven;
because the trapper looks back over his shoulder as he exits from this
area, we can assume it lies in some proximity to the village proper. This
aids the viewer in establishing how close the rescue party is to saving the
woman when they pass back through the space at the time of shot thirty-
seven. (One can note again that they look and react in shot thirty-seven,
which confirms that they have the woman in view.) Second, Griffith motivates the trapper's decision to appeal to the Natives by showing him already engaged in friendly relations with them in shot three. The director
increases suspense when he has the elder leader of the tribe refuse the
request (another realistic touch), but once he leaves, the younger brave
convinces the rest of the tribe to help. In fact, the film introduces a second order of crosscutting here (shots twenty-eight through thirty-two): the
trapper goes off after the elder's refusal and Griffith cuts between his
half-hearted return to the village and the remaining Natives' decision to
join him.

Griffith employs this extended sequence of crosscutting not only to
convey simultaneity of story events but also as a psychological link sol-
dering those events. Enlisting a privileged object (the necklace from the
trapper) helps to underscore the connection the editing conveys. In shot
twenty-seven, the woman, newly brought back to her cell, looks beseechingly at her necklace and then gazes off-frame right. A series of shots depicting the trapper's attempt to gather a rescue party follows directly, be-

fore a return to a shot of the heroine caressing her necklace once again. These recurring shots of the woman with the necklace perform three functions: they motivate the trapper's desperation, remind us that time is running out, and suggest her thoughts of him coincide with depictions of his efforts on her behalf.[4] Griffith had explored linking two spatially separate actions through a character's thoughts as early as 1908, with *After Many Years*. As Tom Gunning has argued in relation to that film, the power of the cut resides in its ability to actively manufacture meaning only latent in the *mise-en-scène* (1991, 114–15).

Griffith's experimentation with psychological editing develops in concert with a mounting emphasis on characters' directional gazes. Characters' glances off-screen help to define the spatial proximity of separated spaces (as when the Puritan looks off from the corner of the cottage in shot fourteen and we next see the shot of the mother gathering flowers, evidently nearby). In other cases, the gaze of a character may direct attention within the frame (as when we see the village officers staring through the window in the background of the cottage in shot seventeen) or may indicate an off-screen sight that a subsequent shot does not represent. The latter occurs in shot thirty-three, when the Puritan forces the woman to look out the prison window at her mother's immolation. We must register the shock of the image through the heroine's reaction; as a title informs us, the Puritan intends for the sight of her mother's torment to weaken her resolve.[5] Tellingly, the woman considers giving in to him but refuses as she catches sight of the necklace.

Overall, characters' looks and editing unite to intensify psychological reactions and clarify spatial relations during the latter part of the film, especially from shot thirty-seven onward, as the rescuers approach the burning site. This, in combination with the increased cutting rate (shots thirty-four through forty-three constitute one-quarter of the film's shots in one-tenth of its running time) and the consistent directionality of the rescuers' route, creates a fully believable chain of linked disparate spaces leading up to the rescuers' destination.

The film's tempo slows for its conclusion, a markedly subdued shot that returns to the space of shot five and the environment previously associated with the young woman.[6] It ends with the trapper touching the necklace a final time, before the heroine nestles into his arm and they walk off together. In keeping with the suppression of a more overt narrational voice in the latter part of the film, Griffith employs no titles to supplement this final shot. (The last had appeared before shot thirty-three, just prior to the acceleration of the film's cutting rate.) Moreover, the highly communicative nature of the narrational strategies abates somewhat for this closing shot. The woman's face registers a degree of muted contentment but remains relatively unexpressive. The viewer receives no cues concerning the couple's future together. They thank the brave for his help, but other loose ends produced by the narrative (such as the fate of the Puritan) remain that way. Given the leisurely pace of the film's final shot, one should not ascribe the tentative nature of the conclusion to time constraints. The narrational posture adopted seemingly abdicates responsibility for guiding our understanding after the rescue's completion; in many of his Biographs, Griffith trades on fairly uncommunicative endings to produce a bounded ambiguity.

Cupid's Monkey Wrench (Powers, April 1911)

When his car breaks down outside a hotel, the driver is mistaken for a repairman by the female proprietor. Later, they both attend a party thrown by a mutual friend. Now aware of her mistake, the woman expresses embarrassment, and the two strike up a romance.[7]

Cupid's Monkey Wrench substitutes a comedy of mistaken identity for the complications of a wrongfully claimed object which had fuelled *The Forgotten Watch*, but the films still share some pertinent formal traits: both rely on staging in depth, both employ one noticeably more closely scaled shot in conjunction with a telephone call, both use a pivotal object to foreground the irony of misrecognition, and both feature that object in their titles. Moreover, both contain a similar number of shots, but this does not offer grounds for arguing similarity, since the later film's running time doubles that of the earlier one. *The Forgotten Watch*'s practice of staging complicated actions within a single space so dominates *Cupid's Monkey Wrench* that several shots run well over a hundred feet. On the other hand, the dependence on editing to forge spatial relations and produce suspense, which typifies *Rose O'Salem-Town*, barely figures in *Cupid's Monkey Wrench*. Instead, considerable attention to comic bits of business gains prominence, oftentimes abetted by manipulation of props. (Whatever intertitles *Cupid's Monkey Wrench* contained in its original version have gone missing; even allowing for this omission, the film remains fairly easy to follow.)

Despite the lack of extensive editing, *Cupid's Monkey Wrench* begins in a manner similar to *Rose O'Salem-Town* by establishing the two protagonists in disparate locales before bringing them together. In this case,

Figure 6.1. Humorous incidents play upon viewer knowledge in *Cupid's Monkey Wrench* (1911).

Figure 6.2. The viewer knows more than the character.

however, the filmmaker sets forth the preconditions for the mistaken-identity plot immediately. A man dressed appropriately for automobile driving, Jack, is introduced as his vehicle overheats, forcing him and another of the car's occupants to go off in search of help. The film then shifts to an elaborate and fairly deep interior set, where a woman, Dolly, burns herself on the radiator featured in the right foreground. Though the filmmaker does not visually reinforce the parallel of the malfunctioning radiators in the two situations (via rhyming close shots, for example), title cards might have underscored the similarities in the full version. The implied simultaneity of these sets of actions soon leads to convergence: Dolly's call for someone to service the radiator coincides with Jack's wandering into the space of shot three after his friend has been conveniently drawn away by another man just outside. Because of Jack's apparel and the monkey wrench he carries, Dolly mistakes him for the repairman and asks him to fix the radiator.

After she has directed Jack to the kitchen, a series of comic set pieces ensues wherein the film trades heavily on the discrepancy between the viewer's knowledge and Dolly's. Much of the humor derives from the ironies attendant in her inappropriate treatment of Jack, as when she hides the silver from him while asking him to fix the sink in the kitchen (fig. 6.1) and examines his bag and hat once she has returned to the room with the radiator (fig. 6.2). Jack decides to extend the charade until he can meet Dolly under other circumstances that will reveal her mistake. Jack conspires to have his friend invite him to a party Dolly will be attending; he outlines his plans in a note (shown as an insert), which the friend in turn shows to her. The particulars of the note establish the setting for the film's final section while also identifying the friend who will reappear in the film's final shot. The protracted denouement effects little more than a reunion of the couple while the film ends with a comical flourish as Jack proffers another wrench.

The strategic repetition of a prop (its centrality signaled by the film's title) points to the emphasis on *mise-en-scène* that characterizes the entire film. Different planes of the sets come into play, demonstrating that filmmakers had begun to emulate Vitagraph's experiments with depth staging. In the set of the hotel sitting room, the filmmaker uses the décor to draw attention to the space in the immediate foreground: for example, a chair is placed with its back to the camera, close enough to the lens to render only the top half visible. The radiator also occupies the foreground plane at extreme frame right, while the telephone sits near the windows in the mid-ground, ensuring that characters will move into different portions of the playing space. At the same time, a second area beyond room-dividing curtains extends the space into the far background as well (fig. 6.3). The filmmaker promotes a sense of verisimilitude by providing sufficient detailing of décor, though portions of the deepest region of the set have been painted in. Even so, at one point Dolly goes into this space to select a book from the faux bookcase (fig. 6.4).

The set for the party proves far less elaborate, but the filmmaker deploys extras to sustain the sensation of a deeper playing field established in the other set. While the protagonists dance in the mid-background, other partygoers are arranged at the front, flanking the sides of the frame to provide a centered view of the dancers. The staging does not fully adopt the Vitagraph practice of positioning characters with their backs to the camera but does place one of the women at a three-quarter turn away (fig. 6.5). The placement of these figures achieves balance in an otherwise underfilled frame while also telescoping visual interest toward the central depths of the image.

Features which amalgamate transitional and primitive attributes offset the relatively developed staging strategies. I have already mentioned the realistically detailed set's inclusion of a painted-in piece of furniture. Another such example involves the temporal overlap that attends the film's sole use of a cut-in. Following the cut-in itself (which fails to retain consistent character positioning from the master shot but employs the background from the set), the return to a fuller shot shows Dolly still on the phone (fig. 6.6; also fig. 6.3). However, when we return to the space after several intervening events over the next two shots—one of which clearly indicates that Dolly's call must be finished—Dolly remains on the phone, suggesting shots three, five, and eight probably all derive from a single master shot that the filmmaker has not edited properly for ellipses.

Figure 6.3. The main set features considerable depth in *Cupid's Monkey Wrench* (1911).

Figure 6.4. Elements in the far background are painted in.

Figure 6.5. Framing the central action while creating depth.

Figure 6.6. A cut-in to a close shot for a telephone conversation.

A similarly uncertain handling of temporal relations between shots occurs near the end, when Jack pulls back the curtains to exit onto the balcony (fig. 6.7): in the following shot, meant to depict the space on the other side of the curtains, Dolly stands anticipating his arrival, but the curtains and door are still fully closed (fig. 6.8). Rather than execute a straightforward match-on-action, the filmmaker produces another example of temporal overlap.

The film's sole cut-in is notable for other reasons than the editing anomalies it produces. Like the closer view used for the policeman's phone call in *The Forgotten Watch,* the cut-in here seems dictated by a logic favoring viewer orientation: the phone call depicted takes place in the mid-ground of a visually busy frame, and the tighter framing eliminates unnecessary surrounding space. Even so, the medium close-up used for this purpose stands out as a surprisingly close shot scale for the period. Given the strong opposition to closer views at this time, one wonders what might have motivated the filmmaker's choice of a shot-scale

Figure 6.7. Preparing to exit the room in   Figure 6.8. . . . results in an instance of
Cupid's Monkey Wrench (1911) . . .   temporal overlap in the subsequent shot.

Figure 6.9. Direct address punctuates the
comic mode of performance.

criticized for promoting a sense of the grotesque. In part, this choice might
stem from the continued formal adventurousness that the problem of representing phone conversations seemed to promote among filmmakers, resulting in such solutions as the split screen, crosscutting, and closely
scaled shots.

The film's performance style evidences a developing generic distinction. For the most part, the actors adopt a fairly light, if often stylized,
mode of performing, indebted largely to verisimilar models over histrionic.
The actors also integrate props into their performances, though more to
provoke laughter than deepen characterization (the express purpose of
props in dramas). Nonetheless, isolated instances of direct address to the
camera occur (fig. 6.9), which suggest a growing awareness that comedy
allows its own approaches to acting (and by extension narration) distinct
from those appropriate for more serious (and less self-conscious) forms of
narrative. By the time slapstick comedy regained prominence as the chief
form of comic storytelling a few years later, filmmakers such as Mack
Sennett at Keystone would borrow formal tendencies evident in *Cupid's*

Monkey Wrench, particularly the use of props and the hybrid acting style, and combine them with a rapid cutting rate to produce a predictable generic approach.[8]

Belle Boyd, a Confederate Spy (Selig, May 1913)

When Union troops planning an attack on Confederate forces occupy Belle Boyd's home, she takes advantage of a hole in the ceiling overlooking their plans and spies on them. Later, she successfully makes off with one of their maps and carries it to the Confederate army in the midst of battle.

By 1913, many filmmakers customarily broke down filmic space in a fairly analytical fashion, resulting in increased shots per reel and multiple camera setups per locale. Others adhered to a more conservative aesthetic, rarely engaging in any intrascene editing at all. *Belle Boyd, a Confederate Spy* commands interest because it represents both tendencies in one film. The first half, depicting Belle's actual spying activities and procurement of the Union troops' plans, incorporates a variety of shot scales and rudimentary scene dissection; for the second half, when she delivers the plans, the filmmaker relies only on more static long-shot framings and links spaces in a fashion that recalls chase films of an earlier period. Though the two parts occupy almost the same amount of running time, the first encompasses twenty-eight shots, while the second only requires nine. If the filmmaker had maintained the approach of the first half throughout, the film's shot total would be closer to the 1913 average; instead he reverts to a logic that treats space as integral blocks of action in the second portion of the film, even though he uses exterior shooting throughout this section.

Indisputably, the heroine's discovery of the Union plans constitutes the crucial event in *Belle Boyd*'s narrative. Its depiction entails the film's most intricately edited sequence, totaling one-third of the film's shots but only one-fifth of its running time. Moreover, the filmmakers apparently devised the discovery to foreground the repeated use of an unusual overhead shot showing the troops at a table below. Even as late as 1913, one can identify films designed for the purpose of privileging a single set piece or distinctive employment of a device. To cite one other example, Kalem's *By the Aid of a Lariat* (1911) revolves around the climactic feat of stretching a lariat across a canyon to rescue a woman from Indians. One can understand this strategy as a holdover from the cinema of attractions, when a novel situation or technique animates an entire film, except in the transitional examples, filmmakers must construct coherent narratives to motivate the novelty.

Belle Boyd begins by establishing Belle's allegiance to the Confederate cause and positing the Union forces as a menace. The film starts in a state of equilibrium with a title informing us that "Belle Boyd and her girl friends repair the battle-torn uniforms of their Confederate sweethearts." Beyond providing a rationale for Belle's subsequent actions, the title and shots to follow verify that troops are waging battles nearby. The initial image remains one of repose, reinforced by a gazebo-like structure in the foreground that frames the activity within. The subsequent shot introduces a disruption, however, as the locale shifts to the woods: a Confederate rider near the camera circles and exits after looking off left; his departure anticipates the emergence of troops in the background, filing across the frame in a leftward direction. The rider enters into the space of shot one in the next shot, while a dialogue title informs us of what we already witnessed in the previous shot—"The Yanks are coming."

The filmmaker charts the Union officers' advance toward Belle's front door through progressively closer framings of the space initially established in shot one. By shot ten, only the doorway is visible, at which point the soldiers enter. One of the officers, who will prove instrumental to the narrative's development later, distinguishes himself from the others in shot eight by shooting down a flag hanging outside Belle's home. He displays the flag pointedly in shot ten before placing it within his uniform; this action helps to emphasize the flag, which will also assume significance later in the narrative.

In anticipation of the sequence depicting Belle's spying efforts, the officers select a table at which to confer; one of the officers notices an object protruding from the ceiling and pulls on it, causing a portion of the ceiling to come down. Just like the watch's placement in the bedroom (in *The Forgotten Watch*), the mother's medicinal practice (in *Rose O'Salem-Town*), and Jack's possession of a wrench (in *Cupid's Monkey Wrench*), the wreckage of the ceiling functions as a seemingly incidental occurrence included deliberately to render subsequent narrative events more believable and properly motivated. In this case, the script has adequately prepared for the officer pulling on the broken ceiling board: we know that battles are taking place near Belle's home, so we can assume the house might have sustained some damage; further, the officers' previous actions have established them as impetuous and presumptuous, so we accept that one of them would pull on a distracting object without thought of the outcome or possible damage. This act of creating a hole in the ceiling lends credibility to Belle's subsequent ability to spy on the officers below; it would seem too coincidental if they happened to pick a spot where Belle already had a previously constructed viewing hole cut out from the floor above.

Once the Yankees clear off the table, the officer who shot the flag offers it to Belle. This gesture helps to indicate his interest in her, which will prove relevant later, but it also motivates Belle's spying efforts by inflaming her sense of patriotism. As if to signal this, Belle still clutches the flag in the subsequent shot, when she goes off to an adjoining room and indicates she has a plan (conveyed by a touch to her head and a finger pointed upward).

The film's narration does not remain consistently communicative during this portion. After the shot where Belle announces her plan, an overhead shot of the officers in consultation follows. The viewer must decipher whether the shot of the officers depicts Belle's idea or merely confirms that a hole now exists above them. Confusion is compounded in the next shot, when the officer who had expressed interest in Belle looks up and then moves toward the stairs in the background. What has caused his suspicion? Is he aware that the upper floor affords a view of the table? Subsequent shots do not fully explain the officer's behavior, although when the following shot shows Belle in the room above, it becomes clear that she has just arrived and has not yet had occasion to look through the hole, still covered by a rug. This shot initiates a brief crosscutting sequence wherein the officer searches the upstairs, and Belle hides when he enters her room. Because the viewer cannot ascertain how much the officer knows, however, suspense is somewhat mitigated.

Once he has left the room, Belle lifts back the carpet to peek. The first of the overhead shots to incorporate Belle's head within the image occurs. Because Belle appears within the composition, these are not optical point-of-view shots, but they convey within a single framing Belle's act of spying on the officers below, replete with the splinters of the floorboard marking off her view. The officer has returned to the space of shot eighteen, a hallway that adjoins Belle's room, but he responds to a call, heading back down and ending this phase of the crosscutting sequence. After one more overhead shot, the view reverts to the earlier framing of the officers from the ground level, as all except the recently returned officer begin to pack up their plans and exit.

At this point in the narrative, the functional value of the officer's interest in Belle becomes most apparent. Presumably, her view of the activity downstairs has informed her that only the one officer remains. Still upstairs, she covers the hole and grabs a roll of paper from a dresser drawer; just prior to exiting the room, she takes a bunch of flowers from a vase, arranging them to obscure the paper from view. No title explains the reason for her actions, though the subsequent shot renders her motivation clear. She arrives downstairs and drops the flowers, knowing that the officer will pick them up for her; when he does, she switches her roll for the map still on the table. Having accomplished her goal, Belle gives the officer a flower but resists his advances by backing away toward the front door. The next shot returns to the outside of the house through a match-on-action of Belle backing through the entrance. Once the officers have left, Belle dispenses with the flowers, opens the map, gestures that she has another plan, and exits. After securing a horse in the next shot, Belle rides back into the space of shot twenty-six, initiating her attempt to deliver the map, which will constitute the film's second half.

The remainder of the narrative consists primarily of Belle's ride to the battlefield, followed by her progress on foot once her horse has been stolen. The filmmaker conveys the theft in an abrupt and confusing fashion, failing even to explain why Belle dismounts. Except for a shot that shows soldiers blowing up a bridge (presumably part of the Union plan), the remainder of the film shows Belle wandering through numerous casualty-strewn battle sites before she delivers the map in the third to last shot. Subsequently the officer in charge pantomimes orders while holding the map, and a title (one of only four in the entire film) informs us that "Belle's bravery has saved the day for General Jackson." The final shot shows Belle and two other officers walking through the carnage prior to turning away from the camera.

Arguably, the film's narratively simple second half does not require the more elaborate communicative devices employed in the first. Nonetheless, the filmmaker seldom clarifies points of possible confusion: What do the plans say? Once the Confederates have gained knowledge of the plans, how does this help them to thwart the Union troops' strategy? Would it have mattered had Belle arrived any sooner or later? Some of these questions derive from the intermittently uncommunicative aspects of the film's first half. First, though the filmmaker goes to considerable lengths to showcase Belle's spying activities (including the adequate motivation of how the hole becomes available and how the heroine gains access to the plans), he never bothers to specify what the plans entail. A cut-in to the papers themselves or a title explaining the nature of the Union strategy would specify how Belle's delivery of the plans might aid the Confederate cause. Without such information, the bridge destruction incident of shot thirty-two fails to have much impact, because it can't be placed within the context of an overarching military strategy. Second, though the filmmaker has established from the outset that Belle and her friends have a personal stake in the outcome of the battle (given the involvement of their "sweethearts"), he does not exploit that connection once Belle obtains the plans. The viewer must speculate about what a Confederate loss might mean for Belle personally and can only guess if any temporal pressure exists, spurring the heroine to reach her destination as quickly as possible. The film never achieves the level of redundancy evident in *Rose O'Salem-Town*, from nearly three years earlier, nor does it create as coherent a sense of diegetic geography once Belle leaves her home. The selective adoption of stylistic elements designed to improve viewer comprehension in *Belle Boyd* results in an inconsistently communicative narrational stance that makes the film seem less formally advanced.

Suspense (Rex, June 1913)

An intruding vagrant menaces a woman left alone in her remote home with only her baby. The woman's husband learns of the break-in during a telephone conversation with her, and he steals a car in order to rush to her salvation. With the police in pursuit, the husband reaches the home just in time to save his wife and child.

In keeping with its title, which succinctly announces its intended effect on the viewer, *Suspense* is an exercise in narrational self-consciousness. The directors, Phillips Smalley and Lois Weber, seem intent on filling the film with flashy stylistic flourishes. In part, the film's overly familiar subject matter facilitates such virtuosity: *Suspense* patterns itself on earlier filmic variants of André de Lorde's play *Au téléphone* (1901), such as Edison's *Heard over the Phone* (1908), Pathé's *A Narrow Escape* (1908), and Biograph's *The Lonely Villa* (1909). Moreover, the script scarcely modifies the stock narrative ingredients of a wife imperiled in a remote location while her husband rushes to the rescue after learning of her plight over the telephone. Because the filmmakers could count on audiences already knowing what to expect from the film, producing the titular suspense provides a challenge; Smalley and Weber meet this by heightening tension and intensifying the film's psychological dimension through manipulation of style. Sprinkled liberally throughout with touches that encourage spectatorial involvement without ever damaging narrative clarity, *Suspense*

Figure 6.10. A tripartite mask for a telephone conversation in *Suspense* (1913).

emerges as one of the most stylistically *outré* films of the transitional period.

As befits a film designed to engender apprehension, *Suspense* adopts an omniscient narration that constantly keeps the viewer more informed than any one of the characters. The clearest example comes in the novel depiction of the phone conversation between husband and wife. Using a triangular mask, the filmmakers divide the frame into three sections, with the husband at the base, the wife in the upper-right portion, and the thief at the left. This configuration permits the directors to convey a sense of three-way simultaneity while also rendering concrete the couple's ignorance of the thief's proximity to their home (fig. 6.10). While effective as a means of telegraphing three-way action (and potentially less confusing than constant crosscutting), this approach probably proved too narrationally self-conscious to influence many future filmmakers.[9]

The tripartite mask stands as one of the film's more striking deviations from a narrational norm, but as we saw in *Cupid's Monkey Wrench* and *The Forgotten Watch*, telephone conversations often invited inventive representational strategies from filmmakers.[10] The distinctiveness of *Suspense* resides in how consistently it devises novel means of representing familiar situations. A few of its methods even hearken back to practices from the primitive era, although their self-conscious use here points more to a retooling of outmoded devices than unwitting anachronism. We might cite the triangular version of the phone conversation again in this context, though a more clear-cut example is the keyhole mask used to frame the maid's view of the mother and baby at the beginning of the film (figs. 6.11 and 6.12). The expressly communicative function that point-of-view performs here differentiates its deployment from earlier versions: the masked shot specifies the intended recipient of the note the maid will compose in the following shot and establishes the identities of the other occupants of the house. Moreover, it situates the nursery as adjacent to the kitchen, which will aid in the viewer's spatial orientation when the tramp breaks into the house later.

The maid's note supplies information about the remoteness of the house, reveals that the maid's departure will leave mother and child unaccompanied, and indicates that her back-door key will be left under the mat. Moreover, by revealing the maid's actions to the viewer but not to the

Figure 6.11. Setting up a point-of-view shot in *Suspense* (1913) . . .

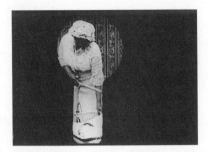

Figure 6.12. . . . via an anachronistic use of a keyhole mask.

Figure 6.13. The overhead shot of the maid's departure.

wife, the narration places the spectator in a position of superior knowledge, which already instills fear in the viewer for the safety of those remaining at the house alone. When the maid leaves, the filmmakers position the camera from a striking overhead perspective, not motivated as point of view (fig. 6.13). Besides drawing attention to itself as a bravura shot, the distinctiveness of the framing helps associate this vantage point with the location of the entry door, so that when the filmmakers repeat it in shot twenty, the viewer can ascertain the tramp's whereabouts. (In other words, this strategy operates as a more flamboyant version of the practice pursued by Griffith in *Rose O'Salem-Town*.)

A long shot of the maid coming down an incline with the house in the distance confirms her written report of the home's isolation. The shot scale also allows the tramp to enter even as the maid exits frame right. He retraces her steps up the hill, but over the next series of shots, the filmmakers only allude to his actual location vis-à-vis the house. The aforementioned telephone conversation occurs the first of two times with the burglar's proximity suggested but left somewhat unspecified because of the small portion of space devoted to him in the upper left part of the frame. Nonetheless, the phone call only heightens suspense: the content of the conversation (relayed through a dialogue title) reveals to us that the husband will not be home for some time, while the representation of the call suggests that the tramp may have heard this information as well.

Once the wife has hung up the phone, she moves to the kitchen and finds the note. At this point the wife still lags behind the audience in the amount of information she possesses, which allows the filmmakers to extend the suspense by not showing the intruder for six shots (shots ten through fifteen), while the wife checks on the baby and locks the door. In shot sixteen the tramp is visible through the nursery window, but the wife does not see him; she collects the baby and moves upstairs, unwittingly increasing the distance between herself and the intruder. The film then begins to alternate between sets of shots of the tramp moving around the house and the wife's activities inside. In shot twenty-one, a closer framing of a space already established in shot eighteen, she hears a noise and looks out her window. The second of the film's point-of-view shots follows: the filmmakers build on the self-consciousness of the earlier overhead shots by staging it so that the tramp's foot and hands come into view before his head, which eventually tilts back to reveal him looking up toward the wife (and the camera) (fig. 6.14). Besides the distinctiveness of the camera position and the deliberate manner in which the tramp enters the shot, the use of point-of-view to intensify the shock of the wife's discovery demonstrates how style can encourage viewer involvement. At this moment, the film engages in a highly subjective form of narration that not only conveys the moment of discovery through the wife's optical point of view but also suggests her psychological reaction by stretching out the revelation of the intruder's presence.

The wife's discovery prompts the second telephone conversation, and a trio of (somewhat redundant) dialogue titles charts the tramp's progress. The titles still perform a necessary narrational function, for they measure the wife's knowledge against what the audience sees. In the first title, she merely states that "a tramp is prowling around the house," but in fact he has already discovered the key that the maid left under the mat. (A self-consciously framed shot of the tramp's hands and feet in the upper left hand of the frame reveals this detail [fig. 6.15].) The second title reveals that the wife's knowledge now matches the tramp's actions, since she describes them accurately. When the third dialogue title indicates an interrupted observation—"Now he is in the . . . "—the image of a dangling phone cord in the tramp's sector of the frame establishes that he has cut the line. Both the husband's and wife's reactions (a startled jump upward

Figure 6.14. Use of a point-of-view shot to intensify the wife's shock in *Suspense* (1913).

Figure 6.15. Framing reveals the tramp's discovery of the key.

Figure 6.16. Conveying proximity via a rearview mirror during the chase.

and a worried glance off-screen, respectively) confirm the termination of the call, and the action now shifts temporarily to the husband initiating a rescue attempt.

From this point onward, consistent crosscutting dominates *Suspense:* initially, alternation occurs between the husband driving toward home in a stolen car and the wife back at the house (shots twenty-seven through twenty-nine); this quickly gives way to a far more complex parallel structure incorporating the husband's pursuit by the police and the tramp's mounting progress toward the upstairs bedroom. Again, the filmmakers avoid the canonical approach to such multipronged last-minute rescues that merely multiplies the number of spaces the editing puts into alternation. Rather than cutting from the husband bent on rescue to the police chasing him, the filmmakers devise a characteristically flamboyant but narrationally effective way to consolidate the information. In two different shots (thirty-four and forty-two), the camera, mounted within the husband's car, shoots a close-up of his vehicle's rearview side mirror (fig. 6.16). The framing typically includes the outline of his concerned face in prominent close-up at frame left and the police in pursuit reflected in the mirror. In effect, the filmmakers have hit upon an innovative method for implying proximity within a single shot. Much like the overhead point-of-view shot, this virtuoso solution violates selected norms (in this case, those of shot scale and composition) and distinguishes itself further by mounting the camera on a vehicle, still a relative rarity at this time. The filmmakers compound the level of ingenuity by sandwiching the inverse of the mirror shot between its two appearances: shot thirty-nine shows the husband's automobile from the vantage point of the moving police car. This time the composition features the profile of a police officer looming in close-up in the left foreground as he looks ahead toward the husband's vehicle, shown within the depth of the right-hand side of the frame (fig. 6.17). This shot also intensifies the momentum of the chase by collapsing the distance between the two vehicles when the police car virtually pulls up beside the husband's car (fig. 6.18).

The filmmakers constantly interrupt the progress of the chase/rescue by returning to the house. Several shots demonstrate a concerted inventiveness in depicting the wife's mounting fear and the tramp's increased proximity. Shot thirty-three begins with the camera aimed into the corner of the bedroom, the wife shown in the reflection of a dresser mirror to the left of the frame (fig. 6.19). As she approaches, her body finally moves into the camera's range, at which point she pulls the dresser into a position in front of the door to act as a barricade. What begins as a flashy reflecting shot that effectively emphasizes the wife's vulnerability while she crouches in the opposite corner of the bedroom, turns out to be a framing that also foregrounds the object of primary narrative importance—the dresser. Moreover, this shot prefigures the function of the following shot, when the car mirror makes its first appearance during the chase: in both cases, reflection embodies causality, insofar as the mirror incorporates an off-screen figure whose presence has a direct bearing on the action depicted onscreen.

Shot forty-three initiates a series of shots designed to stress the mounting intensity of the wife's endangerment. Though not an actual point-of-view shot, it recalls the earlier overhead framing: with the camera positioned at the top of the stairs, the tramp climbs toward it until his face looms in extreme close-up, and eventually he passes beyond the camera's range (figs. 6.20 and 6.21). In 1913, characters rarely advance toward the camera in this manner; no doubt the filmmakers employ this effect to elicit shock. The fairly close framings of the next two shots compound the menace conveyed in shot forty-three. Combining rapid cutting rates with these

Figure 6.17. An inversion of the chase's mirror shot in *Suspense* (1913) eventually incorporates . . .

Figure 6.18. . . . movement within the shot which measures the diminishing distance between the two vehicles.

Figure 6.19. Using the dresser mirror to reflect the wife's predicament.

Figure 6.20. The tramp advances toward the camera . . .

Figure 6.21. . . . until his face looms as an extreme close-up.

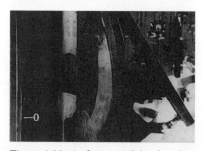

Figure 6.22. A close-up of the door key and part of the dresser in *Suspense* (1913) . . .

Figure 6.23. . . . prepares for the violent gesture of the tramp's forced entry . . .

Figure 6.24. . . . leading to the closest scaled shot of the wife, shown screaming.

progressively closer shot scales renders the tense situation even more suspenseful. Shot forty-four begins as a close-up of the door key and a portion of the dresser before the tramp's arm smashes through (figs. 6.22 and 6.23). This synecdochic representation of his presence recalls the earlier shot of his hands and feet at the kitchen mat; just as that image was succeeded by the image of the severed phone cord, the violent thrust of his arm gives way to the closest shot yet of the wife, shown screaming (fig. 6.24).

These shots constitute the film's climax, and with the film's tension at a high point, the narration again shifts back to the rescue, with the arrival of the husband and the police shown in rapid succession. Here the filmmakers exploit crosscutting's potential for temporal expansion, for in the time it takes to depict the arrival of the rescuing party, no discernible intervening time has elapsed in the bedroom. A brief shot whose framing features the tramp in the left foreground and the wife in the right background (the first time the two have actually shared the same space) yields to a shot of the police running up toward the house, shooting. The sound from that space causes the tramp to leave the bedroom, as depicted in the next shot, and the final two shots of the film show the intruder and the husband engaged in a struggle before the police intervene and contain the tramp, allowing the husband to reunite with his wife and child in the bedroom. The filmmakers invest little effort in reestablishing a mood of domestic tranquility; the rather preemptory conclusion scarcely dissipates the residual anxiety created by the film's effective marshaling of distinctive formal strategies.[11]

Despite its extremely self-conscious approach to narration, *Suspense* is rarely less than fully communicative. Owing in part to the familiarity of the narrative, the film proves quite easy to comprehend, but the filmmakers' studied refusal to use any expository titles (and only four brief dialogue titles and one letter insert) demonstrate their commitment to conveying story information largely through other means. The battery of stylistic methods employed derives primarily from editing (a rapid cutting rate, far above the industry norm, and a marked reliance on different forms of crosscutting, with variants introduced for the telephone conversation and during the chase) and cinematographic properties (a consistently varied shot scale and, perhaps most unusual for the period, a variety of distinctive camera positions and framings, including overhead shots, moving camera, and close-ups of various body parts). *Suspense*'s stylistic expressiveness, while it never compromises its narrational competence, so exceeds the norms of the period that the film emerges as an anomaly.[12] In its expert manipulation of diegetic space, its sustained involvement of the spectator in the emotional plight of its protagonists (through subjective narration and numerous close-ups, among other strategies), and its unrelieved production of suspense via a narrational stance that rarely withholds information, *Suspense* serves as a model for the classical practices of a few years hence. However, the film's persistently inventive style, too self-conscious to allow complete subordination to narrative demands, simultaneously marks *Suspense* as a transitional film whose narrational distinctiveness distances it from classical norms.

As these six case studies demonstrate, a broad range of stylistic usage and narrational strategies spans the period encompassing both *The Boy Detective* and *Suspense*. The formal changes involved clearly point away from primitive cinema and toward classicism. Yet, the narrational self-assurance of *Suspense* might mislead us into equating mature transitional filmmaking with classical practice. Here the corrective of *Belle Boyd* helps demonstrate that the variety of approaches still employed by 1913 distinguishes the transitional period from later years. The myriad changes style and narration undergo from 1907 to 1913 definitely confirm an ongoing trend toward more systematic narrativization of available devices. However, even though one can observe filmmakers consolidating stylistic and narrational tendencies by the end of the transitional period, they have not yet achieved codified employment of a limited range of devices. Once the transitional period ended, filmmakers continued to refine and regulate the variety of options available to them even as extended running times posed new problems of narrative structure and narrational expedience. Within a few more years, a considerably more predictable type of storytelling practice emerged out of this process. Nonetheless, after 1913 never again would one find such a diverse range of narrational norms within a seven-year period of American filmmaking.

7

Conclusion

Is THE TRANSITIONAL PERIOD a distinct phase within the formal history of American filmmaking or merely a way station between the primitive and the classical? The transitional period's salient characteristic—its constant engagement of change—renders any definitive description particularly difficult. Yet the thoroughgoing nature of the alterations involved so demonstrably affected film form, I believe we must accord these years their status as a unique period. Overall, the halting but substantial recasting of formal operations increased film's narrativizing capacity in ways that no one could have imagined at the outset of the period. Concepts of narrative structure, narrational norms, the articulation of temporal and spatial relations, the deployment of stylistic devices—all these underwent significant transformations during the years in question. As I have argued, such shifts occurred within a context of defined and observable changes to industrial structure and production practices. Moreover, the institutionalization of trade press response provided a forum for self-appointed experts to comment on the experiments taking place and attempt to shape change by setting standards and voicing objections.

How, exactly, might filmmakers have pursued the explorations in formal development that characterize this period, given the industrial conditions of the time? We know the solutions they devised to different narrational problems emerged slowly and sporadically; even so, by 1913 the collective impact of these experiments resulted in a filmmaking practice more heavily narrativized than ever before. Specific problems—increased demand for films, promotion of viewer comprehension and engagement—guided filmmakers in their choice of goals, while certain constraints—the set durational limit of the thousand-foot reel, trade press standards—shaped the kinds of solutions which could emerge. Finding workable ways to solve the narrational problems they faced could lead filmmakers to emulate other media or art forms where applicable (principles of set design from theater or certain temporal articulations from lantern slides), but for the most part, they probably relied on an intuitive system of trial and error.[1]

The rapidity with which companies churned out films during the period contributed to the problem-solving process in both positive and negative ways. High demand meant that producers had little time to worry over representational problems at length; such solutions as they did devise often emerged in a piecemeal fashion and not as part of an ongoing plan to transform film form systematically. Moreover, the supposed promise of quick and substantial profits would encourage producers to value efficient delivery of finished films over inventive handling of narrational dilemmas.[2] Nonetheless, the repetitive nature of the production process also meant that filmmakers could try out and then revise solutions within a circumscribed time frame; they could reject unwieldy or problematic approaches after a limited number of attempts, just as they could refine promising methods over the course of the next few productions. In the same vein, the large volume of output allowed companies to view the work of the competition with ease and tailor their solutions accordingly: if the press or audiences responded well to a particularly efficacious narrational innovation, other filmmakers could emulate that attempt quite quickly thereafter.[3]

Nonetheless, not all solutions were easily copied, not even successful ones. Numerous complicating factors could militate against the immediate adoption of certain techniques. First, if the trade press registered a negative or even ambivalent reaction toward a distinct approach (e.g., the adoption of a closer shot scale), the perceived drawbacks might dissuade filmmakers from experimenting further. Second, if the method in question involved particular skills or increased expense (as would be the case with altering performance styles or developing more intricate set designs), some companies would resist because of their own inherent limitations. For example, if less-established companies initially resisted the lead of Biograph in developing crosscutting, they probably did so because they feared that whatever complications increased editing introduced to the production and postproduction stages could outstrip its narrational benefits. Accomplished competitors, such as Vitagraph, may have preferred to develop approaches that did not seem indebted to the efforts of a major rival. Finally, the diverse range of talents and interests involved in film producing reduced the odds that the industry would gravitate to singular solutions with speed and certainty. Eventually most manufacturers would opt for preferred methods, but even within individual companies, one can still note inconsistencies of approach; this suggests that some filmmakers remained unconvinced of the advantages in particular experiments.

Because significant formal changes during this period appear most often in the films of acknowledged industry leaders like Vitagraph and Biograph, one can assume that other filmmakers preferred to wait and copy proven techniques rather than risk novelty themselves. This tendency becomes less pronounced by the end of the period, indicating not only that the increased maturity of these competitors lent them more confidence but also that continuity of personnel and establishment of a company-based identity helped to propel lesser manufacturers to devise their own methods. By the tail-end of the transitional period, many companies had expanded operations sufficiently to develop extensive and dependable stock companies and craft departments; directors might have their own units with which they worked repeatedly; script departments existed as separate entities, tailoring scenarios to the company's perceived areas of specialization; and talent might be promoted from within, as when actors graduated to direction.[4] All these tendencies would encourage companies to incorporate reliable methods of storytelling, concurrent with the streamlining of the production process to ensure consistency and dependability. Stability in personnel and establishment of a steady supply of useable scripts reduced the risk in developing uniform approaches to fashioning legible and compelling narratives. Company practices, such as apprenticeship and internal promotion, would help ensure that the organization assimilated whatever solutions might be devised, while the desire to be recognized as industry leaders would spur companies to continue developing successful approaches to mounting narratives.

As much as altered production practices encouraged increased attention to effective storytelling, industrial expansion ensured continued discrepancies in the representational competencies of manufacturers. So while broad standards had established themselves by 1913, the rate of change remained uneven. In the preceding chapter, I demonstrated the range of approaches via comparative analysis of six sample films. As a final synthesis, I will provide a synchronic overview to balance the diachronic portrait sketched out there.

At the beginning of the period, the marked impetus toward telling longer and more complex stories forced a rethinking of approaches to narration. Audience comprehension and narrative complexity threatened to prove mutually exclusive goals, as indicated by the initial increased reliance on extratextual tools (such as lecturers and forms of talking films).

In order to convey more involved narratives with effectiveness, filmmakers had to devise methods to render the stories' complexities understandable. First, this meant choosing narratives whose principles of organization would be amenable to the single-reel format. Extended stories with multiple lines of action proved unworkable; instead, scenarists gravitated toward concentrating on a central narrative incident, the causes for which derived directly from the character traits of the main protagonist. Even if the script honed those traits to a requisite minimal range, filmmakers had to devise means to supply adequate characterization: flashbacks could provide motivation, visions could plumb character psychology, and the verisimilar performance style could allow diverse emotions to play over the actors' faces, captured in sufficient detail by closer shot scale.

Similarly, to articulate time and space properly, filmmakers explored ways to show how spaces related to one another and to communicate temporal gaps or altered temporal order without undue confusion. Methods for working out these problems varied substantially, particularly in the early years of the period. Not all approaches proved equally useful, and some experiments were abandoned. Certain solutions, such as a reliance on titles and inserts to carry the weight of narrative exposition or specify temporal gaps, appealed to filmmakers because of their ease; even so, condemnation by the trade press or the limitations of the single-reel format could render these approaches undesirable. Moreover, any proposed solution would need to meet the increasingly important goal of sustaining verisimilitude, which trade press commentators viewed as essential to a form of entertainment attempting to rival the theater. Unlike the theater, however, film found itself indebted to the reproductive powers of the camera. As Eustace Hale Ball insisted, "The [film] stage is set with scrupulous attention to detail, the properties are all arranged and . . . real ornaments must be obtained instead of imitations which are used on the stage, because the audience of a theatre has not the bitter keenness of perception possessed by the motion camera lens" (1913, 21).

Perhaps understandably, filmmakers showed an initial preference for solutions that required a minimal degree of narrational intervention on the level of shaping the depicted action. Rather than experiment extensively with the properties of editing, move the camera in to a noticeable degree, or alter the style of performance, filmmakers opted for simpler strategies. Unfortunately, many of these solutions proved to be makeshift remedies. Split sets might help convey contiguity, but they resulted in long stretches of undifferentiated narrative action that invited audience confusion.

Repeated instances of wordy inserts to convey narrative information used up valuable footage and risked drawing attention to the mechanics of narration. As the period progressed, filmmakers increasingly turned their attention to the properties of *mise-en-scène* and editing in order to forge longstanding solutions to the problems of increased verisimilitude and narrative complexity.

One solution might well beget another. As filmmakers became more comfortable with the resources of editing, narratives amplified in their spatial scope and temporal range. The use of flashbacks and articulated spaces provided additional ways to communicate character motivation, which strengthened the causal links binding narrative events. Closer shot scales afforded easier recognition of performers' reactions, which permitted actors to demonstrate a wider psychological range. Similarly, details of sets and décor became more noticeable, providing actors with props to embellish and deepen their performances; this also allowed directors opportunities to vary the staging of narrative action, hence maintaining audience interest.

All of these methods emerged slowly during a protracted period of experimentation. Filmmakers formulated crosscutting, staging in depth, or a verisimilar performance style, to name but three formal attributes of the period, in a manner that demonstrates a desire for useable tools over confidence in proven solutions. Filmmakers would test the workability of such procedures and then set about refining them and expanding their narrational range, a process that could involve a number of years. Similarly, filmmakers do introduce approaches to storytelling that still remain underdeveloped as of 1913: the potentialities of narrative space—in the form of such strategies as shot/reverse shot and extended scene dissection—receive a rudimentary testing in the late stage of the transitional period but await their full articulation in the years to follow.[5]

The nature of transition, then, involves filmmakers' slow process of reaction to externally imposed problems. Filmmakers shared a broad-based goal of bending style to the express purpose of telling stories effectively and clearly, but they lacked any firmly held sense of the narrational capacities of cinema's stylistic elements. The ongoing testing of solutions, performed within a developing and distinct industrial context (defined by particular production practices and trade press reactions) produced the relevant formal changes. These changes involve manipulating the properties of the medium to promote viewer comprehension while fashioning narratives dependent on character and causality.

The preceding portrait of how narrational change occurs during the transitional period leads us to the threshold of the classical cinema and the end of this book. Before concluding, I would like to indicate a few areas of inquiry proceeding directly out of this book's project that deserve mention. First, my emphasis on the formal functioning of American cinema during the transitional years invites comparison with complementary developments in other national cinemas of the time. In particular, scholars have tended to contrast the editing-based style of U.S. films with a deep-staging aesthetic prevalent in European productions. As Richard Abel's work reminds us, such differences can result in distinct periodizations; beyond that, these formal discrepancies might translate into divergent narrational strategies as well and influence the way in which particular national cinemas developed.

Second, my account has stressed changes endemic to the transitional period, but a study of the continuities across the early cinema era might prove productive as well, especially as it relates to general principles, such as focusing viewer attention or maintaining engagement. A third avenue for continued research involves the years directly following the transitional era—the initial period of feature filmmaking. As I pointed out in chapter 1, these films constitute a body of work distinct from the achievements I have detailed, but the relationships among transitional one-reelers, the first features, and early examples of classicism warrant extensive examination. Moreover, the first multiple-reel films, which American companies experimented with in 1909, began to emerge with some regularity by 1912–13 (usually in the form of two-reelers) and also deserve separate analysis. I have alluded to these films only occasionally in this study, in part because their length differentiates them from the single-reel film to the extent that one must view them as separate formal entities. Stylistically, they function similarly to the films I have described here, but their increased length invites different approaches to narrative structure.[6] With the imposed compactness of the 1,000-foot running time removed, two-reelers offer varied narrative formulas: some films simply pad the story in order to extend a single reel's worth of action over two reels; others increase the number of climaxes (Thanhouser's *Under Two Flags* [1912]) or principal characters (Kalem's *The Siege of Petersburg* [1912]).[7] Still others follow a climax with additional story-extending actions (Essanay's *The Death Weight,* from 1913, offers a fight *and* a chase subsequent to the predicament described in the title). Griffith uses the extra half-reel of *The Mothering Heart* (Biograph 1913) both to deepen characterization and provide spectacle (in the form of dance performances). Extended length could allow a company to translate increased expenditure into brand-name enhancement, through more running time devoted to impressive sets, photogenic locales, or larger-scaled action sequences. This notion of distinct company identity also merits more attention than I have accorded it here: it strikes me as crucial to furthering our understanding of how to connect industrial performance and formal trends. My research only underscores the significance of the work of scholars such as Charles Musser on Edison, Tom Gunning on Biograph, and Herbert Reynolds on Kalem and the continued need for more company-based studies of this nature.

The remaining issue involves the dangling cause of culture: at the outset, I preempted consideration of cultural concerns, citing the scholarly tendency to wield them as overly broad determining factors. If we reintroduce culture into the mix, it should entail careful integration of developing formal norms and the ideological realm. The formal features I have investigated often attach themselves to scenarios that seem designed to capitalize on concerns relevant to the age. We must cautiously forge productive connections between the ongoing attempt to construct a legible formal system and the meaning-laden stories this system supports. This need not translate into investing individual devices with a cultural significance they cannot support. Instead, it means finding points of contact where the form gives shape to prevailing ideas or produces some intriguing tension.

Let me introduce an example extracted from my own study. The increased reliance on visions as a means of revealing character psychology during the transitional cinema represents an instance where filmmakers marshaled stylistic devices to promote a sense of subjectivity. As my analysis of *'Twixt Love and Ambition* demonstrated, such efforts could result in sufficient ambiguity to produce a degree of textual instability. Faced with the need to develop the psychology of characters, filmmakers might devise methods that would cause different problems of comprehension or render the narrational process overt. In combination with ideologically charged narrative material (such as scenarios concerning female independence or worker insurrections) these methods could result in films whose relevance to the cultural context of the day we must understand in part through their formal operations. The emotional intensity of *Suspense,* for example, derives from the manner in which formal ingenuity weds itself to a subjectively rendered anxiety over female endangerment. Tom

Gunning has argued that one of the distinctive features of Griffith's Biograph films is that they display "both the foundations of the later classical style (its narrativization), as well as alternatives to that style through their flaunting of the rhetorical presence of the filmic narrator" (1991, 296). This, it seems to me, is a fruitful way of tying meaning and the cultural realm to formal analysis. Filmmakers, when searching for ways to satisfy demands for verisimilitude and narrative legibility, might devise methods that either open up the possibility for obvious intersection with contemporaneous cultural concerns or render the narrational process self-evident in a way that invites more direct viewer engagement. Neither of these possibilities, however, can be understood properly—or adequately—without a corresponding sense of the operative norms of the period in question.

By studying transition in the manner I have done here, I do not mean to preclude understanding of how cultural concerns might inform or be inflected by formal trends within a given historical juncture. Instead, I have designed this project to remind us that any such conjectures regarding these relationships must remain cognizant of how and why formal tendencies arose when they did. In my view, a historical poetics of transition should not eliminate the value of contextualized understandings of cultural artifacts such as films, but rather, force such understandings to account for their assumptions and connections and not ascribe to form a broad-based meaning it cannot sustain. Only then can the nature of transition emerge with the specificity it requires to expand our understanding of film history.

I will close by indicating how a historical poetical account of transition can enhance our understanding of other periods in film history wherein formal change warrants attention. Admittedly, the transformation of style and narration in the American cinema from 1907 to 1913 represents a formal shift more dramatic than one is likely to find in other periods of comparable duration; nonetheless, this method justifies its applicability on the basis of describing change, not merely isolating its most prominent exemplary instances. The specific developments I have charted are unique to a particular context, but the broader questions and general approach recommend themselves to an understanding of different periods defined by transition. The type of transition could vary: I can imagine similar studies examining the adjustment to a new technology (like sound or widescreen), the intervening years between significant movements within a nation's cinema (such as Italy in the 1950s or France or Russia in the early 1930s), or the initial stages in an emergent nation's establishment of an indigenous filmmaking practice. In each instance, a historical-poetical examination would identify the distinctive formal qualities of periods previously relegated to the backwaters of film study, either because they lack the aesthetic distinctiveness of more celebrated highpoints or fail to achieve the stability enjoyed by more durable era-spanning modes of film practice.

Linking transitional eras like the one I have studied to subsequent and relatively familiar periods represents more than an exercise in "connect-the-dots" history. Defining transition enriches our sense of context; knowing what precedes the eventual norm not only provides it with an illuminating prehistory but also allows us to see how the shifting ground of experimentation eventually becomes sufficiently predictable to form the foundation of a coherent system.

APPENDIXES
NOTES
FILMOGRAPHY
WORKS CITED
FILM INDEX
GENERAL INDEX

APPENDIX A: NOTES ON METHOD

As the research portion of this project included studying a large number of the available extant films from the period, I should provide some explanation regarding selection and viewing procedures. Even though the number of titles of relevant American films held by archives constitutes only a small percentage of the total output of this period, more exist than I could hope to see, given my own restrictions of time and money and the detailed viewing procedures I followed for each print studied. Even so, I wanted my sample to be broad and representative of the output of the period (insofar as current holdings allow); for that reason, I often deliberately restricted my choices from production companies that offer a relative surfeit of extant titles (Biograph being the most obvious example), while attempting to see all available releases of those manufacturers whose remaining output seems scarce in comparison.

In table A.1, I have itemized the titles seen, with a breakdown according to year of release and production company. For the most part, titles viewed were full (or nearly full) prints, with fragments viewed only when necessary (as in the case of an underrepresented year or production company). Given the exigencies of film acquisition and preservation, not all titles exist in equally viewable condition, nor can one possess full certainty that subsequent distributors have not altered the print in some fashion. Obviously, any tampering with a print would tend to compromise certain findings such as shot count and running time, but for the most part, these have not caused substantial problems for my calculations.

For each title viewed, I followed a consistent set of procedures: while watching the film on a Steenbeck viewing table, I performed a shot-by-shot analysis, which included keeping track of running times for each shot, as well as changes in shot scale and camera position and notes concerning any significant elements of the *mise-en-scène*. When possible, I photographed still frames from the viewed films directly off the Steenbeck screen to record notable instances of representative stylistic traits.

The early years, in particular, rarely provided an excess of available titles. However, because the number of production companies proliferated in the tail-end of the period under study, it became more difficult to see all available prints for those years, even in the case of smaller firms. In the case of the larger companies,

Table A.1. Sample devised by year and production company

PRODUCTION CO.	1907	1908	1909	1910	1911	1912	1913	TOTAL PER CO.
Edison	8	6	4	5	7	9+1v	7	47
Biograph	20+1v	34+9v	06+12v	30+8v	10+9v	3+9v	7v	158
Vitagraph	5	7	11	17	9+1v	11+1v	5	67
Lubin	1v	1	19	5	6	10+1v	2+1v	46
Selig	2+1v	1	0	2	12	9	1+1v	29
Kalem	1	1	0	1	15	10	2+1v	31
Essanay		0	6	7	9+1v	10+1v	3+1v	38
IMP			3	7	16	8	3	37
New York MP			3	4	3	9	0	19
Powers			0	4	1	4	5	14
Thanhouser				5	2	6+2v	6	21
American				2	2	10	5	19
Nestor				0	5	2	1	8
Reliance				1	2	2	2	7
Solax					2	4+1v	1+2v	10
Am. Kinema.					2	3	0	5
Rex					1	6	2	9
Keystone						1+1v	1+8v	11
Miscellaneous			1	2	3	9	11	26
Total per yr.	39	59	65	100	118	143	78	602

Note: I have designated titles viewed outside an archival context as "v" for video. In cases where I have viewed fewer than three titles of a company's output, I have grouped the films together under "Miscellaneous."

especially Vitagraph and Biograph, I was forced to be particularly stringent. Biograph posed special problems. The output of that company exists in disproportionate plenitude relative to the rest of the industry. And because at least three recent book-length studies of Griffith's work at Biograph have taken advantage of the availability of his films made there, I saw no point in privileging Biograph titles to the point where they would dominate my sample out of proportion to the company's position within the industry. The problems with Biograph do not end there. Because we know more about Griffith and Biograph than any comparable filmmaker and company of this period, we must resist the temptation to let them stand as representative. At the same time, one cannot ignore the inestimable contribution director and manufacturer made to the period's developments. For this reason, I have selected Biograph titles at random, folding the films viewed into the general sample, allowing them their rightful place, but not overplaying their status. Moreover, because this study foregrounds the ordinary film over the works of certain gifted auteurs, I have not emphasized the achievements of Griffith (or those of other identified and notable directors), except when it serves to make a point regarding norms within the period.

APPENDIX B:
SHOT-BY-SHOT ANALYSES FOR CHAPTER 6

Legend for Shot Scales

els   extreme long shot (camera at considerable distance from human figure)
ls   long shot (human figure shown in totality)
mls   medium long shot (human figure shown from knees up)
ms   medium shot (human figure shown from waist up)
mcu   medium close-up (human figure shown from chest up)
cu   close-up (camera sufficiently close to show only a small object, or the human head)

The Boy Detective (1908)

[Except where noted, shot scale is long shot, with substantial space at the top of the frame. Camera position is level, though in several of the exterior shots, the camera is placed at an oblique angle in relation to the action.]

Shot one: (exterior) The boy detective and a friend (in a messenger's uniform) play in the foreground of frame left. The friend gives the boy detective a (toy) gun. A young woman walks into the center of the frame, followed by two men. When she pauses to go into a store, the men hide behind the two boys until she has returned, when they follow her out of the frame. The boy detective quits playing and quickly follows.

Shot two: (exterior) The woman from shot one enters, followed by the two men; the boy detective follows behind.

Shot three: (exterior) The woman enters first and turns toward stairs at frame left. The camera pans left slightly to follow her and then adjusts itself back to its initial position as the men pause to watch. As they walk on toward the background the boy tries to interest them in buying a newspaper.

Shot four: (exterior) The two men go into a building. The boy enlists his friend to go in; the friend receives a note which he shows to the boy. The boy reacts by running off.

Shot five: (exterior) A cart goes by before the boy runs through the space.

Shot six: (exterior) As the boy rounds a corner, he knocks a man down.

Shot seven: (exterior) The boy runs through, away from the camera.

Shot eight: (as shot three) The boy enters from the depth of the image and runs up the stairs at left, with the camera panning slightly to follow.

Shot nine: (interior) The woman from shot three is at the far left; a maid announces the boy's presence. The woman listens as the boy explains the situation. She makes a call, after which the boy begins to dress in her clothes. The three exit to the left and then return as the boy parades about in his new outfit. The friend arrives with a message and then leaves. The remaining three all look out the window and the maid and boy then exit. The woman remains at the window.

Shot ten: (as shot eight) The boy, still in the woman's clothes, descends the stairs; the camera pans right to show a carriage parked in the street as the boy mounts it.

Shot eleven: (exterior) On another street outside the city, the carriage is stopped by the two men. When the boy emerges from within, he intercepts them at gunpoint and holds them while the police arrive in the background. The boy offers a police officer a cigarette from the gun. The carriage and police vehicle ride off.

Shot twelve: (ms/interior) The boy detective, no longer in his disguise, aims his gun and emulates shooting. He then laughs, taking a cigarette out of his gun and smoking it before slapping the gun as if to underscore the joke.

The Forgotten Watch (1909)

[All shots are in long shot, except where noted. Typically, characters' heads touch the top of the frame and their bodies fill it. In most interior shots, when characters move to the very front of the frame, the scale comes close to medium long shot (mls).]

Shot one: (interior) The judge, surrounded by three women, prepares to leave; the maid remains active in the background for much of the shot.

Shot two: (exterior) The judge leaves by a doorway.

Shot three: (mls/interior) The wife comes in to the bedroom and notices that the watch is missing.

Shot four: (as shot two, but slightly closer framing) The wife checks for the judge, but he has already gone.

Shot five: (exterior) A streetcar arrives and the judge enters via left foreground.

[Title: The judge thinks a pickpocket has stolen his watch]

Shot six: (exterior) The trolley stops and a few passengers dismount, including the judge. He discovers his watch missing, and starts to chase after the man who exited prior to him. [splice]

Shot seven: (exterior) A chase ensues with a large group chasing after a running man.

Shot eight: (exterior) The chase continues until the man is caught; a fight ensues until the police arrive and end it.

Shot nine: (exterior) Outside the police station, the two parties are brought inside as the crowd follows.

Shot ten: (interior) In front of a sergeant, the judge demands his watch. The sergeant orders the accused man to give up the watch in his possession. He is then led away.

Shot eleven: (as shot one) The judge explains what happened. His wife then shows him that his watch is still there. The judge goes to the phone in mid-ground and places a call.

Shot twelve: (closer scale [ms] of portion of shot ten) The sergeant answers the phone.

Shot thirteen: (as shot eleven) The judge hangs up and tells his family.

Shot fourteen: (interior) In a hallway, the judge apologizes to the thief about the false accusation and is then relieved of his own watch. Once the man has left, the judge discovers his loss.

Rose O'Salem-Town (1910)

[Shot scale is typically a cross between long shot and medium long shot, with the majority of shots featuring characters cut off above the ankle, but with some space remaining at the top of the frame. The camera angle is straight-on, except where noted.]

[Title: The Sea Child]

Shot one: (exterior) A seashore with rocks and water ebbing in and out. A woman enters from frame right and looks about; she points to the right and exits.

Shot two: (exterior/overhead high angle) From the rocks above, the woman enters from left and is seen gazing below.

Shot three: (exterior) In a Native village, a trapper completes a deal. He and one of the Native leaders go off together.

Shot four: (as shot two) The woman exits frame left.

Shot five: (exterior) At the shore, the men enter. The trapper signals as though he has heard something. First the Native leaves, and then the trapper, who exits right.

[Title: The trapper meets the pretty maid of the sea]

Shot six: (exterior) At another part of the shore, the woman is frolicking. The trapper comes upon her and they strike up a conversation. He kisses her, but when he attempts a second, she leaves.

[Title: The Puritan hypocrite attracted by the girl]

Shot seven: (exterior/slightly high angle) The corner of a cottage is visible in the left foreground. The Puritan comes in from the center background, while the woman enters from the right shortly thereafter. He approaches her but is rebuffed.

Shot eight: (interior) Inside the cottage, the woman's mother is at left, giving (medical) help to a man. The woman enters from the right.

Shot nine: (as shot seven) The Puritan looks into the cottage and shakes his fist menacingly. He then signals that he has an idea.

[Title: Next Day / The Puritan's advances repulsed by the girl, he vows revenge]

Shot ten: (as shot eight) The Puritan takes the woman's arm and strokes it presumptuously. When rebuffed, he uses a two-fingered gesture and exits. The woman seeks the comfort of her mother.

[Title: He declares the girl and her mother witches]

Shot eleven: (interior) In a meeting room, four men are arranged at the left. The Puritan comes in and stands at the right. The men agree to send one of their party to accompany him.

[Title: Love's token]

Shot twelve: (as shot nine) The trapper gives the woman a necklace; they part.

Shot thirteen: (as shot ten) The mother advises a woman about her sickly child, but tells them to keep it secret. After they exit, she goes to the door as well.

Shot fourteen: (as shot twelve) The mother goes out; the men who have been hiding around the corner point off in the direction she has exited, as if to see . . .

Shot fifteen: (exterior) The mother, amidst flowers, goes off after picking. The men move into the foreground as the Puritan interprets her actions.

[Title: The old mother's kindness purposely construed to be witchcraft]

Shot sixteen: (as shot fourteen) The men return and approach the cottage with two others.

Shot seventeen: (as shot thirteen) The men, visible through the window at right, look into the cottage, as the two women are shown inside.

Shot eighteen: (as shot sixteen) The men enter exterior doorway from frame left.

Shot nineteen: (as shot seventeen) The men come into the cottage from left. The Puritan finds cards on the table and has the mother taken away. A man gestures at the woman with a rope as she recoils; he then pulls her toward the door.

Shot twenty: (as shot eighteen) They emerge on the other side, followed by the Puritan.

[Title: Her sweetheart learns of her impending fate]

Shot twenty-one: (exterior) The trapper is asking directions of some men in the background, as the women are brought in to a building just in front. He is told of the charges and reacts with widened eyes, points in recognition, and then moves off to right.

Shot twenty-two: (interior) The woman is dumped into a cell and sits at the left foreground. Finally, she begins to sob.

Shot twenty-three: (exterior) The trapper runs out, pauses to look back over his shoulder and continues into the background.

[Title: Condemned by a prejudiced jury]

Shot twenty-four: (as shot eleven) The room is full as the mother is held at the right foreground. She faints and is dragged out.

Shot twenty-five: (as shot twenty-two) After waiting, the woman is dragged out by a group of men.

Shot twenty-six: (as shot twenty-four) The woman is condemned. She lunges accusingly at the Puritan, but is restrained and led out.

Shot twenty-seven: (as shot twenty-five) She is returned to her cell. She looks beseechingly at her necklace, and looks off frame right.

Shot twenty-eight: (as shot three) The trapper begs the Natives for help; the elder refuses. Trapper exits left.

Shot twenty-nine: (exterior) The trapper runs into a different part of the forest, from left, clearly agitated.

Shot thirty: (as shot twenty-seven) The woman sits staring in her cell.

Shot thirty-one: (as shot twenty-eight) The elder exits; the younger brave from shot five elects to help and enlists others. They go off frame left.

Shot thirty-two: (as shot twenty-nine) The Natives enter from background and offer to help the trapper.

[Title: Shown her mother's fate to weaken her determination]

Shot thirty-three: (as shot thirty) The woman caresses her necklace. The Puritan comes in and forces her to the window, where she looks out and recoils. She considers giving in to him but refuses as she gets sight of the necklace.

Shot thirty-four: (exterior) The rescuers run up a path.

Shot thirty-five: (as shot thirty-three) Men come in to take the woman out. She holds her necklace and makes a declaration before being led out.

Shot thirty-six: (exterior) She is tied up to a stake.

Shot thirty-seven: (as shot twenty-three) The rescuers approach, look out, and react.

Shot thirty-eight: (as shot thirty-six) More straw is added to the burning site.

Shot thirty-nine: (exterior) The rescuers rush forward.

Shot forty: (as shot thirty-eight) The fire is lit.

Shot forty-one: (exterior/slightly high angle) The rescuers mount an embankment.

Shot forty-two: (as shot forty) The rescuers come in, causing the villagers to disperse. The woman is freed and taken away. After the rescuers have departed, a few villagers point upward.

Shot forty-three: (as shot five) The trapper and the woman thank the brave, who departs right. The trapper touches the necklace, his chest, and then the woman, before pointing off. She stares out blankly then nestles in his arm before they walk off together.

Cupid's Monkey Wrench (1911)

[Shot scale is similar to that employed in *Rose O'Salem-Town*. Characters are often placed at some depth within the set.]

Shot one: (exterior) An overheated car is pulled over at the side of the road.

Shot two: (exterior) The car is being pushed; two of the occupants, including the driver, go off via frame left.

Shot three: (interior) A young woman looks for a book then goes over to the radiator and burns herself on it. She calls the maid in and then goes to the background to use the phone.

Shot four: (mcu of space within shot three) The woman on the phone.

Shot five: (as shot three)

Shot six: (interior) In a workroom, a man adjusts some tools and then looks to the left, calls out and exits. An older man answers the phone, finishes the call, grabs some tools and exits.

Shot seven: (exterior) The two men from shot two are about to enter when another man intercedes and draws one away, leaving the driver to go in alone.

Shot eight: (as shot five) The woman hangs up. The driver wanders in and is mistaken for a repairman. He happens to have a monkey wrench with him. When he has successfully completed the job, he is whisked out via frame left by the woman.

Shot nine: (interior) Entering the kitchen, she asks him to fix the sink. His friend enters but keeps his identity a secret. The woman offers the "repairman" lunch while trying to hide the silver. She exits, and the two men concoct a plan, writing a note.

Shot ten: (insert/note) "Dear Frank: Stranded at this infernal hotel. Car broke down, can't get away until tomorrow. Hear you have party tonight at your house. May I come? Yours, Jack."

Shot eleven: (as shot nine)

Shot twelve: (as shot eight) The woman scrutinizes Jack's bag and hat. Frank enters and shows her the note.

Shot thirteen: (as shot ten)

Shot fourteen: (as shot twelve) The woman exits.

Shot fifteen: (interior) People are dancing in a large open room. Jack enters and the woman registers her embarrassment, but they dance together. After she exits via the left and he looks for her before going out the same way. Frank then exits in the same direction.

Shot sixteen: (as shot fourteen) The woman goes out the French doors. Jack comes in and does the same.

Shot seventeen: (interior) The woman stands on the balcony, soon joined by Jack. Frank comes out, sees them together, and produces a huge wrench.

Belle Boyd, a Confederate Spy (1913)

[Title: Belle Boyd and her girl friends repair the battle-torn uniforms of their Confederate sweethearts]

Shot one: (exterior/ls) Belle and her friends converse with their soldier boyfriends while enjoying refreshments the servant brings.

Shot two: (exterior/ls) In the woods, a rider looks off left. He then circles his horse and rides off. Troops file by in the background.

Shot three: (as shot one) The rider from shot two comes in via the background.

[Title: "The Yanks are coming"]

Shot four: (as shot three) The soldiers ride off via frame right, as the women go into the house in the background.

Shot five: (interior/ls) The women come into the living room and look out the window.

Shot six: (ls of space visible within the background of shot four) Yankee soldiers come into the frame from the left. The women can be seen on the other side of the window at the far right. The soldiers dismount and one points toward a flag fluttering just at the right frameline.

Shot seven: (as shot five)

Shot eight: (as shot six) The soldier shoots his gun at the flag.

Shot nine: (as shot seven) The women react with horror.

Shot ten: (still closer framing of the doorway from the space of eight/mls) The soldiers knock at the door while the shooter displays the flag he has obtained. The servant is opposed to their entering, but Belle welcomes them inside.

Shot eleven: (as shot nine) The soldiers come in and decide they need the table at the center of the room for a work station. An object protrudes from the ceiling which hangs over the table; one of the soldiers pulls on it, dislodging a portion of the ceiling. The servant cleans up the mess, while the soldier who had fired the gun offers Belle the flag and then bows.

Shot twelve: (interior/mls) In an adjoining room, the women stand in front of a fireplace and look off frame right. The servant and Belle enter from the direction of their glances. Belle clutches the flag she has been given and then signals that she has an idea. She points above and exits to the right.

Shot thirteen: (interior/high angle overhead ms of Yankee officers in consultation) The shooting soldier looks up.

Shot fourteen: (as shot eleven) He rises and points above, while Belle is visible in the background ascending the stairs. He proceeds to the stairs and climbs them soon after.

Shot fifteen: (interior/ls) Belle tiptoes over to where the hole is.

Shot sixteen: (interior/mls) The soldier comes up the stairs toward frame left and pauses at the top. He looks to the door in the background, opens it and then goes off further left.

Shot seventeen: (as shot fifteen) Belle reacts to the noise and hides in the closet. The soldier comes in and checks behind the curtains. He then goes over toward the hole as she leaves the closet and goes behind the curtains while his back is turned. He then checks the closet before leaving.

Shot eighteen: (as shot sixteen) He looks out a window.

Shot nineteen: (as shot seventeen) Belle lifts back the carpet to look through the hole.

Shot twenty: (interior/overhead high angle mls of the soldiers, from a different perspective than that in shot thirteen) Belle's head is at lower frame center, with officers visible below through splinters in floorboard.

Shot twenty-one: (as shot eighteen) The soldier responds to a call from below and heads back down.

Shot twenty-two: (as shot twenty)

Shot twenty-three: (as shot fourteen) The soldier returns and the others pack up their plans and begin to exit.

Shot twenty-four: (as shot nineteen) Belle covers the hole over, then obtains a roll of paper from her dresser that resembles the plans. Before leaving the room, she thinks to grab flowers from a vase which help to obscure the roll.

Shot twenty-five: (as shot twenty-three) As she arrives, she drops the flowers, which the soldier picks up. She switches the rolls while he is bent over. She gives him a flower, but resists an advance and backs out of the entry door.

Shot twenty-six: (as shot eight, but over slightly to frame left, with the window at right no longer visible) In a match on action, Belle is seen exiting. The soldier follows directly behind her. The Yankees are on the steps, awaiting their horses. When they are brought up, they mount and ride off frame left. Belle hands the flowers to a friend, opens the map, signals that she has a plan and goes off via frame left.

Shot twenty-seven: (exterior/ls) Belle rides out through an open stable door.

Shot twenty-eight: (as shot twenty-six) Belle rides off frame right.

Shot twenty-nine: (exterior/els) Belle rides in from the background.

Shot thirty: (exterior/els) She rides in, but turns back when soldiers emerge from the background shooting.

Shot thirty-one: (exterior/ls) Belle dismounts and places her horse behind a gate. A man rushes in, pushes her away and jumps on the horse, riding away. She exits on foot via frame right.

Shot thirty-two: (exterior/els) Soldiers march by on a bridge, followed by soldiers on horses. One of the last in the procession jumps off, sets an explosive and watches as part of the bridge blows apart.

[Title: Through the battle-field]

Shot thirty-three: (exterior/els) Belle enters a battlefield. Smoke rolls over, obscuring the view, but eventually clears. Belle goes off right, but the camera remains at the scene for some time after.

Shot thirty-four: (exterior/ls) Belle enters another casualty-torn site from right. She offers succor to a man in the foreground and then leaves.

Shot thirty-five: (exterior/ls/els) Belle runs in from behind the camera. Smoke billows out, all but obscuring the action of Belle delivering the map.

Shot thirty-six: (exterior/ls) An officer is holding a map in the center of a clearing. Belle is brought in nearer the foreground; he approaches her and then gives his men their orders based on the information she has delivered.

[Title: Belle Boyd's bravery has saved the day for General Jackson]

Shot thirty-seven: (exterior/els) Belle, the general, and another soldier walk through carnage. The general gestures to Belle as though to indicate what she has accomplished, and the three then turn and face toward the back of the frame.

Suspense (1913)

Shot one: (interior/mls) A maid comes in with a suitcase and a disgruntled look. She sets the case down and looks through the keyhole of an interior door.

Shot two: (interior/masked mls) A mother is leaning over her baby's crib.

Shot three: (as shot one, but camera somewhat farther back, though still mls) The maid thinks to write a note and grabs some paper.

Shot four: (insert) "I am leaving without notice. No servant will stay in this lonesome place. I will put the back door key under the mat. Marie."

Shot five: (as shot three) She leaves via a door in the back left of frame.

Shot six: (exterior/high angle overhead ls) Seen from above, and through the exterior backstairs, the maid leaves.

Shot seven: (exterior/els) The maid is seen coming down an incline and then exits to the right. A vagrant enters from the left and looks toward the maid's progression off-screen. He then heads up the hill toward the house.

Shot eight: (interior/triangular masked ms) The husband is visible in the bottom portion of the shot, making a phone call.

[Title: "I won't get home until late. Will you be allright?"]

Shot nine: (as shot eight, but now the other two portions of the mask are filled in) At the top right, the wife can be seen on the other end of the line, while the vagrant is shown listening at the top left.

Shot ten: (as shot one) The wife enters from frame right and spots the note.

Shot eleven: (as shot four)

Shot twelve: (as shot ten) The wife is distressed and goes back out through the door by which she entered.

Shot thirteen: (interior/mls) A match-on-action of the wife coming into a bedroom. She goes toward the phone, then decides against it. Instead, she bends down over the crib.

Shot fourteen: (the right half of the room depicted in shot thirteen) A cut on the wife's movement allows her walk over to the window to be shown; she shuts the window. She exits frame right.

Shot fifteen: (interior/ls) In a hallway, the wife walks toward the front door and locks it, then goes back the way she came.

Shot sixteen: (as shot fourteen) The vagrant is visible in the background on the other side of the window. The wife re-enters, and then passes by in the foreground with the baby toward frame right without noticing the vagrant.

Shot seventeen: (as shot fifteen) She takes the baby upstairs.

Shot eighteen: (interior/ls) In another bedroom, the wife sits with the baby.

Shot nineteen: (exterior/ls) The tramp climbs down off a ledge.

Shot twenty: (as shot six) He approaches the door.

Shot twenty-one: (closer framing of a portion of shot eighteen, now mls) The wife is in front of the window; she hears a noise and looks out.

Shot twenty-two: (exterior/overhead high angle pov mcu) The tramp's feet and hands come into view before his head, which he tilts back to look up at the wife.

Shot twenty-three: (as shot twenty-one) The wife pulls her head back in.

[Title: "A tramp is prowling around the house"]

Shot twenty-four: (as shot nine) The wife (depicted at the right) comes in from the right to get the phone as the tramp (depicted at the left) grabs the key under the mat. The husband is on the phone at the bottom.

[Title: "Now he is opening the kitchen door"]

Shot twenty-five: (as shot twenty-four) The tramp comes in via the kitchen door; the other two segments of the triangle remain as before.

[Title: "Now he is in the . . . "]

Shot twenty-six: (as shot twenty-five) A cut phone line is show at the upper left; at the upper right, the wife looks off toward the right; at the bottom, the husband rises and exits right.

Shot twenty-seven: (exterior/els) At the foot of a building, a car sits. The driver gets out to look at the back; while he is checking, the husband, who has come out of the building, jumps into the front.

Shot twenty-eight: (as shot twenty-one, with a shot scale between that of shot eighteen and shot twenty-one) The wife is distraught.

Shot twenty-nine: (as shot twenty-seven) The husband drives off. The driver draws the attention of the police; he joins them in pursuit of the husband.

Shot thirty: (as shot twenty-eight)

Shot thirty-one: (space of shot twelve, but with a different framing/mls) The tramp puts down the knife. He finds food in the cupboard.

Shot thirty-two: (exterior/els) The cars careen around a corner, one after the other.

Shot thirty-three: (corner of the bedroom from shot thirty/mls) The wife is shown via reflection in a mirror within a dresser at the left of the frame. She then moves toward the door, becoming visible to the camera and pulls the dresser in front of the door.

Shot thirty-four: (exterior/cu/traveling shot) A rearview mirror showing the police car in pursuit is at the right of the frame; the husband's profile appears intermittently at the left.

Shot thirty-five: (as shot thirty-one, but ms) The tramp goes through the door.

Shot thirty-six: (exterior/ms) A man stands in the middle of a road, smoking, and a car comes up suddenly from behind.

Shot thirty-seven: (exterior/ls/slight high angle) From a hill to the side of the road, the husband appears to be checking something (the man from shot thirty-six?) and then rides off frame left. The police car follows, driving by without stopping.

Shot thirty-eight: (as shot sixteen) The tramp looks around, carrying the knife.

Shot thirty-nine: (exterior/ms/traveling shot) A passenger in the pursuing police car, at the left foreground, looks ahead toward the pursued car ahead at the right. The police car gains on the pursued vehicle and pulls close, with the cars' relative positions within the frame changing accordingly.

Shot forty: (as shot thirty-eight) The tramp exits frame right.

Shot forty-one: (resembles shot eighteen, but mls) The wife stands with the baby.

Shot forty-two: (a variation on shot thirty-four, but in a different location)

Shot forty-three: (interior/high angle) With the camera positioned above an upper portion of the stairs, the tramp climbs up toward it, coming into a looming close-up, before passing beyond.

Shot forty-four: (as shot forty-one) The wife goes to the back of the bed near the window.

Shot forty-five: (portion of shot thirty-three/cu) The door and key and a small part of the dresser are shown until the tramp's arm breaks through.

Shot forty-six: (as shot forty-four, but in mcu) The wife is at the window, screaming.

Shot forty-seven: (exterior/els) The husband's car rushes by; he jumps out.

Shot forty-eight: (as shot forty-five) The tramp opens the door.

Shot forty-nine: (the space of shot forty-seven, but from a different perspective, with the camera moved about 90 degrees) The police car drives up.

Shot fifty: (as shot forty-one) The tramp comes in at the left foreground and sees the wife in the right background.

Shot fifty-one: (exterior/els) The police approach from below, shooting.

Shot fifty-two: (as shot fifty) The tramp hears gunshots and runs back out of the room. The wife falls on the bed.

Shot fifty-three: (as shot forty-three, but with the camera positioned to show more of the left side of the space) The husband enters from the left underneath, as the tramp is running down. He attempts to attack the husband with the knife, but the police come in and overwhelm him. The husband runs upstairs.

Shot fifty-four: (as shot fifty-two) The driver of the stolen car enters, and understands the motivation for the husband's actions. The husband comforts his wife.

[The film ends abruptly, possibly before its proper conclusion.]

NOTES

Chapter 1. Introduction

1. For the most concise overview of neoformalism and its application to film, see Thompson (1988), 3–44.

2. The original use of the term "narrativization," as coined by Stephen Heath, entails "the constant conversion to narrative, catching up the spectator as subject in the image of narrative and in the film as its narration" (1981), 107; critics following Heath tend to stress the ideological import of how the viewing subject becomes figuratively subsumed into the processes of narrative structuration. I prefer Tom Gunning's version, which downplays any Lacanian component. (This allows an understanding of the importance of spectatorial address without raising the issue of subjectivity to the level the original formulation would demand.) Simply put, narrativization involves the increased "subordination of filmic discourse to narrative purposes" (Gunning 1991), 42.

3. For an overview of the Brighton Project, see Bowser (1979), 509–38; and Thompson (1984), 139–43.

4. For an assessment of the contribution of the Vitagraph retrospective to early film scholarship, see Krämer (1988).

5. See Thompson (1985b), 155–230 and Salt (1983), 83–131.

6. See Jesionowski (1987), Gunning (1991), and Pearson (1992); Bowser (1990); deCordova (1990); Sloan (1988); Uricchio and Pearson (1993); and Hansen (1991), Staiger (1995), and Stamp (2000). The most telling indication of the shift the scope of early cinema scholarship undergoes during the 1980s emerges when one compares the two summarizing anthologies published as virtual bookends for the decade. The earlier collection, entitled *Film before Griffith*, from 1983, ends as its title suggests, with essays considering the status of cinema circa 1907–8, whereas the final section of *Early Cinema: Space, Frame, Narrative* (1990), is entitled "The Continuity System: Griffith and Beyond."

7. Moreover, Russian formalism has often underwritten both their approaches: Thompson has invoked this theoretical tradition quite explicitly, particularly the work of Eikhenbaum, while the conceptual debt appears far less pronounced for Gunning, who shows a preference for Todorov, a descendant of the original "Russian

school." By this, I do not mean to imply that there are not substantive differences in the two scholars' approaches, nor do I mean to suggest that they have pursued equivalent goals in how they have examined transition. Nonetheless, each has contributed immeasurably to our understanding of the relationship between narration and style within this period. Other scholars have offered a different assessment when comparing these two authors. Abel, for one, argues that Thompson's work shares with Barry Salt's an inherent binarism that also valorizes the classical system toward which all preceding style ostensibly leads. He distinguishes the work of Gunning (and Gaudreault) from that of Thompson by noting the former's openness to seeing transition in "dialectical" terms (1994), 102–3. This assessment strikes me as somewhat unfair. While Thompson's account of narrational shifts in *The Classical Hollywood Cinema* keeps the ramifications for classicism firmly in view, she still devotes ample attention to the singular achievement of transitional cinema, particularly in the context of a book aiming to explicate the features of the later mode; see, as one example, Thompson (1985b), 194. Nonetheless, Gunning's analysis of the nature of transition probably stands as the more fully elaborated of the two models, though Thompson (1997) bears comparison.

8. In his recent and invaluable account of early cinema in France, Richard Abel has provided yet another, more detailed periodization, chiefly constructed to account for changes in the French cinema, but perhaps more pointedly, designed to demonstrate how scholars have marginalized non-American cinemas within their periodizing schemas. Abel contends that we should understand the transition from the cinema of attractions to a fully narrative cinema as occurring in four stages, beginning with the years 1894–1904 (encompassing the cinema of attractions), followed by 1904–7 (representing the "transition to a narrative cinema"), then 1907–11 (the dominance of the "pre-feature, single-reel story film"), and ending in the 1911–14 period (and the "rise of the feature film") (1994), xv. I would dispute neither the notion that any account of American (or international) cinema during the formative years must at least implicitly acknowledge the influence of French filmmaking practice nor that developments in France may differ in some crucial ways from the circumstances which obtain for American practice. I will address this issue further later in the chapter.

9. The question of when narrative filmmaking achieved dominance within the American marketplace has occasioned considerable scholarly debate, chronicled in Allen (1979), Musser (1984a), and Allen (1984).

10. Even though Charles Musser has argued that domination of the American market by fiction films occurs as early as 1904, he still cites 1907 as a pivotal year; see Musser (1983). Moreover, Musser chooses to end his history (1990) of the first stage of early cinema at 1907.

11. For more detailed accounts of these phenomena, see, respectively, Loughney (1984) and Musser (1991b). I will examine the latter issue at greater length in the following chapter.

12. For an overview of these developments, see Bowser (1990), 217–24. In chapter 2, I will expand upon the issue of the MPPC's significance.

13. As Rick Altman has pointed out to me, changes at the exhibition level further confirm the significance of 1913 for industrial developments. The installation of a second film projector in projection booths, the elimination of ancillary entertainments like song slides from the bill of fare, and implementation of distinct architectural principles in the construction of new theaters all mark the end of this period; see also Bowser (1990), 121–36.

14. For more on how the script structure of the early feature differs from that of the one-reeler, see Brewster (1991b) and Thompson (1998).

15. A mere sampling of the recent works on the subject of exhibition and/or reception confirms the uncontestable value of this vein of early cinema research; outstanding examples include Musser and Nelson (1991), Waller (1995), Fuller (1996), Rabinovitz (1998), and Singer (2001).

16. The extensive debate on this question involving Ben Singer and Robert Allen et al. indicates how contentious the issues remain and how wide-ranging the research possibilities. For the full scope of the debate, see Singer (1995; 1996), Allen (1996), Higashi (1996), and Uricchio and Pearson et al. (1997).

17. The most useful discussion of the concept appears in Bordwell (1983), 5–18. One can find subsequent elaborations in Bordwell (1988), especially chapter 1; Bordwell (1989a), 369–98; and Bordwell (1989b), especially chapter 11.

18. By perusing the texts listed in the preceding endnote, one can glean the nature of the criticisms leveled at film study approaches reliant upon methodologies other than neoformalism. Responses to some of those criticisms and critiques of different aspects of Bordwell's work appear in Gunning (1991), especially 289–95; Andrew (1989), 157–64; and Nichols (1989), 487–515, among others.

Chapter 2. "Boom Time in the Moving-Picture Business"

1. Eileen Bowser argues that the substantial growth in nickelodeon openings stabilizes by the end of 1908 (1990), 6. In the middle of the period under investigation, *Moving Picture World* estimated that there were 12,000 theaters in the United States "where motion pictures are exhibited" (6, no. 7, 19 February 1910), 247.

2. Charles Musser supplies a convincing argument for how and why Griffith was allowed the degree of autonomy he was at Biograph by comparing that company's situation to Edison's in 1908 (1991b), 56.

3. Two of the more extensive recent overviews of the American industry at this time can be found in Bowser (1990) and Gunning (1986). I base my account of the formation of the MPPC on their accounts and reports in trade papers of the day.

4. America's relationship with foreign producers and markets receives a thorough examination in Thompson (1985a), 1–48. Abel (1999) speaks to the crucial role Pathé played within the American market in the period under discussion.

5. As Janet Staiger has suggested, "The organizing of the Patents Company seemed to indicate a stable business climate, and the individual firms, assured of regular unrestricted national and international sale of their products through the Patents Company, began to run off up to one hundred copies of each negative rather than the ten to twelve previously struck. The increased income provided capital for expanding their operations" (1980), 15.

6. As Abel (1999) points out, Pathé had already established a regular release schedule by 1906–7. Its implementation by the MPPC signals an industry-wide acceptance of the practice.

7. A considerable body of literature devoted to the establishment of the Trust and the opposition of the Independents exists; aside from the sources listed in endnote 3, Keil (1993) provides a recent overview of many of the issues and a representative bibliography.

8. Even so, if a demonstrably cheap film was made during the final years of this period, invariably it would be an Independent production.

9. A helpful overview of industry developments in the few years directly following the move toward increased film length can be found in Bowser (1990), 217–33.

10. See Abel (1999) for a detailed account of how the industry squeezed out and discredited the most prominent foreign producer during this period, France's Pathé Frères.

11. Janet Staiger has addressed this apparent dichotomy in economic terms: "Standardization was a dual process—both a move to uniformity to allow mass production and a move to attain a norm of excellence. Standardizing stylistic practices could make the production fast and simple, therefore profitable. However, differentiation was also an economic practice . . ." (1985b), 108–9.

12. Both Anderson (1979) and Abel (1999) provide information on the production and marketing of westerns during this period. Bowser (1990) argues for the distinct generic identity of Indian and Civil War films; Altman (2000) critically examines the genealogy of the western and the claims made for its status as a genre in the early cinema period.

13. The trade press complained constantly of the perceived inferiority of Independent films at this time, particularly during the first years of Independent production. Even taking into account the biases of journals that favored the MPPC, one can detect consensus concerning the shortcomings of early Independent productions. Lux Graphicus provides a typical pronouncement in 1909: "Broadly speaking, Independent pictures are not the equal in quality of those which older firms have been making for years past . . . The Independent manufacturers must get up to the recognized standard in the work . . ." (*Moving Picture World* 5,

no. 14, 2 October 1909), 448. For additional comments regarding industry concern about the quality of Independent product, see Anderson (1979), 24. Viewing extant early efforts from new Independent producers confirms that these films often lack the production values or narrative coherence of many of their MPPC counterparts.

14. Charles Musser has documented that Trust members tacitly agreed not to engage in any competitive tactics involving personnel: "The MPPC provided a framework within which licensed manufacturers reached informal or secret understandings and acted in concert. Manufacturers agreed not to hire personnel away from other licensed producers, nor to hire those that had been discharged for 'justified reasons' or simply left" (1991a), 456. Nonetheless, this did not render the Trust companies any less vulnerable to employee raids by the Independent companies.

15. It is a matter of conjecture as to why Biograph suffered repeated losses from its ranks of featured performers more than from other departments and to a greater degree than other companies. Beyond Pickford and Johnson, Charles Inslee, Marion Leonard, Florence Lawrence, Owen Moore, and Henry Walthall all defected, leaving Biograph to replenish its stock company at different junctures. Such departures created the circumstances for Griffith's three most celebrated late-era Biograph stars—Lillian Gish, Mae Marsh, and Blanche Sweet— to gain prominence. (Pickford and Walthall both returned to Biograph in 1912.) Vitagraph, on the other hand, seemed to enjoy relative stability with its stock company, and such stalwarts as Florence Turner and Maurice Costello remained stars at the company throughout the entire period (see Graham et al. 1985; Slide 1987). Though both companies received critical acclaim for the performances associated with their films, Biograph's reputation was arguably greater, which might account for why it was targeted more consistently. Beyond that, Biograph's resistance to identifying its actors (a policy Vitagraph did not share) could have prompted some of its stars to leave for a company that would promote them by name. This might explain in part why Griffith gravitated toward such young and relatively inexperienced actors as Gish et al. in the later Biograph years.

16. See *Moving Picture World* (5, no. 22, 27 November 1909), 779; *Moving Picture World* (7, no. 12, 17 September 1910), 630; *Moving Picture World* (9, no. 9, 9 September 1911), 688; *Moving Picture World* (16, no. 12, 21 June 1913), 1273 (the last-named figure includes multireels, which increases the total substantially).

17. Both Balshofer and Dwan claim responsibility for the negative cutting on the films they shot on the West Coast, though the negatives were then sent back East, to the "girls who assembled the positive prints . . . The joiners, as they were called, cut the individual scenes from each roll . . ." See Balshofer and Miller (1967), 56, 66; Bogdanovich (1971), 24. This concurs with Staiger's findings; she determined that it was not until the early teens "that cutters had taken over part

of the director's work and assembled a rough cut following a continuity script . . ." (1985b), 152.

18. James Morrison's recollections concerning his first year at Vitagraph indicate that the company allowed experimentation at times, but that even an organized studio like Vitagraph failed to incorporate efficient solutions to certain technical problems consistently; see Brownlow (1968), 16. Musser's portrait of Edison's concerted move toward a "factory"-like system of production control, spearheaded by newly hired studio chief Horace Plimpton in March of 1909, allows that such cost-efficiency measures still did little either to reduce expenditures or to improve the quality of the films (1991a), 453–56.

19. Prior to this, as the introduction to the film section of George Kleine's *Illustrated Catalog of Moving Picture Machines, Stereopticons, Slides, Films* from 1905 indicates, most subjects were well over the previous industry standard of fifty feet, "the duration upon the curtain depending upon the action." This entry goes on to suggest that exhibitors were urging producers to provide longer subjects because the public showed a preference for films "from 400 to 700 feet in length" (repr. in Pratt [1973], 40–41). The choice of the thousand-foot length, as Epes Winthrop Sargent would later explain, was "merely a measure of convenience, the amount of film conveniently held in a machine at one time and a convenient standard of quantity for the exhibitor. A thousand-foot reel should run 18 to 20 minutes" ("Technique of the Photoplay," *Moving Picture World* 9, no. 2, 22 July 1911), 108.

20. As Richard Abel has pointed out, each of these journals adopted its own editorial position, which necessarily included support of a particular faction during the developing licensing wars: "by late 1908, an American trade press for moving pictures was fully constituted and spread across a spectrum of industry interests" (1999), 84.

21. Roberta Pearson has argued, for example, that the trade press's seemingly prescient support for a particular performance style several years before it became established practice was probably motivated by a desire to align film with the voices of progressive reform, which had expressed reservation about the type of entertainment found in nickelodeons circa 1905–8. Trade press condemnation of acting styles associated with the socially stigmatized melodrama functioned not merely as aesthetic judgment, but as a calculated attempt to upgrade cinema's status as a form of respectable entertainment; see 1992, 128–39.

22. Though, as Kristin Thompson has pointed out to me, it is likely filmmakers *were* paying attention to the trade press at this time, if only because their extensive use of it as a forum for self-promotion and discussion (once they became identified by name in the mid-teens, as actors had earlier) indicates a familiarity with and appreciation of the trade press's usefulness.

23. After consulting a broad range of trade journals published during the period, including *Billboard, New York Clipper, Variety* and *Views and Film Index*, I

decided to concentrate on three journals as the basis of my research into the trade press: *Moving Picture World, New York Dramatic Mirror* and *Nickelodeon/ Motography. Moving Picture World* is arguably the most influential journal of the period and certainly the most detailed. If I rely on selections from it to a greater degree than the *Mirror*, I do so to avoid any privileging of Griffith or the Biograph Company, to whom the *Mirror*'s main reviewer/commentator, Frank Woods, had direct links. Moreover, my selection also reflects whatever diversity may derive from the journals' origination in different production centers (the *World* and the *Mirror* in New York, *Nickelodeon* in Chicago).

24. For an account of how uplift arguments applied to "working and immigrant audiences" which still stresses the economic advantages to the trade press, see Uricchio and Pearson (1994), 48.

25. Accordingly, certain columnists would write under pseudonyms which played up their role as representatives of the audience: Woods called himself "Spectator," while *Moving Picture World* featured an unsigned column called "Observations by Our Man about Town."

26. A typical strategy employed by writers when they wished to impress their readership with their superior knowledge was to invoke a background in another field, as in these introductory comments by Thomas Bedding: "I have had many many associations with the theater and with those who make the theater their business . . . May I also, at the risk of being thought too egotistical, tell the reader that besides being a novelist, I am and also have been dramatist [*sic*] . . ." ("The 'Dramatic Moment,'" *Moving Picture World* 6, no. 10, 12 March 1910), 372.

27. *Nickelodeon* amended this list slightly later the same year: "In criticizing a film there are four major features to watch. Opinions differ as to the relative importance of these features, which are acting, photography, production and story" ("Film Criticism," 4, no. 7, 1 October 1910), 176. Though the change is a slight one, it recognizes the distinct difference between the story per se and its elaboration via its film treatment (or "production").

28. For a representative example of such a complaint, see *Moving Picture World* (9, no. 4, 5 August 1911), 294.

29. Robert Anderson has argued that such attributes account in part for the early positive response to westerns: "The success of the Western did establish the Selig and Essanay companies in the vanguard of American cinema as the realism, action and authenticity of their on-location pictures repeatedly attracted the accolades of the national trade magazines" (1979), 24.

30. Occasionally, reviewers would assess qualities deemed photographic in terms antithetical to realism. In a review of *The Story of Rosie's Rose*, the critic observes that "the first scene of this picture seems cramped. If a bit more background had been shown, it might have had more atmosphere and looked more like life and less like a photograph" (*Moving Picture World* 9, no. 11, 23 September

1911), 891. One assumes that in this instance the writer employs the word "photograph" to designate a picture that draws attention to its qualities as a (deficient) rendering, rather than a reproduction which reinforces the qualities of the subject recorded.

31. The week following the appearance of Graphicus's column the *World* had supplied a complimentary caption reading "a specimen of good photography and excellent pictorial composition" for another obviously posed still from Kalem's *The Legend of Scar Face*. This second mistake undoubtedly fueled the journal's "campaign" against production stills; see *Moving Picture World* (7, no. 6, 6 August 1910), 293.

32. Later in his article, Hulfish does amend his position somewhat by conceding that artistic use of the medium can occur, not only by alteration of the camera's lens and position but by tinting as well.

33. This helps to explain why some found the term "realism" unacceptable: it denied the transformative role of fiction. Louis Reeves Harrison, for example, took issue with advocates of realism by arguing that of all "false grounds taken by critics none is more common than that of realism. There are dramatic moments in all lives, but to group and intensify these within the limits of a pictured story is not realism, but its artful semblance" ("Superior Plays: The Important Elements of Their Construction," *Moving Picture World* 8, no. 22, 3 June 1911), 1234.

34. Questions of motivation inevitably required proper consideration of character psychology, as this review of Thanhouser's aptly titled *The Crisis* demonstrates: "It is a fault in many photoplays that they demand our acceptance of incidents which may be natural but which are not convincing merely because time and space were not taken to make us familiar with the mental peculiarities that make the events natural" (*Moving Picture World* 9, no. 8, 2 September 1911), 629. This review suggests that character psychology could easily be assimilated to notions of realism as long as it was properly explained. In effect, proper delineation of psychology would render resultant actions "natural."

35. Writing in 1909, Archer McMackin states that "now, nearly all the film companies have organized scenario departments, presided over by a dramatic editor, who devotes his entire time to receiving and reading manuscripts and continually soliciting ideas" ("How Moving Picture Plays Are Written," *Nickelodeon* 2, no. 6, December 1909), 171.

36. Staiger and Thompson agree that companies did not rely upon amateur writers for very long, and that the vogue for soliciting such scripts probably ended once feature films became the dominant form; see Staiger (1985b), 138 and Thompson (1985b), 165.

37. Recall the earlier quote by David Hulfish, which viewed "motography as merely the means for placing before the audience *the thoughts of the author of the picture*" [emphasis mine].

38. As David Bordwell has noted, one finds the tenets of classicism reiterated within "Hollywood's own discourse, that enormous body of statements and assumptions to be found in trade journals . . ." (1985a), 3. The scenario instructions merely anticipate what would become doctrine a number of years later.

39. For a representative critique of a film lacking climaxes, see *Moving Picture World* (4, no. 22, 29 May 1909), 713–14; a less common occurrence is the complaint that a film contains too many: "One climax follows another so closely that they actually crowd together in the mind, making it impossible in some instances to separate them sufficiently to understand where one begins and the other ends" (*Moving Picture World* 5, no. 10, 11 September 1909), 316. George Rockhill Craw, among others, speaks to the structural value of the climax in "The Technique of the Picture Play—Structure," *Moving Picture World* (8, no. 4, 28 January 1911), 178–80.

40. Not coincidentally, companies like Chronophone and Cameraphone, among others, experimented with versions of sound film on a fairly extensive basis in 1907–8 as well; see Musser (1983), 8–9.

41. In March 1908, *Moving Picture World* reported the favorable response that the "talking pictures" approach elicited for a screening of *Francesca di Rimini* (2, no. 12, 21 March 1908), 233; in an editorial from September of that same year, the *World* advocates expanded use of lecturers to explain what films mean because of unclear narratives (3, no. 13, 26 September 1908), 231. But by year's end, the *World* indicates that "talking pictures are losing their hold on popular favor" (3, no. 22, 28 November 1908), 419, while reviews are stating that films "should be made clear so [they can] be understood" (*Moving Picture World* 4, no. 3, 16 January 1909), 69.

42. Similarly, other potential aids to intelligibility, like music or sound effects, were never accorded the same primacy as textually based means, precisely because they relied on the individual exhibitor. Nonetheless, they persisted as devices that exhibitors could employ to encourage comprehension (or, more typically, to create atmosphere), unlike the short-lived phenomenon of "talking pictures."

43. For more on how the trade press championed film acting at the expense of the theater, see Brewster and Jacobs (1997), 99–100.

44. Mae Marsh would echo these sentiments over a decade later: "The value of good business cannot be overrated. It goes a long way toward making up for the lack of voice" (1921), 53.

45. As Kristin Thompson has pointed out, one cannot overestimate the influence of the mass-market short story, particularly on screenwriters, but also, one can assume, on trade reviewers; see (1985b), 163–73. Nonetheless, the general aesthetic absorbed from the short story or theater or some combination of the two shared certain classically based principles; this aesthetic, in turn, required amendment before it could apply usefully to a new medium.

Chapter 3. "A Story Vital and Unified in Its Action"

1. André Bazin dismisses "the two industrialists Edison and Lumière" as having little bearing on what cinema would become. Bazin may well be correct, but not for the reason he supplies (i.e., their failure to recognize that "the guiding myth . . . inspiring the invention of cinema" is the realization of "an integral realism" inherent to the medium). See Bazin (1967), 17–22.

2. For a concise (and representative) account of how cinema fit into a "tradition [of] display of new technologies as entertainment," see Gunning (1995), 88.

3. Charles Musser, among others, has documented the types of films that were projected during cinema's first years; such screenings "emphasized movement and lifelike images at the expense of narrative" (1990), 117.

4. André Gaudreault has argued that a type of narrativity has always defined cinema. In "Film, Narrative, Narration," he differentiates between two levels of narrativity, that which is a feature of the individual shot (by virtue of "iconic analogy") and that which the process of editing produces. Because the first broadly applies to any single-shot film, Gaudreault claims that cinema has been "doomed to tell stories 'for ever'" from its inception. He goes on to say that "this special feature of the cinema, that of having always been narrative right from the beginning, explains why this art . . . so quickly found its vocation of storyteller" (1990), 71. But one can identify cinema's eventual narrative role as "predictable" without asserting that it was envisioned as a narrative medium from the outset. (One could also argue that this predictability lay no more in cinema's inherent narrative capacities than in an industry-based desire to shift from novelty status to a competitive form of narrativized entertainment rivaling the theater.) As I will go on to demonstrate, the introduction of the second level of narrativity that Gaudreault refers to was essential for film to *tell* stories.

5. Charles Musser attributes the "new phase of rapid expansion" within the American film industry in 1903 to the "popularity of story films" (1990), 335. Richard Abel (1999), building on the research of Robert Allen, predates the commercial impact of multishot narratives by pointing to the importance of Méliès films within the American market.

6. Tom Gunning has convincingly shown that the earliest comedies, which he labels gag or mischief films, should be viewed as distinct from the "more linear and narrativized form of the comedy chase" (1995), 96. While the former demonstrate a "rudimentary narrative structure," Gunning claims that they "are not simply a primitive story on which later narrative films will build, but rather a unique structure, differing considerably from the narrative forms introduced by the dramatic films which become dominant around 1907 to 1908" (1995), 94. The discontinuous nature of most gag films, coupled with their typical brevity (often one-shot comedies), militates against their contributing to cinema's narrative development in the way the chase film does.

7. Edward Branigan provides an incisive overview of this conception of narrative (1992), 4–8. Branigan's discussion and my own are indebted substantially to Todorov's examination of these issues, particularly 1971, 1977a, and 1977b.

8. The link between the chase format and narrative tendencies has been made by numerous scholars, foremost among them Donald Crafton (1995) and Noël Burch (1990b), both of whom have developed the issue in ways distinct from what follows.

9. This is not the same as saying that Méliès's work is inherently theatrical or does not avail itself of editing of a particular kind. For more on this issue, see Gaudreault (1987) and Gunning (1989). Abel provides a comprehensive overview of the Méliès *féerie* (1994), 68–78.

10. Musser examines the existence of chase elements in *The Great Train Robbery* (1991a), 259–60.

11. Both Riblet (1991), 10 and Jesionowski (1987), 61–62 make mention of what they call the "accumulation chase," but their emphases are different from mine.

12. As Kristin Thompson has pointed out to me, another type of story film reliant on causality developed at roughly the same time as the chase film. Its structure inverts that of the chase: whereas chase films offer an initiating cause leading to an extended series of effects, these films allow causes to accumulate until a final effect provides the conclusion. Examples include *Mary Jane's Mishap* (1902), where a variety of gags establish the title character's lackadaisical nature, culminating in her mistakenly pouring paraffin into the stove and causing a fatal explosion, and *A Policeman's Love Affair* (1905), where the assignation between cop and maid is played out for some time before they finally are discovered and the cop is ejected from the home. In films like these, the linking of similar causes prolongs the action; arguably, this model would possess applicability for scene structure in later one-reelers.

13. A. Nicholas Vardac refers to the play as *A Race for Life* (1987), 57, while Charles Musser entitles it *A Race for a Wife*, which is also the title of a 1906 Vitagraph parody (1991a), 542, endnote 142. Vardac's citation is correct, as a listing of Kremer's works in Parker confirms (1908), 255. Bordman characterizes *A Race for Life* in negative terms, claiming that "[Kremer's] type of play had to be content with the customary one-week booking at a combination house" (1994), 545.

14. For a succinct statement of the situation, see Bowser (1990), 53–54. The "uplift movement" took aim at cinema to improve the quality of films viewed by immigrant and working-class audiences. But by encouraging cinema to absorb cultural values of the middle class, advocates of uplift rendered film more palatable to that audience as well. For more on this issue, see Gunning (1991), 88–92.

15. Appropriately, Eileen Bowser (1983) entitles her analysis of another dramatic film from the same year "Toward Narrative, 1907: *The Mill Girl*."

16. Abel outlines how French filmmakers, faced with similar problems, opted for comparable narrative structures at this time; see Abel (1994), 181.

17. For examples of such criticism, see *Nickelodeon* (3, no. 7, 1 April 1910), 179; *Nickelodeon* (4, no. 7, 1 Oct. 1910), 176; *Moving Picture World* (5, no. 22, 27 Nov. 1909), 751; *Moving Picture World* (6, no. 13, 2 April 1910), 517.

18. Of course, most films spend comparatively less time on introductions and conclusions than on what they bracket. But because one-reel films are so brief, this emphasis on the "core" of the narrative action becomes more pronounced. In contrast, early multireelers often take a more leisurely approach to introducing characters before initiating any crucial narrative events; see *The Siege of Petersburg* (Kalem 1912), *The Guiding Light* (Lubin 1913), and *The Death Weight* (Essanay 1913), all two-reelers which feature more extended introductions. Thompson (1997) discerns an even more disproportionately lengthy introduction in the single-reel *The Tiger* (Vitagraph 1913).

19. Romance often figures prominently, either as a desired goal (*Back to Nature*) or as an established state of affairs imperiled by narrative developments (*Path of Duty*).

20. Eustace Hale Ball warns against including any unnecessary complicating actions: "Avoid all actions or characterizations which are not definitely needed in the removing of obstacles to the completion of the story . . ." (1913), 36.

21. An exception that proves the rule is Lubin's *The Missing Finger* (1912), which does not introduce its female protagonist until one-third of its narrative is complete. Significantly, the introduction of her character coincides with a spatial shift, as the film changes its locale for the remainder of the story.

22. A *Moving Picture World* review argues for the logic of the model in terms of maintaining audience interest: "If a love story was told from beginning to end without anything to disturb its delightful charm, no doubt it would be so commonplace that it would be lacking in interest. Consequently, various disturbances are interlarded to add to the interest . . . or hold the attention of the audience which is watching a picture" (6, no. 7, 19 February 1910), 257.

23. I will discuss the function of temporal gaps at greater length in chapter 4.

24. Abel (1994), 199–201 demonstrates how this device functions in *L'Homme aux gants blancs* (1908), an adaptation of a de Lorde play.

25. This model of narration derives primarily from Bordwell (1985b), particularly 57–61, and Bordwell and Thompson (1997), 101–8. Bordwell has acknowledged Meir Sternberg's exploration of these concepts in relation to literature as a source for his own theories; see Sternberg (1978).

26. Tom Gunning (1988) has suggested that these earliest instances of point of view testify once again to the power of the "attraction," though as early as films like *A Search for Evidence* (1903), a narrativizing tendency is apparent. Russell Merritt has argued that "the most glaring feature of the [early] dream film is the persistent undercurrent of ethical and social didacticism implicit within the

vision"; he goes on to note that American filmmakers rarely moved "inward to explore the psychological relationships between dream and reality" (1986), 71. Richard Abel observes that around 1906–7, Pathé films such as *Aladdin* and *Cinderella* use dreams for narrative purposes; even so, these dreams function within the context of fantasy films, whose primary appeal tended to be visual spectacle. Abel prefers to see spectacle serving "a double function, one in which its effect as an attraction comes close to being subordinated to, and redirected to accommodate, the demands of a parallel strand of narrative" (1994), 176.

27. As Thompson (1997) stresses, the lack of narrational intervention via editing and shifting shot scale meant the chief cues were provided by "acting, décor, staging, framing, and occasional written material in the form of intertitles and inserts" (413).

28. Bowser (1990), 139–46; Salt (1983), 120–21; and Thompson (1985b), 183–86 have all covered the use of titles during this period; Abel (1994) discusses how they function in various French films from the same time. Inserts have garnered far less attention, with Bowser and Thompson each discussing them briefly.

29. Many of the Biograph titles from 1908 exist without their original titles. And, as Eileen Bowser warns, the problems extend beyond just the absence of titles: "if the print is a reissue or was preserved in another country . . . the titles are not often the original ones" (1990), 144.

30. As one might expect, Pathé established the narrational value of employing titles (and inserts) to render dramatic scenarios comprehensible somewhat earlier than its American counterparts; see Abel (1994), 155.

31. In his advice to prospective screenwriters in 1911, Epes Winthrop Sargent advises that titles (or "leaders" as they were often called) be both "brief" and "fluent": "'For his sister's sake Dick is silent' expresses the fact as definitely as 'Dick does not deny the crime in order that he may keep from Nell the knowledge of her brother's crime,' and uses seven words against twenty" ("Technique of the Photoplay," *Moving Picture World* 9, no. 5, 12 August 1911), 363.

32. Not surprisingly, two of those titles refer to the film's sole insert—a note of warning. This indicates the equally crucial role inserts were to play as narrative messengers, especially from 1909 to 1911.

33. Nonetheless, practical constraints prevented filmmakers from substituting titles too often, especially lengthy ones. As Eustace Ball warned, each word amounts to a foot of film; excessively verbose titles could constitute one-fifth of a film's entire footage (1913), 24–25.

34. As chapter 2 demonstrated, the trade press consistently championed maintaining a sense of verisimilitude during this period. Bowser has suggested that "intertitles could interfere with the illusion of reality by reminding the spectators that they were being told a story instead of actually seeing it happen"

(1990), 140; Thompson implies the same (1985b), 184. In an article from 1911, Robert Grau writes in anticipation of a time when scriptwriters "will eliminate to a great extent the very primitive methods now in vogue in indulging in "explanations" on the screen, also in transcribing on the screen letters and telegrams for the purpose of clarifying the spectator's mind, but which is inconcrete in its effect, and disillusionizing" ("The Photo Play of Tomorrow," *Moving Picture World* 8, no. 19, 13 May 1911), 1058.

35. One can find other instances of ambivalent comments regarding titles and their employment in *Moving Picture World* (6, no. 18, 7 May 1910), 736; *Moving Picture World* (6, no. 19, 14 May 1910), 777; and *Moving Picture World* (7, no. 18, 29 October 1910), 982.

36. An exception that proves the rule is this title from a musically themed comic film from 1912, *Canned Harmony* (Solax): "Bill is forcibly impressed with the fact that life is composed of bars and feet of discord."

37. Both Bowser (1990), 143–44 and Thompson (1985), 184–85 elaborate on this point; the trade press was torn as to whether placement before or during might prove more disruptive.

38. While he does not allude to the usefulness of titles per se, Clarence Sinn does indicate that accompanists would benefit from any cues supplied them: "We have no rehearsals; we know nothing of the pictures until we see them at the first show, during which we must 'play something' and at the same time determine on the most fitting music" ("Music for the Picture," *Moving Picture World* 7, no. 23, 3 December 1910), 1285. A letter sent to the same journal, dated 5 March 1911, is more explicit, indicating that titles preceding actions are necessary to cue pianists for tonal shifts, etc. and suggests that a synopsis sent ahead would be helpful ("'A Blue Note' by the Pianist," *Moving Picture World* 8, no. 12, 25 March 1911), 661.

39. Janet Staiger claims that manufacturer provision of cue sheets was a "standard service for the exhibitors in the early 1910s" (1985b), 153.

40. A random sampling of various films from 1910 indicates that substantial diversity still marked the use and frequency of titles and inserts, despite their universal adoption by American companies: *Jean and the Waif* (Vitagraph, December)—27 shots, 14 titles, 0 inserts; *Playing at Divorce* (Vitagraph, December)—25 shots, 5 titles, 0 inserts; *The Bandit's Mask* (Selig, January)—25 shots, 9 titles, 2 inserts; *Path of Duty* (Lubin, September)—24 shots, 1 title, 2 inserts; *Under Western Skies* (Essanay, August)—26 shots, 4 titles, 1 insert; *Daddy's Double* (Thanhouser, April)—28 shots, 8 titles, 1 insert; *The Newspaper Error* (Powers, April)—25 shots, 9 titles, 5 inserts; *The Pugilist's Child* (Powers, September)—26 shots; 9 titles; 3 inserts.

41. The most egregious case of excessive inserts I have come across is IMP's *[Margharita]* (1911), which relies on no fewer than seven.

42. Detailed characterization could also provide verisimilitude, as Eustace Hale Ball suggests: "Every scenario [can invite] an audience's interest [by directly expressing its theme], maintaining that interest with suspense and sympathy, and making it "real life" by character depiction" (1913), 38.

43. I will postpone discussion of flashbacks until the next chapter because of the temporal issues involved.

44. As Bowser (1990), 62 and Brewster and Jacobs (1997), 66 have argued, the typical manner of presenting the vision—superimposed within a portion of the frame left "empty"—is probably indebted to the stage melodrama's "vision scene." Vardac discusses this theatrical technique at various points (1987), including 17 and 34–45.

45. Abel demonstrates how Pathé films from the 1906–7 period, like *Pauvre Mère* and *Pour un collier!*, were already developing character psychology through visions; see (1994), 135–36, 151.

46. As Brewster has argued, *A Friendly Marriage* evinces little interest in the sustained investigation of informational hierarchies that point of view can promote. A more appropriate example might be Vitagraph's *Out of the Shadows* (1912), which also provides a pleasing symmetry: just as the heroine becomes convinced of her fiancé's dalliance with her adopted daughter through a falsely interpreted view of the couple, so too is she persuaded to change her mind when she sees her daughter with the latter's real beau. In narrational terms, the gap between character knowledge and audience knowledge is eventually collapsed; in terms of narrative structure, point of view both triggers the plot's disruption and effects the plot's resolution.

47. Gunning has warned against understanding the emphasis on display as a "monolithic definition of early cinema, a term that forms a binary opposition with the narrative form of classical cinema" (1993b), 4. I am not ignoring the distinctions Gunning wishes to see observed within the schema he has devised. When I argue that one cannot reconcile Gunning's concept of attractions easily with the model of narration I have proposed, I refer to the concept in its purest form. I would agree with Gunning that attractions function as the "dominant" within cinema until the transitional era, when significant changes have begun to occur.

48. Ben Brewster has argued that examples of narrativization remain sufficiently rare in pretransitional cinema that when a film does employ a device for narrative purposes, "the attraction [might be] narrative itself" (1991a), 9.

49. Gunning extends this notion into the classical period: "By describing narrative as a *dominant* in the classical film I wish to indicate a potentially dynamic relation to non-narrative material. Attractions are not abolished by the classical paradigm, they simply find their place within it" (1993b), 4.

50. Tom Gunning cites one such instance in a *Variety* review of *The Greaser's Gauntlet* (Biograph 1908): "Here a clever bit of trick work is introduced

to bring about an intensely dramatic situation" (1 August 1908, 13; quoted in [1991], 72).

Chapter 4. "An Immeasurably Greater Freedom"

1. The passage from Linda Arvidson Griffith's memoirs has been much cited and debated; see Jacobs (1968), 103 and Gunning (1991), 109. I include it here not to validate the actual recollection, but rather to indicate the prevalence of spatiotemporal concerns within industry thinking.

2. Among the many books to explore the way in which technology affected the conception of time and space at the turn of the century, two of the most illuminating are Kern (1983) and Schivelbusch (1986).

3. See Musser (1990) for more detail about the technological roots of cinema and the advertising strategies for early screenings.

4. For extended discussions of the motion film, see Gunning (1983) and Keil (1991). Kirby (1997) forges links both historical and theoretical between cinema and railway travel.

5. In his examination of early film's use of photography, Tom Gunning elaborates on the medium's appropriateness as a tool of narrative development: "Three interlocking aspects of photography—its indexical evidence about a referent; its iconic image which allows immediate recognition; and its detachable nature which allows it to refer to a referent that is absent, separated from it in space and time, make the photograph the ideal tool of the process of detection, the ultimate modern clue" (1993c), 2.

6. In the case of *The Story the Biograph Told*, such envelopment is literal: the incriminating evidence, projected to the diegetic audience as a single-shot attraction recalling *The May Irwin Kiss*, occupies the structural center of this five-shot film.

7. The categories of temporal organization cited derive from Genette (1980) and have been applied to film by numerous scholars, chief among them Bordwell (1985b), 77–88. The schema for understanding spatial strategies derives from Noël Burch, as relayed by Gunning (1981), 17.

8. For an insightful explication of the significance of "a unified viewpoint of the action" to early cinema's concept of continuity, see Gunning (1989).

9. For one of many accounts of this phenomenon, see Bowser: "The chase film consisted almost entirely of diagonal movements from the distance to a close exit at one or the other side of the frame. This movement would be repeated in each following shot, from the distance to the foreground. . . . Such shots were quite long, giving time for the participants to run completely through the shot, from the leading actor to the last straggler" (1983), 334.

10. Earlier attempts at constructing spatial relations of any complexity typically result in temporal overlap, wherein the movement from one space to another, contiguous one results in the repetition of action. Examples of this practice abound in early narratives, but the *locus classicus* remains the rescue scene from *The Life of an American Fireman* (Edison 1902), primarily because one archival version of the film featured the shots reedited in such a way that they emulated the crosscutting variant that would come into vogue later. For a discussion of the relevance of overlap to a consideration of early cinema, and the case of *Fireman* in particular, see Musser (1979), 32–33 and Gaudreault (1983), 314–23. *The Boy, the Bust and the Bath* avoids overlap in part due its care in establishing the close confines of the film's narrative space.

11. The possible influences of such forms as comic strips on cinema have been examined extensively; for representative examples, see Lacassin (1972) and Fell (1974; 1980; 1986). Don Crafton provides some cautionary advice against overstating the formal similarities between the two media (1990), 221–38.

12. For some intriguing suggestions concerning Vitagraph and the development of editing within various genres during the period of 1906–9, see Brewster (1987), 292–95. Brewster also suggests that (Vitagraph) comic films retain and foreground particular formal devices much more often than do dramatic films (305); from this, we might extrapolate that the comic films discussed would function as an ideal site for spatial exploration. Abel detects similar strategies of spatial analysis through contiguity at work in several French comedies; see (1994), 221–27.

13. Brewster ties trade recognition of Vitagraph's "realistic comedies" to a *Moving Picture World* review of *Romance of an Umbrella*, which cites it as a "new type of 'charming comedy'" (1987), 306. Biograph's *Jones and His New Neighbors*, from 1909, represents an attempt to fuse the domestic observational comedy with contiguity-based confusion. In 1911, reviewing the John Bunny/Flora Finch "comic character picture" *Subduing Mrs. Nag, Moving Picture World* claimed it was "better than average, but . . . not to be compared with the real comedies that this company produces every now and then" (9, no. 3, 29 July 1911), 210.

14. André Gaudreault has noted "an insistence on temporality is a phenomenon which grows in importance in 1907"; see (1983), 326.

15. Other films from this time span that employ clocks in similar ways include *Cupid's Pranks* (Edison 1908), *The Suburbanite's Ingenious Alarm* (Edison 1908), and *Lonesome Junction* (Biograph 1908).

16. Based on reviews mentioning such plot structures, an accepted variant became the employment of a prologue taking place a number of years before the main narrative action. In the *Moving Picture World* review of Kalem's *A Child of the Sea*, which features just such a structure, the critic precedes his comments by stating, "Kalem stories are never involved or intricate" (4, no. 23, 5 June 1909), 753. Two such examples of this structure I have seen from 1910 are Selig's *A Tale of the Sea* and Powers's *The Pugilist's Child*. The latter uses strategies to mark

time's passage similar to those that I will describe in conjunction with *A Range Romance*.

17. As an example, one could cite *The Army Surgeon* (Kay-Bee 1912), which features two deadlines (the title character's sweetheart refusing to respond to his proposal until the night of a party in her honor, and a Native tribe leader threatening an attack unless a doctor is sent to tend to his ailing wife). The second deadline interferes with the surgeon's ability to meet the conditions of the first when he agrees to go to the Native camp. Note as well that the deadlines no longer serve merely to advance the narrative; instead, they now function as demands deriving from the needs or whims of characters. This results in a more pronounced degree of causality. Interwoven causal lines propel the narrative forward, with the chief's needs affecting the doctor's ability to meet his own.

18. Though I have come across only one example of a film relying on this strategy earlier than 1911, *Moving Picture World* contains a review of Lubin's *The Dead Letter*, from 1910, which remarks that "the details of the picture are worked out with considerable care and a semblance of the flight of time is given by the change in looks and environment" (7, no. 27, 31 December 1910), 1538.

19. Instead of a flashback, some films apparently used a two-tiered time frame, connecting one story set in the past to another from the present; in this variant, the psychology of an individual character does not link past to present. While I have not been able to see an extant version of such a film from the early transitional period, *Moving Picture World* does make mention of this approach in its review of Lubin's *The Old Hall Clock* (4, no. 20, 15 May 1909), 636–37. Note the film title's emphasis on temporality. *Moving Picture World* also makes mention of a temporal shift in Vitagraph's *The Empty Sleeve*, when noting that "the change from an old couple walking down the street to the young couple of forty years ago is excellently managed [as is] the change back" (4, no. 23, 5 June 1909), 753. Unfortunately, neither this review nor the one in *New York Dramatic Mirror* specifies whether this shift is rooted in the couple's consciousness or not (61, no. 1590, 12 June 1909), 15.

20. The third example, from the final shot of Lubin's *The Yiddisher Boy*, features a single flashback depicted as a superimposed image within the frame's upper-left corner. Because a dialogue title ("You helped me 25 years ago. I am glad to help you now.") precedes it, the flashback image within the final shot may well be the visual equivalent of what the recalling figure is recounting.

21. Uricchio and Pearson provide a discussion of the flashback structure of the film; see (1993), 152.

22. A *Moving Picture World* review of *Backward, Turn Backward, O Time in Your Flight*, an Edison film of 1909, provides evidence of another early flashback film: "A basket of fruit is brought to them and a big red apple recalls memories of an escapade of apple stealing in which they figured when children, and the scene is reproduced, while they rehearse the story" (5, no. 13, 25 September

1909), 414. In this case, however, the flashback apparently comes from shared memories, triggered by a valued object.

23. Occasionally, some scenarios featured more complex temporal ordering, as in the case of Thanhouser's *Just a Shabby Doll* (1913), which places a flashback within a flashback; in such cases, filmmakers would have to attempt some imaginative blending of approaches, such as depicting the enfolded flashback as an inset superimposition. Thompson (1985b) and Salt (1983) generally concur on the development of flashback form during this period.

24. For an explanation of the difference between recounting and enactment, see Chatman (1978), 32.

25. Ben Brewster has labeled such films examples of multiple diegesis, and he argues that they became the "preferred way of telling long-time-period stories in one-reel films" (1991b), 49. Given the difficulties filmmakers experienced accommodating stories with an extensive time frame (in films like *An Alpine Echo* or *A Friendly Marriage,* Brewster's cited example), I think this a reasonable assumption, which further explains increasing visibility of multiple diegesis films at a late stage in the development of the one-reeler.

26. Defending the "photoplay" as a distinct form of artistic expression, Münsterberg argued that "the photoplay is not music in the same sense in which it is not drama and not pictures. It shares something with all of them. It stands somewhere among and apart from them and just for this reason it is an art of a particular type which must be understood through its own conditions and for which its own esthetic rules must be traced instead of drawing them simply from the rules of the theatre" (1970), 73.

27. In part, one can attribute Münsterberg's acceptance of editing to the later date of his writing. Critics in the trade press reduced resistance to crosscutting only after its widespread adoption as industry practice around 1914–15. But even after that point, one finds objections to excessive crosscutting. For more on negative trade press reaction to rapid cutting, particularly as evidenced by Griffith's Biograph films, see Pratt (1973), 100–105; Bowser (1990), 258–59; and Thompson (1985b), 212.

28. I will postpone any further discussion of molded space until the next chapter, primarily because it does not involve temporality to the degree articulated space usually does.

29. As cut-ins typically involve a marked change in shot scale, I will discuss them at length in the following chapter, after introducing relevant aspects of cinematographic properties.

30. Brewster cites the employment of split sets within a number of Vitagraph films from 1907–8 as well, based on an examination of fragments held by the Library of Congress (1987), 292.

31. Split sets never entirely disappeared as an option for filmmakers, but their occasional later use typically represents a narrationally self-conscious depiction of space, as in *The Ladies' Man* (1961).

32. Abel identifies a similar cutting strategy in Pathé's *Les Forbains* (1907); see (1994), 188–90.

33. For a discussion of the changing norms of contiguity/simultaneity's representation within the context of assessing relative narrational self-consciousness, see Thompson (1997), 413.

34. Tom Gunning cites *The Guerilla* as Griffith's first use of a "three-pronged editing pattern found in his later last-minute-rescue films" (1991), 133.

35. Tom Gunning discusses this issue at greater length, particularly in reference to the 1909 Biograph *The Drive for Life* (1991), 190–95. Sternberg has demonstrated how such retardatory procedures are especially effective in cinema, which he describes as a "time-art": "When the action is abruptly broken off at an exciting point and the scene shifts, nothing in the spectator's power can do away with the impeding material . . . Whether he likes it or not, he is compelled to sit it out, waiting for the piece to revert to the suspended strand and resolve his suspense" (1978), 162.

36. Joyce Jesionowski has pointed out another spatial aspect of the last-minute rescue worth considering: when the villain approaches the family's apartment the first time, he maps out the distance between the street and the apartment, which indicates to the viewer the amount of space the father will need to traverse when he attempts the rescue (1987), 155. Such efforts also affect the viewer's sense of how much time the father will take in reaching the apartment once he reaches the familiar space of the exterior entrance, demonstrating the interdependency of time and space within the rescue format. What Jesionowski does not mention is that *The Cord of Life* fails to develop equally helpful spatial cues for the route the father travels from the apartment exterior to where he will meet up with the villain. (In fact, he takes a thoroughly different route back home after the villain has revealed his plan.) In future films, Griffith will often map out these other intermediary spaces systematically as well (as in *The Musketeers of Pig Alley* [1912]).

Chapter 5. "The Modern Technique of the Art"

1. For an overview of the changes in Griffith's reputation as more recent research has further contextualized his achievements, see Thompson and Bordwell (1994), 51–52, which also assesses the 1913 advertisement's role in establishing the Griffith myth.

2. I am not ruling out the value of assessing the style of certain directors (in the cases where preservation of their work allows such assessment). Rather, I am saying that an author-based approach to considering style within this period will not take us very far in the way of general observations. Moreover, this era imposes other limitations on studying films in terms of a director's oeuvre: many of the works have come to us as unauthored, either due to industry practice (a refusal

to name the director) or the condition of existent prints (exacerbated by insufficient documentation which would aid in determining the identity of unnamed directors).

3. For another application of the "problem-solution" model, see Bordwell (1997), esp. 149–57.

4. In an editorial from 1910, *Moving Picture World* let its preferences be known and suggested that inferior producers were learning to copy the achievements of recognized producers: "The Biograph releases are distinguished by a certain pictorial quality which is the outcome of patient systematized work in the photographic department . . . they have a standard of quality . . . which other makers are laudably endeavoring to emulate" ("The Qualitative Picture," 6, no. 25, 25 June 1910), 1089. For another overview of American companies which assesses their respective styles, see "Earmarks of the Makers," *New York Dramatic Mirror* (60, no. 1560, 14 November 1908), 10. Abel (1999) documents how the American trade press used its critical influence to discredit the "foreign" nature of Pathé's productions.

5. Abel (1989) makes a similar point when introducing an analysis of French films from the post-attractions era.

6. For a provocative argument about "how the theatre served as one of the nodal points for conceptualizing 'the pictorial' and hence provided a more general guide for cinematic mise-en-scène," especially from 1913 to the end of the decade, see Brewster and Jacobs (1997).

7. For more on these prestige-laden adaptations and historical films, see Abel (1994), 246–77.

8. Uricchio and Pearson (1993) discuss and reproduce the sources for several individual shots from these Vitagraph films. The *New York Dramatic Mirror* singled out filmmakers at the company for "the fidelity with which they almost invariably provide costumes, scenery and accessories for their pictures, in strict harmony with the country and time in which the scenes are to have occurred" (60, no. 1545, 2 August 1908), 7.

9. Numerous commentators would point to cinema's ability to use real locations as an obvious advantage over theater's lack of verisimilitude: "The abolition of the painted scenery of the backdrop gives to the drama a sense of reality, a solidity, that it never had before. The mountains and clouds do not now show spots of threadbare canvas. The tumbling waves do not throw up dust . . ." ("The Drama of the People," *New York Independent;* repr. in *Moving Picture World* 7, no. 16, 15 October 1910), 865. Louis Reeves Harrison pointed to a director whose "presentation was stagey and therefore artificial" in order to argue the following: "Now the advantage photoplays have over those on the stage is that they can *do away with artificiality.* They appeal to the brain entirely through the eye, and most effectively by means of moving images, events and scenes closely approximating those of actual existence. This naturalness is one of the greatest charms of the

pictural drama, and venerable traditions of the older art should not be allowed to mar this delight" ("The Pictural Drama as a Fine Art," *Moving Picture World* 7, no. 18, 29 October 1910), 1042. The *New York Dramatic Mirror* went even further, claiming "the moment that motion picture dramas were offered to [audiences] showing natural surroundings instead of painted scenes, the popular price public deserted the melodrama theatre and put it out of business" (61, no. 1589, 19 June 1909), 16.

10. For more on the construction of angled sets, see Bordwell (1997), 178 and Brewster and Jacobs (1997), 180–81.

11. In part, one can attribute the trade press's desire for a high degree of verisimilitude to a similar enthusiasm within the theater, which dates back at least to the 1860s and finds its most famous exponent in David Belasco. Discussion of increased realism in theatrical set design and decoration, including the incorporation of the box set, can be found in Vardac (1987), 15–16; Thompson (1985b), 217; and Pearson (1992), 31–32.

12. In this regard in particular, the trade press often acknowledged the superior achievements of French producers like Pathé and Gaumont. Commenting in 1910, Louis Reeves Harrison praised Gaumont at the expense of American producers: "The interiors as well as the exteriors . . . are beyond comparison with our own. . . . In these picture plays, the French give attention to minute details while our producers slam on a lot of stage furniture very unlike the real thing and neglect the little graces that give a room the restful spirit of home life" ("An Aesthetic Tragedy," *Moving Picture World* 7, no. 11, 10 September 1910), 569.

13. Nonetheless, even location shooting was subject to certain strictures. As H. F. Hoffman advised, prospective location scouts should have "learned by dint of personal application just what objects and conditions in nature make for art and those that do not. [They] should be grounded in the laws of composition, such as balance, light and shade, rhythm, contrast, repetition, leading line, massing subordination, simplicity, form, detail, tone quality, etc." ("Motion Picture Backgrounds," *Moving Picture World* 7, no. 6, 6 August 1910), 287. I doubt quite so much forethought as Hoffman proposes informed the choice of locations at this time, but still, one can discern increased attention to the pictorial quality of locales by at least 1909: this is often a salient feature of the companies which depend upon exteriors, like Selig. Eustace Hale Ball indicates that only the "large studios, in some instances, have "location men," whose specialty is to seek locations for exterior dramatic work" (1913), 16.

14. Even so, achieving maximal verisimilitude within sets still eluded certain manufacturers as late as 1913, particularly newer companies with reduced means. The hotel lobby set for Crystal's *The Innocent Bridegroom* (1913), for example, features painted-on pigeon holes and alarm bell.

15. *Moving Picture World* provided a more detailed explanation of this position in its review of Selig's military drama, *The Heroine of Mafeking:* "Possibly

soldiers would see little things that are not as they are carried out in actual military practice, but it must be remembered that the average audience looks at these films as pictures, and the *suppression of detail helps rather than harms* what appears on the screen" (emphasis mine) (5, no. 26, 25 December 1909), 920.

16. In this regard, the precepts of the trade press during the transitional period anticipate those that guide later classical practice. For a fuller account of how realism is subordinated to the needs of narrative, see Bordwell (1985a), 19–21.

17. Those companies that could not afford sufficiently detailed sets would do well to avoid inadequate substitutes, or else find themselves charged with dramatic inconsistency and "unnaturalness." C. H. Claudy's complaints are typical: "A play [i.e., film] goes from outdoors, where everything is natural, to an interior that they'd laugh out of a Bowery playhouse. Rich society people have their habitat in rooms so small they can barely turn round, and furnished with ten-dollar-a-week taste" ("It 'Went Over,'" *Moving Picture World* 8, no. 5, 4 February 1911), 231.

18. Barry Salt employs the term "space behind" to describe this aspect of set design (1983), 113. While Salt correctly associates the "space behind" approach most strongly with the French, it does exist in American films as well and is not always accompanied by a cut-in to the rearground action as he states when describing Vitagraph's handling of this form of staging.

19. Some uncertainty surrounds the actual meaning of the term "staging" during the transitional period, because it appears to have had two different connotations within the trade press for a time. For example, in 1909, *Moving Picture World* states that "by staging we mean correctness as regards details of scenery, dress, furniture, etc." ("The Staging of the Picture," 4, no. 26, 26 June 1909), 874. A few years later, this earlier understanding of staging (i.e., the care demonstrated when mounting the film) had ceded to the alternative meaning—the arrangement of actors in front of the camera.

20. *Moving Picture World* made the connection clear in a 1909 editorial: "Many . . . films are, as it is commonly said, "as pretty as pictures;" in other words, in composition, lighting, sentiment and treatment, they comply with the principal canons of pictorialism" (4, no. 21, 22 May 1909), 665. Not coincidentally, the editor of *Moving Picture World* prided himself on his photographic knowledge; see Bowser (1990), 96.

21. Ideally, crowd scenes could incorporate actual people caught unawares, but this presented its own problems: first, filmmakers would have to arrange the filming of crowds to prevent a visually confusing randomness; and second, if members of the crowd became conscious of the camera, their acknowledgement of its presence would destroy any advantages of illusionistic verisimilitude their incorporation had produced in the first place. A *Moving Picture World* review sums up the benefits of the successful use of "real people" for crowd scenes:

"Real street scenes with slum crowds passing unconsciously were used as background; nothing could be more realistic" (9, no. 3, 29 July 1911), 209.

22. See Brewster and Jacobs (1997), 170–71. A 1911 discussion of the filmic "stage space" corroborates such an assessment: "It is well to bear in mind that the actual stage is fan-shaped rather than rectangular, growing broader as the distance from the camera increases" (Epes Winthrop Sargent, "Technique of the Photoplay," *Moving Picture World* 9, no. 2, 22 July 1911), 108. See also Ball (1913), 18–19.

23. Ball concurs with these figures in his description of the field of action suitable for filming (1913), 19.

24. Besides, filmmakers staged most of these "quality" productions to take full advantage of their spectacular qualities. The response to the opulence of Selig's multireel *Cinderella* by *Moving Picture World*'s reviewer indicates the degree to which spectacle could become almost perceptually overwhelming: "There is such a wealth of setting, both outdoor and interior; such a great variety of properties and costumes, selected with the utmost care, so much of action and heart interest throughout these 3,000 feet of film that one cannot possibly take in at one sitting more than a small fraction of the actual values" (10, no. 9, 2 December 1911), 704.

25. As Reynolds has pointed out, the adherence to Tissot's illustrations promotes the establishment of considerable depth within interior sets and often creates dynamic perspectives within a film notable otherwise for a fairly conservative style. See Reynolds (1992); for comments on the film's style, see Keil (1992). A selection of contemporary critical reactions to *A Corner in Wheat* can be found in Slide (1982), 23–25. Eileen Bowser has also noted the correlations between fine art and film during this period; see (1990), 267–71.

26. For more on this strategy in late-era Griffith Biographs, see Keil (1989) and Bordwell (1997), 196.

27. European filmmakers, particularly the French, employed deep staging more consistently than Americans. For various accounts of the prevalence of deep staging practices in European films, see Brewster (1990); Salt (1983), 111–16; and Gunning (1993a). David Bordwell (1995) has provided a comprehensive analysis of staging strategies in the films of Louis Feuillade which suggests that the director used cutting as a supplement to staging; Abel (1997) analyzes this aspect of Feuillade as well.

28. Proper centering of the action was already established before 1907; David Bordwell argues that even those primitive films which may not offer perfectly centered compositions still direct the viewer's eye to salient elements (1997), 165–68. Eileen Bowser points to *The Mill Girl* (Vitagraph 1907) as an early transitional film which has thoroughly assimilated centering principles, and I have not noted any trade press complaints about improper centering of dramatic action (as opposed to crowded staging). The principle of centering had become so

sufficiently ingrained that filmmakers experimented with deliberately asymmetrical compositions in the later transitional years as a form of artistic variation or dramatic emphasis (see Bowser [1990], 101, 252–53). In most instances, the filmmaker would provide strong visual cues to reinforce the narrative center of interest, as in the depicted example from *Love Hath Wrought a Miracle* (Vitagraph 1912 [fig. 3.20, p. 78]).

29. For an extended examination of how staging in-depth functions within early cinema, see Bordwell (1997), 158–98.

30. Janet Staiger (1985a) has also tied shifts in cinematic performance style to developments within the theater, though she claims that the Delsarte method encouraged greater attention to facial movements.

31. Brewster and Jacobs expand on this point by itemizing all the differences between theatrical acting and film acting circa 1908 (no spoken dialogue, no live audience, relatively long shot scale, and short screen time) to provide a context for actors' performances: "In response to these conditions, a theatrically trained actor moving into film at this time might well have been motivated to develop a more emphatic style than he had formerly employed on stage" (1997), 106.

32. I should also point out that adopting the verisimilar mode of acting promoted further changes to style as much as stylistic developments affected performance; Janet Staiger has argued, "the [verisimilar] acting style affected camerawork, editing and blocking. It is important to note, however, that the specificity of film—its ability to change camera/character distances, the flexibility of spatial manipulations through editing—certainly must, likewise, have allowed the acting style to develop" (1985a), 22.

33. Though individual films, particularly comedies, have combined different acting styles up to the present, discrepancies appear more pronounced in the transitional period. Moreover, as Kristin Thompson has pointed out, comedy provides a generic rationale for retention of performance styles considered outmoded in other contexts: "During the teens, pantomime acting primarily in long shot shifted its function; with modifications it became generically motivated in the work of silent comedians"; see (1985b), 192.

34. Brewster and Jacobs (1997), 108 address the issue of how the brief format of single-reelers "contributed to the relatively swift pace of film acting."

35. One *Moving Picture World* commentator went so far as to oppose the two trends, naming one the "School of Action" and the other the "School of Acting," and associating Selig with the former and Biograph with the latter. Ideally, he argued, a company must fuse the two qualities, which is exactly what happened as film scenarios progressively tailored story action to emerge out of the traits of goal-driven characters (Hans Leigh, "Acting and Action," 5, no. 13, 2 October 1909), 443–44.

36. Admittedly, the trade press could demonstrate inconsistency when applying standards of verisimilitude to acting. In the interview with the stage di-

rector, repose is identified as "one of the strongest methods of obtaining an effect" in the theater, whereas in the "Motion ad Nauseam" article, the author understands repose as a cessation of unnecessary movement. These discrepancies render such descriptive adjectives as "restrained" less stable than one might normally assume, but still do not justify Brewster and Jacobs's characterization of trade press demands for subtle acting as "amorphous"; see (1997), 101.

37. Sample criticisms of actors taking note of the camera's presence can be found in *Moving Picture World* (5, no. 14, 2 October 1909), 451; *New York Dramatic Mirror* (64, no. 1657, 21 September 1910), 31; *Moving Picture World* (9, no. 2, 22 July 1911), 124; *Moving Picture World* (9, no. 6, 19 August 1911), 462. Selig's "Pointers on Picture Acting" expressly warn against performers "glancing toward the camera" (repr. in Lahue [1973], 63). For an intriguing reaction to the *Mirror*'s insistence that actors not look at the camera, see "A Little More on Camera Dodging," wherein the *Film Index* takes actors to task for the opposite tendency: "there have been pictures in which we have observed the movement of the players mainly up and down the stage, so to speak, thus presenting a full rear view too frequently" (6, no. 1, 4 January 1910), 3.

38. Nonetheless, as Pearson has argued, critics would apply these adjectives to a wide range of performance styles, because the "press had reason to valorize the verisimilar code even before it became dominant. While reviewers may have used such terms as 'natural' or 'true to life,' they rarely detailed the expressions and gestures that led them so to characterize the performance" (1992), 164.

39. Pearson sees this as a deliberate strategy on the industry's part to upgrade the status of film by aligning it with more respectable arts like the theater (1992), 128–39. Manufacturers imported actors and scenarists from the theater as one of the more obvious ways to assure cinema's equality with drama. This approach proved fairly unsuccessful, however: only those stage-trained performers who could adapt to the emerging verisimilar style managed to extend their screen careers past a few films.

40. Several of Selig's "Pointers on Picture Acting" stress the importance of sustaining a sense of "realism" (repr. in Lahue [1973], 63–64).

41. Vitagraph, one of the early exponents of the verisimilar style, began exploiting this notion in its advertising in 1910, when it described its films as "life portrayals."

42. Richard deCordova (1990) examines the emergence of the phenomenon of stardom in American film in detail and argues that from 1909 up until 1913, actors were viewed primarily as "picture personalities"; that is, their actual performances determined their personae, and not their private (or public) lives.

43. Eileen Bowser (1990), 145–47 provides more examples of this practice (extending past 1913), but states that it does not begin until 1911, no doubt overlooking the 1910 *Moving Picture World* reference.

44. One can find numerous detailed analyses of the performance style employed in these and other representative Biographs, most of which contextualize the performances within larger stylistic systems evident in Griffith's films during this period. See, in particular, Pearson (1992), Jesionowski (1987), and Gunning (1991), but also Merritt (1976) and Keil (1989) and Brewster and Jacobs (1997), 129–31, who study Griffith's performance style in relation to European tendencies. For further comments on performance style at Vitagraph, see Salt, who argues that the company led the way in "restrained naturalism of the acting," as part of an overall strategy to identify the company's style with naturalistic detail (1987), 184–85.

45. Both Salt (1983), 89–100 and Thompson (1985b), 223–27 and 270–75 provide detailed accounts of the technological developments that accompanied changes in lighting procedures.

46. In an article entitled "Silhouetted Moving Pictures," *Moving Picture World* commented, "the silhouette moving picture may probably receive some impetus from a recent release of the Rex Company. Here many of the figures are shown just as detailless shadows with sharp outlines. Some interesting moonlight effects appear in this Rex release, which is called *By the Light of the Moon*" (8, no. 10, 11 March 1911), 518. Kalem had been singled out the year before for a silhouette effect in *The Engineer's Sweetheart*, which the reviewer claimed "shows a commendable attention to detail on the part of the producers" (*Nickelodeon* 4, no. 8, 15 October 1910), 226. As Kristin Thompson has suggested, lighting effects proved sufficiently novel (while usually remaining realistically motivated) to warrant praise and serve as a form of product differentiation (1985b), 224.

47. Additional details on Griffith's experiments with lighting at Biograph, particularly in 1909, appear in Salt (1983), 89–91 and 93; Jesionowski (1987), 30–32; and Gunning (1991), 171, 176–77, and 181–82. Brewster (1987), 295–98 and Salt (1987), 186–90 supply carefully observed comments regarding Vitagraph's lighting practices, both indicating that the company developed involved procedures from the beginning of the period.

48. Bowser discusses appearances of open door shots as well; see (1990), 241.

49. For an analysis of the lighting in *Proving His Love*, see Gartenberg (1984), 22.

50. Both Salt (1983), 84–87 and Thompson (1985b), 264–67 provide extensive information about cameras during this period.

51. Thompson cites the various possible prohibitions against camera movement (1985b), 227–28.

52. Later, in another positive appraisal of Reliance's cinematography, a reviewer attributes the clarity to a new film stock, though he doesn't elaborate: "The change in the film used by the firm is shown in the sharpness of the pictures and the stereoscopic relief which characterizes their appearance on the screen" (*Moving Picture World* 8, no. 13, 1 April 1911), 720. The consistent praise of

Nestor for its quality of photography suggests perhaps that it used a slightly different lens or stock as well, but writers never mention this.

53. For criticism of blurry moving figures, see *Moving Picture World* (5, no. 14, 2 October 1909), 450; an assessment of how a short focal length lens could produce problems is provided in "Too Near the Camera," *Moving Picture World* (8, no. 12, 25 March 1911), 633.

54. Griffith employs this tactic most dramatically in two late Biograph films, *The Musketeers of Pig Alley* (1912) and *The House of Darkness* (1913). Tom Gunning explains the extra effort in focus-shifting such shots entailed, as well as discussing their expressive power (1991), 275. See also Bowser (1990), 101; Jesionowski (1987), 35; and Keil (1989), 30.

55. Barry Salt, following Jean Mitry, refers to noticeable instances of high and low angles as exemplifying "the cinematographic angle" for precisely this reason. Salt's examples indicate that marked use of "the cinematographic angle" was restricted to European filmmaking practice during this period, in particular, to the Danish cinema (1983), 103. In a later article on Vitagraph, Salt amends his claim to include some examples from that company that also employ angled shots in 1910–11 (1987), 185–86.

56. One can find this shot reproduced in Thompson (1985b) as illustration 16.22.

57. See Salt (1983), 106–8 and (1987), 181–83. Salt attributes Vitagraph's changed camera position, which he labels "the Vitagraph angle," to the influence of such French films as *La Mort du Duc de Guise* (1908). Both Salt and Bowser (1990), 95 allude to reviewers who mention the effect of characters appearing "heroic"; for another such reference, this one from the writer of a letter, see *Moving Picture World* (9, no. 6, 19 August 1911), 469.

58. For representative reviews of films constructing off-screen space through character glances, see *Moving Picture World* (4, no. 10, 6 March 1909), 268; and *Moving Picture World* (7, no. 15, 8 October 1910), 813.

59. This use of off-screen space prefigures the more systematic deployment one finds in such late Griffith Biographs as *The Musketeers of Pig Alley* (1912) and *The Lady and the Mouse* (1913). (For more on this aspect of Griffith's style, see Keil [1989], 25.) The availability of Griffith's entire Biograph output confirms his inventive development of certain framing principles. But without a similarly extensive sampling of other companies' films, one cannot know whether examples like those from Essanay and Kalem are imitative of Griffith, part of their companies' own respective development of the technique, or even an industrywide trend, in which case they may have influenced Griffith. The fact that Powell employs off-screen space self-consciously by 1910 might lead us to identify Griffith as the logical source of influence, but again, we cannot know this with certainty, as many of Powell's films demonstrate a fair degree of individuality and ingenuity.

60. Others have pointed to a later instance of independent camera movement in Edison's *The Passer-by*, from 1912; see Salt (1983), 87.

61. The actual percentages per year are as follows: 1907, 19 percent; 1908, 16 percent; 1909, 39 percent; 1910, 16 percent; 1911, 27 percent; 1912, 36 percent; and 1913, 52 percent. I removed the highest and lowest percentages to calculate a period average. The percentage for 1909 is probably high because of the disproportionate weighting of Lubin films—which rely on pans extensively—in the sample for that year; conversely, underrepresentation of Lubin films for 1910 and 1911 might account for those years' lower rates.

62. I have seen extensive use of pans (some of them narrationally revelatory) in a French film from as early as 1904 (Pathé's *Indiens et cow-boys*); Abel (1994) comments on this aspect of Pathé's output, 123–24 and *passim*, as does Salt (1993), 78.

63. However, even in this regard, the argument remains suspect. Initially, Griffith may have developed the possible uses of the pan beyond basic reframing far less consistently than other features of style, but it held interest for him nonetheless. Virtually everyone points to the lyrical rhyming pans which begin and end *The Country Doctor* (1909), but one can cite numerous other instances of distinctive camera movements from late 1908 onward; see Gunning (1991), 210–18; and Jesionowski (1987), 32–33.

64. Other notable examples include the revelation of an open window that subsequently allows a character to escape in Vitagraph's *Victims of Fate* (1910); a rival whose presence is unknown to the couple he has been following revealed by a pan in IMP's *The Lighthouse Keeper* (1911); and the aftermath of an accident shown via a pan in Edison's *Dangers of the Street* (1913). American's 1913 *Trapped in a Forest Fire* features two narrationally intriguing pans. In the first, after a character leaves the room, the camera pans right to reveal another character who has been present the entire time. In the second, a character exits because of a fire, and the camera then picks up a figure in the background as it pans left; we learn that this figure, who eventually moves to the position occupied by the first prior to his departure, is the woman whom the exiting character had arranged to meet. Abel points to an early example of a particularly ostentatious ninety-degree reverse pan in Pathé's *Les Forbains* (1907); see (1994), 189.

65. Thompson (1985b) provides frame enlargements illustrating this example; see illustrations 17.46–47.

66. Abel cites a similar and roughly contemporaneous example in Film d'Art's *Werther* (1910); see (1994), 261–62.

67. Other films to feature a relatively high number of pans and/or tilts are *The Ranchman's Nerve* (American 1911), *An Old Appointment* (Edison 1912), *The End of the Feud* (Essanay 1912), and *With the Mounted Police* (Thanhouser 1912). Based on the admittedly limited evidence available, it appears that aside from Lubin, both American and post-1911 Thanhouser found fixed axial camera movements a particularly reliable stylistic option.

68. Though shot scale can involve both variations in camera distance within an individual film and the dominant selected distance, I will cover only the latter aspect in this section and discuss the former in the context of editing.

69. Ben Brewster has explained it thus: "[The position circa 1909] has a literal, theatrical conception of the represented space, where the screen is a window immediately behind which the principal characters stand a measurable distance away from the spectators" (quoted in Elsaesser [1990], 28).

70. For representative expressions of these concerns, see "The Size of the Picture," *Moving Picture World* (8, no. 10, 11 March 1911), 527; *Moving Picture World* (9, no. 4, 5 August 1911), 294.

71. Kristin Thompson has pointed out to me that the trade press's position might possess a logic I have not considered: possibly, commentators believed the disruption introduced by enlarged figures could distract viewers from attending to the narrative flow.

72. Well-known examples of each type occur in, respectively, Edison's *The Great Train Robbery* (1903) and *The Gay Shoe Clerk* (1902).

73. Tom Gunning has noted how the emblematic close-up functioned as a "more economical equivalent" to the apotheosis ending popularized in early French films: "[A] sense of finality [is offered] not through a narrative resolution but through an intensification of spectacular visual display, a climax of the film's attractions" (1987), 231. Abel (1994) argues that French filmmakers began to employ cut-ins as aids to narrativization as early as 1904–6.

74. For extended discussion of what appears to be the last extant manifestation of the emblematic close-up, in Vitagraph's 1910 *Playing at Divorce*, see Gunning (1987), 237–38; and Bowser (1990), 96.

75. Virtually all the examples I have seen from 1909—Vitagraph's *An Alpine Echo*, Essanay's *A Ranchman's Rival* and *Two Sides to a Story*, and Bison's *Faithful Wife* and *Reunited at the Gallows*—employ such shots at the end of the film; only Lubin's *Sporting Blood* does not.

76. Abel discusses a representative example of this type of cut-in in *L'Homme aux gants blancs* (1908); see (1994), 199–200.

77. Prior to this, the press had occasion to mention "alternate scenes" or "shifts in scenes" in reviews of various films—often Biographs—but they offered no consistent criticism of the practice. For a sampling of representative comments on editing and its effects, see *Moving Picture World* (4, no. 10, 6 March 1909), 268; *Moving Picture World* (6, no. 15, 16 April 1910), 599; *Nickelodeon* (4, no. 8, 15 October 1910), 226; *Nickelodeon* (5, no. 5, 4 February 1911), 138.

78. For example, in "Scenario Construction," published over a year earlier, the following figures are mentioned: "The number of scenes in full reel films vary anywhere from ten to as high as thirty-five. The average is about fourteen" (*Moving Picture World* 8, no. 6, 11 February 1911), 294.

79. A few words on the calculation of these figures is in order. First, I excluded Biograph films from the sample group to demonstrate the differences

between cutting rates at that studio and the rest of the industry. (I excluded non-Griffith titles as well, because films by other directors at the studio generally featured fairly high cutting rates. Biograph's cutting rates prior to Griffith's arrival are consistent with other production companies. Data concerning cutting rates at companies other than Biograph must be considered provisional, because the proportion of surviving titles is so much lower.) Second, I only included those titles whose original release length exceeded 800 feet; the vast majority of these were films between 950 and 1,000 feet. Third, I tried to count only complete films, though some titles may be missing a few shots. Finally, I elected to exclude intertitles from my shot counts because they are not reproduced consistently in the prints available for study and their inclusion can artificially increase shot counts for certain studios. In this, my approach remains consistent with Gunning's and thus renders a comparison of our figures workable. (Because both Barry Salt and Kristin Thompson include intertitles in their shot counts, comparison with their figures will reveal very little, though the trends cited should be consistent; see Salt [1983], 128–29.) For Gunning's original table, see (1991), 264. Gunning's table also serves as the source for the Griffith-related data in table 5.2.

80. Thompson (1985b) supplies an extended discussion of these two editing procedures, particularly as they develop throughout the teens; see 207–10.

Chapter 6. Analyzing Transition

1. Let me preface the actual analyses with a few words about print sources and viewing procedures. I viewed all the films initially as 16 mm or 35 mm prints, derived from the collections housed at the Museum of Modern Art, the Library of Congress, and the Wisconsin Center for Film and Theater Research. When necessary, I checked films after archival screenings by watching video copies. The plot descriptions listed at the beginning of the analyses are the stories of the films as I have come to understand them from viewing the prints. Wherever it seemed advisable, I have provided supplemental synopses as supplied by the production companies to the trade press.

2. Audience foreknowledge undoubtedly played a role in the film's intelligibility, since the main character was based on a newspaper serial character known as Swipsey; see Niver (1968), 117.

3. Commentators widely frowned upon coincidence, seeing it as a violation of verisimilitude. In his scriptwriting manual, Eustace Hale Ball stressed that "coincidence is the make-shift of a writer who cannot make the characters of his plot work out the story" (1913), 35–36.

4. A title naming the necklace "Love's token" asserts its status as a valued object prior to its first appearance in shot twelve. The necklace also functions in ways beyond those already mentioned. The young woman clutches it when the

Puritans drag the heroine and her mother away in shot nineteen, reminding us that the trapper exists as a means for her rescue. Moreover, the necklace appears to be a trinket that the trapper might use in his interactions with the Natives, which indirectly links the young woman and her eventual agents of salvation.

5. It appears that this off-screen representation of violence occasioned some controversy at the time of the film's release. In its review of the film, *Moving Picture World* reported: "The idea of the deacon compelling the daughter to behold from her cell window the burning of her mother, is somewhat repulsive; it would seem that the young girl should have been treated equally with the audience in allowing imagination to fill its purpose, rather than an actual view of the tragedy so mercifully saved from the public. It is not surprising that exception has been taken to this part by the public press" (7, no. 15, 8 October 1910), 813. Critics responding negatively to a *character* being subjected to an unpleasant visual display tacitly recognizes that vicariously experienced violence (via a character's reaction) could prove almost as unsettling as its actual depiction.

6. Because he restricts spaces to a limited number of disparate settings, Griffith can forge connections between different characters and the places they inhabit. While the young woman is associated with the sea, the Puritan is tied directly to the town. The forest remains the space most consistently associated with the trapper, which connects him to the Natives, but he also appears at the sea, which the Puritan never does. In this way, the film's spatial logic underscores the assertion that the trapper is the ideal mate for the young woman.

7. The summary I have provided derives from my own understanding of the film, based on the depicted action and the sole insert. Comparing my version to the synopsis furnished by the manufacturer reveals the elaborated narrative detail one cannot extrapolate from the current print: "Jack Talbot, a dashing American, is automobiling when his car breaks down on a country road. The chauffeur informs him that it will take a day to repair the damage. Jack spies a country hotel in the distance and decides to stay overnight. On his way to make arrangements, he meets Fred Moore, a former college chum, who, upon learning of the difficulties, invites him to spend the night with him. Upon their arrival at Fred's house, one of the neighbours calls to Moore to go with him. Moore tells Jack to go in the house and make himself at home. In the meantime, Dolly Moore, the pretty sister of Fred, has discovered a leak in the radiator and 'phones for the plumber to hurry to her assistance. Jack enters a few minutes later and she takes him for the plumber, as he happens to have a monkey wrench in his hand. Jack realizes that he can have some fun and allows Dolly to show him the radiator, which he repairs. She also decides as long as he is there he can fix the pipes of the sink. Fred discovers Jack at his task and at Jack's request, decides to keep the joke up. Fred's folks are giving a dance and they send Fred's old chum an invitation. At the affair he is introduced to Dolly, who realizes the mistake she has made, but before the evening is over Jack and Dolly are engaged, Fred coming

upon the scene with the lucky monkey wrench" ("Stories of the Films," *Moving Picture World* 8, no. 13, 15 April 1911).

8. For more on the development of Keystone's formal traits, see Riblet (1995).

9. Split-screen representations of multiple actions resurface sporadically, in French films of the 1920s, for example, and those of the post-classical Hollywood era. Only stylistically self-conscious directors like Brian De Palma rely on the technique more than occasionally, however.

10. I have already noted the moderate deviations from shot-scale norms that representing of telephone calls produced in both *The Forgotten Watch* and *Cupid's Monkey Wrench*. For more detailed investigations of this phenomenon, see both Bowser (1985) and Tsivian (1994).

11. Given that the prints of *Suspense* I have viewed cut off the action rather suddenly at the end, I think it possible the conclusion we now have is a truncated one, or even that a final shot has gone missing from the current version.

12. Only once in *Suspense* does the narrative action not emerge clearly. Shot thirty-six depicts a man standing in the middle of the road, smoking a cigarette. A car comes up behind him quickly, producing a remarkably abrupt depiction of the man being hit. (Only if one views the film in slow motion is the act fully visible.) The ensuing actions of the subsequent shot also prove rather difficult to comprehend. The camera position has changed, resulting in a vantage point removed from the road; one cannot discern easily what happens, but it appears that the husband checks to see what has occurred, gets back in his car, and then exits, followed directly by the police car, which never pauses. The filmmakers do not reveal the fate of the man, who may have been hit, nor do they render his body visible in the second shot. The filmmakers probably included this interlude to provide an impediment to the progress of the rescue; whether one can attribute the hurried and largely unintelligible representation of this shot to the shooting circumstances or whether viewer uncertainties derive from intentionally uncommunicative narration, I cannot say.

Chapter 7. Conclusion

1. As Robert Spadoni (1999) indicates in his perceptive account of how Vitagraph developed techniques that may have led to the practice of shot/reverse shot, filmmakers would occasionally lay the groundwork for the emergence of solutions they themselves had not anticipated. Moreover, some solutions addressed multiple problems. By limiting myself to the formal problems confronting filmmakers of this period, I am not suggesting that the solutions devised might not also have addressed other concerns in the bargain. The introduction of intertitles, for example, functioned as a useful narrational tool, but it also permitted pro-

ducers to promote their actors by naming them within the film, and this in turn helped the industry develop a star system during the period.

2. An article that describes the making of a Selig film in 1909 estimates that the film in question cost in excess of $1,000, but that "total sales will probably net $15,000." While this might be an exceptional case given the subject matter involved (a reenactment of Roosevelt's African hunting expedition), it still indicates the substantial profits possible in filmmaking at this time; see "Scientific Nature-Faking" (*Colliers* 43, 3 July 1909), 13 (repr. in Lahue [1973], 53).

3. As David Hulfish pointed out, one could discern audience response with relative ease: "[One] can learn much about [the] show by watching [the] patrons as they come out. It is not necessary to inquire what they think of the show. Comments will pass among them which may be overheard by the manager and the cashier as they pass the ticket window, commenting favorably and unfavorably upon the film pictures they have seen a few minutes before. . . . The responsiveness of the audience in the theatre is one barometer of public approval; the attitude and conduct of patrons leaving the theatre is another. The ticket sales will be another, but this last is not so quick in its indications of response" (1970), 31–32.

4. These attributes apply to Selig, circa 1911, as detailed in Eugene Dengler's "Wonders of the Diamond S-Plant" (*Motography* 6, no. 1, July 1911), 7–19. Indications are that most of the larger companies operated in similar ways by the end of the transitional period.

5. For more on this issue, see Spadoni (1999).

6. See my comments in chapter 3, endnote 18. Roberta Pearson touches upon some of these features of the multireeler in her helpful overview of the transitional period; see (1996), 39.

7. Such strategies mirror the advice given by those like Eustace Hale Ball, who suggested that the "technical presentation of a two or three reel subject is virtually the same as that of a single reel, except that there should be a proportionate addition to the number of scenes, and dramatic crises" (1913), 57–58.

FILMOGRAPHY: VIEWED TITLES, 1907–1913

Note: Titles within square brackets are provisional titles assigned to films whose actual titles have yet to be determined.

TITLE	PRODUCTION COMPANY	FORMAT	ARCHIVE
1907			
Cohen's Fire Sale	Edison	16 mm	MOMA
College Chums	Edison	16 mm	MOMA
Jack the Kisser	Edison	16 mm	MOMA
Laughing Gas	Edison	16 mm	MOMA
Lost in the Alps	Edison	16 mm	MOMA
The Rivals	Edison	16 mm	MOMA
Stage Struck	Edison	16 mm	MOMA
The Trainer's Daughter	Edison	16 mm	MOMA
An Arcadian Elopement	AM&B	16 mm	MOMA
Deaf-Mutes' Masquerade	AM&B	16 mm	MOMA
Dr. Skinum	AM&B	16 mm	MOMA
The Elopement	AM&B	16 mm	MOMA
The Energizer	AM&B	16 mm	MOMA
Fights of Nations	AM&B	16 mm	LoC
Fussy Father Fooled	AM&B	16 mm	MOMA
The Hypnotist's Revenge	AM&B	16 mm	MOMA
If You Had a Wife Like This	AM&B	16 mm	MOMA
The Love Microbe	AM&B	16 mm	MOMA
The Model's Ma	AM&B	16 mm	MOMA
Mr. Gay and Mrs.	AM&B	16 mm	MOMA
Mr. Hurry-Up of New York	AM&B	16 mm	LoC
Neighbors	AM&B	16 mm	MOMA
Terrible Ted	AM&B	16 mm	MOMA
Tired Tailor's Dream	AM&B	16 mm	MOMA

1907 (*continued*)

Trial Marriages	AM&B	16 mm	LoC
The Truants	AM&B	16 mm	MOMA
Under the Old Apple Tree	AM&B	16 mm	MOMA
Wife Wanted	AM&B	16 mm	MOMA
The Yale Laundry	AM&B	Video	n/a
The Boy, the Bust and the Bath	Vitagraph	16 mm	MOMA
The Easterner	Vitagraph	35 mm	NFA
The Haunted Hotel	Vitagraph	35 mm	LoC
Liquid Electricity	Vitagraph	35 mm	MOMA
The Mill Girl	Vitagraph	35 mm	MOMA
The Stolen Pig	Vitagraph	35 mm/inc	LoC
The New Arrival	Lubin	Video	LoC
The Bandit King	Selig	16 mm/fr	LoC
His First Ride	Selig	16 mm/fr	LoC
The Girl from Montana	Selig	Video/fr	n/a
Ben Hur	Kalem	Video	n/a

1908

Cupid's Pranks	Edison	16 mm/inc	MOMA
Fireside Reminiscences	Edison	16 mm	MOMA
The Merry Widow Waltz Craze	Edison	35 mm	LoC
Pocahontas	Edison	16 mm/inc	MOMA
The Suburbanite's Ingenious Alarm	Edison	16 mm	MOMA
Tale the Autumn Leaves Told	Edison	16 mm/inc	MOMA
The Adventures of Dollie	AM&B	Video	n/a
After Many Years	AM&B	Video	n/a
At the Crossroads of Life	AM&B	16 mm	MOMA
At the French Ball	AM&B	16 mm	MOMA
An Awful Moment	AM&B	Video	n/a
Balked at the Altar	AM&B	Video	n/a
The Barbarian Ingomar	AM&B	Video	n/a
The Black Viper	AM&B	16 mm	LoC
Bobby's Kodak	AM&B	16 mm	MOMA
The Boy Detective	AM&B	16 mm	LoC
A Calamitous Elopement	AM&B	Video	n/a
The Call of the Wild	AM&B	Video	n/a
Caught by Wireless	AM&B	16 mm	LoC
Classmates	AM&B	16 mm	MOMA
Deceived Slumming Party	AM&B	16 mm	LoC

TITLE	PRODUCTION COMPANY	FORMAT	ARCHIVE
1908 (*continued*)			
Falsely Accused	AM&B	16 mm	MOMA
A Famous Escape	AM&B	16 mm	LoC
The Girls and Daddy	AM&B	Video	n/a
The Guerilla	AM&B	16 mm	LoC
Her First Adventure	AM&B	16 mm	MOMA
His Day of Rest	AM&B	16 mm	LoC
Hulda's Lovers	AM&B	16 mm	LoC
Invisible Fluid	AM&B	16 mm	LoC
The Kentuckian	AM&B	16 mm	LoC
The King of the Cannibal Island	AM&B	16 mm	LoC
The King's Messenger	AM&B	16 mm	LoC
Lonesome Junction	AM&B	16 mm	MOMA
Man in the Box	AM&B	16 mm	LoC
Mixed Babies	AM&B	16 mm	LoC
Old Isaacs the Pawnbroker	AM&B	16 mm	MOMA
'Ostler Joe	AM&B	16 mm	LoC
The Outlaw	AM&B	16 mm	LoC
Over the Hills to the Poorhouse	AM&B	16 mm	LoC
The Princess in the Vase	AM&B	16 mm	MOMA
Professional Jealousy	AM&B	16 mm	MOMA
Romance of an Egg	AM&B	16 mm	LoC
The Sculptor's Nightmare	AM&B	16 mm	LoC
The Snowman	AM&B	16 mm	MOMA
The Stage Rustler	AM&B	16 mm	LoC
A Terrible Night	AM&B	16 mm	LoC
Thompson's Night Out	AM&B	16 mm	LoC
Where the Breakers Roar	AM&B	Video	n/a
The Yellow Peril	AM&B	16 mm	LoC
An Auto Heroine	Vitagraph	35 mm/inc	NFA
A Cowboy Elopement	Vitagraph	16 mm	MOMA
Francesca di Rimini	Vitagraph	35 mm	MOMA
Get Me a Step Ladder	Vitagraph	35 mm	NFA
The Last Cartridge	Vitagraph	35 mm	LoC
Nellie, the Beautiful Housemaid	Vitagraph	16 mm/fr	LoC
Salome	Vitagraph	35 mm/inc	NFA
The Hebrew Fugitive	Lubin	35 mm	NFA
The Cattle Rustlers	Selig	35 mm	NFA
The Renegade	Kalem	35 mm	NFA

1909

The House of Cards	Edison	16 mm	MOMA
The Luck of Roaring Camp	Edison	35 mm	NFA
Three Thanksgivings	Edison	16 mm	MOMA
True Love Never Runs Smoothly	Edison	35 mm	NFA
At the Altar	Biograph	Video	n/a
The Cord of Life	Biograph	Video	n/a
A Corner in Wheat	Biograph	Video	n/a
The Country Doctor	Biograph	16 mm	MOMA
A Drunkard's Reformation	Biograph	Video	n/a
Eloping with Auntie	Biograph	16 mm	LoC
Fools of Fate	Biograph	Video	n/a
The Gibson Goddess	Biograph	35 mm	LoC
The Golden Louis	Biograph	Video	n/a
His Lost Love	Biograph	Video	n/a
Lines of White on the Sullen Sea	Biograph	Video	n/a
The Lonely Villa	Biograph	Video	n/a
Mr. Jones and His Neighbors	Biograph	Video	n/a
The Rocky Road	Biograph	Video	n/a
Those Awful Hats	Biograph	Video	n/a
To Save Her Soul	Biograph	16 mm	LoC
Trying to Get Arrested	Biograph	16 mm	LoC
What Drink Did	Biograph	Video	n/a
An Alpine Echo	Vitagraph	35 mm	NFA
The Forgotten Watch	Vitagraph	35 mm	LoC
From Cabin Boy to King	Vitagraph	35 mm	LoC
An Irish Hero	Vitagraph	35 mm	LoC
Life of Moses	Vitagraph	16 mm	MOMA
The Magic Fountain Pen	Vitagraph	35 mm	NFA
Napoleon: The Man of Destiny	Vitagraph	35 mm	LoC
Oliver Twist	Vitagraph	35 mm	NFA
The Poor Musician	Vitagraph	35 mm	LoC
A Romance of the Umbrella	Vitagraph	35 mm	NFA
The Scales of Justice	Vitagraph	35 mm	LoC
The Call of the Heart	Lubin	16 mm	LoC
The Doctor's Bride	Lubin	16 mm	LoC
The Drunkard's Child	Lubin	16 mm	LoC
The Haunted Hat	Lubin	16 mm	LoC
Her Face Was Her Fortune	Lubin	16 mm	LoC
How Brown Got Married	Lubin	16 mm	LoC
The Hungry Actor	Lubin	16 mm	LoC
Near Sighted Mary	Lubin	16 mm	LoC
The Newest Woman	Lubin	16 mm	LoC

TITLE	PRODUCTION COMPANY	FORMAT	ARCHIVE
1909 (*continued*)			
Professor Wise's Brain Serum Injector	Lubin	35 mm	NFA
She Would Be an Actress	Lubin	16 mm	LoC
Sporting Blood	Lubin	16 mm	LoC
A True Patriot	Lubin	16 mm	LoC
The Two Cousins	Lubin	16 mm	LoC
The Unexpected Guest	Lubin	16 mm	LoC
When the Flag Falls	Lubin	16 mm	LoC
Wifey Away, Hubby at Play	Lubin	16 mm	LoC
The Woman Hater	Lubin	16 mm	LoC
The Yiddisher Boy	Lubin	35 mm	LoC
Broncho Billy Rejected	Essanay	35 mm	NFA
The Neighbor's Kids	Essanay	35 mm	LoC
A Ranchman's Rival	Essanay	35 mm	LoC
The Tell Tale Blotter	Essanay	35 mm/inc	LoC
Ten Nights in a Bar Room	Essanay	16 mm	LoC
Two Sides to a Story	Essanay	35 mm	LoC
Hiawatha	IMP	16 mm	MOMA
His Last Game	IMP	16 mm	LoC
The Two Sons	IMP	35 mm	LoC
Faithful Wife	NYMP/Bison	35 mm	LoC
The Parson's Prayer	NYMP/Bison	35 mm	LoC
Reunited at the Gallows	NYMP/Bison	35 mm	LoC
The Aborigine's Devotion	World Film Manufacturing Co.	35 mm	LoC
1910			
Arms and the Woman	Edison	16 mm	LoC
How Bumptious Papered the Parlour	Edison	16 mm	LoC
Into the Jaws of Death	Edison	35 mm	NFA
Pardners	Edison	35 mm	LoC
The Stolen Father	Edison	35 mm	NFA
The Affair of an Egg	Biograph	16 mm	LoC
After the Ball	Biograph	16 mm	LoC
All on Account of the Milk	Biograph	16 mm	MOMA
The Course of True Love	Biograph	16 mm	MOMA

1910 (**continued**)

Faithful	Biograph	Video	n/a
Happy Jack, a Hero	Biograph	16 mm	LoC
His Last Dollar	Biograph	16 mm	LoC
His Trust	Biograph	Video	n/a
His Trust Fulfilled	Biograph	Video	n/a
His Wife's Sweethearts	Biograph	16 mm	LoC
The Honor of His Family	Biograph	16 mm	LoC
The House with Closed Shutters	Biograph	Video	n/a
How Hubby Got a Raise	Biograph	16 mm	LoC
The Kid	Biograph	16 mm	LoC
A Knot in the Plot	Biograph	16 mm	LoC
Love in Quarantine	Biograph	16 mm	LoC
Love of Lady Irma	Biograph	16 mm	LoC
A Lucky Toothache	Biograph	16 mm	LoC
The Masher	Biograph	16 mm	LoC
Never Again	Biograph	16 mm	LoC
Not So Bad as It Seemed	Biograph	16 mm	LoC
An Old Story with a New Ending	Biograph	16 mm	LoC
Over Silent Paths	Biograph	Video	n/a
The Passing of a Grouch	Biograph	16 mm	LoC
The Proposal	Biograph	16 mm	LoC
The Purgation	Biograph	16 mm	LoC
The Recreation of an Heiress	Biograph	16 mm	LoC
Rose O'Salem-Town	Biograph	Video	n/a
Serious Sixteen	Biograph	16 mm	LoC
A Summer Tragedy	Biograph	16 mm	LoC
The Tenderfoot's Triumph	Biograph	16 mm	LoC
The Troublesome Baby	Biograph	16 mm	LoC
Turning the Tables	Biograph	16 mm	LoC
The Unchanging Sea	Biograph	Video	n/a
Up a Tree	Biograph	16 mm	LoC
The Usurer	Biograph	Video	n/a
When We Were in Our 'Teens	Biograph	16 mm	LoC
White Roses	Biograph	16 mm	LoC
Back to Nature	Vitagraph	35 mm	NFA
Brother Man	Vitagraph	35 mm	LoC
Daisies	Vitagraph	35 mm	NFA
In Neighboring Kingdoms	Vitagraph	16 mm	MOMA
Jack Fat and Slim Jim			
at Coney Island	Vitagraph	16 mm	MOMA
Jean and the Waif	Vitagraph	35 mm	NFA

TITLE	PRODUCTION COMPANY	FORMAT	ARCHIVE
1910 (*continued*)			
A Life for a Life	Vitagraph	35 mm	LoC
The Love of Chrysanthemum	Vitagraph	35 mm	LoC
The Mystery of Temple Court	Vitagraph	35 mm	LoC
Playing at Divorce	Vitagraph	16 mm	LoC
Ransomed, or a Prisoner of War	Vitagraph	16 mm	LoC
Renunciation	Vitagraph	35 mm	NFA
The Telephone	Vitagraph	16 mm	LoC
A Tin-Type Romance	Vitagraph	16 mm	LoC
Twelfth Night	Vitagraph	35 mm	LoC
Victims of Fate	Vitagraph	35 mm	LoC
Where the Wind Blows	Vitagraph	35 mm	NFA
The Almighty Dollar	Lubin	35 mm	LoC
The Dream Pill	Lubin	35 mm	NFA
The Gambler's Charm	Lubin	35 mm	LoC
The New Boss of Bar X Ranch	Lubin	35 mm	NFA
Path of Duty	Lubin	35 mm	NFA
The Bandit's Mask	Selig	35 mm	NFA
A Tale of the Sea	Selig	35 mm	LoC
The Colonel's Errand	Kalem	35 mm	NFA
[The City Cousin and the Cowboys]	Essanay	35 mm	NFA
A Darling Confusion	Essanay	35 mm	NFA
[The Deputy's Duty]	Essanay	35 mm	LoC
Method in His Madness	Essanay	16 mm	LoC
Pals of the Range	Essanay	35 mm	NFA
Under Western Skies	Essanay	35 mm	LoC
Whist!	Essanay	35 mm	LoC
Bear Ye One Another's Burdens	IMP	16 mm	LoC
A Crippled Teddy Bear	IMP	35 mm	LoC
Faithful Max	IMP	35 mm	NFA
Fruits and Flowers	IMP	35 mm	LoC
Mendelssohn's Spring Song	IMP	35 mm	LoC
The Mistake	IMP	35 mm	LoC
A Self-Made Hero	IMP	35 mm	LoC
Cowboy for Love	NYMP/Bison	35 mm	NFA
Flight of Redwing	NYMP/Bison	35 mm	NFA
Girl of the Plains	NYMP/Bison	35 mm	LoC
Love in Mexico	NYMP/Bison	16 mm	LoC

1910 (*continued*)

Aunt Hannah	Powers	35 mm	LoC
How Women Love	Powers	35 mm	LoC
The Newspaper Error	Powers	35 mm	LoC
The Pugilist's Child	Powers	35 mm	LoC
Daddy's Double	Thanhouser	35 mm	NFA
Not Guilty	Thanhouser	35 mm	LoC
Vicar of Wakefield	Thanhouser	35 mm	LoC
Winter's Tale	Thanhouser	35 mm	LoC
Young Lord Stanley	Thanhouser	35 mm	LoC
A Husband's Deception	American	35 mm	LoC
A Troublesome Parcel	American	35 mm	LoC
Where Sea and Shore Doth Meet	Reliance	35 mm	NFA
An Italian Sherlock Holmes	Yankee	35 mm	LoC
A Touching Mystery	Atlas	16 mm	LoC

1911

Between Two Fires	Edison	35 mm	LoC
The Black Bordered Letter	Edison	35 mm	NFA
Freezing Auntie	Edison	35 mm	NFA
A Stage Romance	Edison	35 mm	NFA
A Strike at the Mines	Edison	35 mm	NFA
The Test of Friendship	Edison	35 mm	NFA
The Writing on the Blotter	Edison	35 mm	LoC
Bobby the Coward	Biograph	Video	n/a
The Broken Cross	Biograph	Video	n/a
The Chief's Daughter	Biograph	Video	n/a
Comrades	Biograph	16 mm	MOMA
Enoch Arden	Biograph	Video	n/a
The Failure	Biograph	16 mm	MOMA
Fate's Turning	Biograph	16 mm	WCFTR
Help Wanted	Biograph	16 mm	LoC
His Mother's Scarf	Biograph	Video	n/a
Lily of the Tenements	Biograph	16 mm	MOMA
The Lonedale Operator	Biograph	Video	n/a
The Midnight Marauder	Biograph	16 mm	LoC
Mr. Bragg, Fugitive	Biograph	16 mm	MOMA
The New Dress	Biograph	Video	n/a
The Poor Sick Men	Biograph	16 mm	LoC
The Primal Call	Biograph	Video	n/a
Priscilla and the Umbrella	Biograph	16 mm	MOMA
Priscilla's April Fool Joke	Biograph	16 mm	MOMA
The Sunbeam	Biograph	Video	n/a

TITLE	PRODUCTION COMPANY	FORMAT	ARCHIVE
1911 (*continued*)			
The Clown and His Best Performance	Vitagraph	35 mm	NFA
Davy Jones in the South Seas	Vitagraph	16 mm	LoC
A Friendly Marriage	Vitagraph	16 mm	LoC
Jean Rescues	Vitagraph	35 mm	LoC
Lady Godiva	Vitagraph	16 mm	WCFTR
The Politician's Dream	Vitagraph	16 mm/fr	LoC
Proving His Love	Vitagraph	35 mm	LoC
The Troublesome Secretaries	Vitagraph	16 mm	LoC
Vanity Fair	Vitagraph	Video/inc	n/a
The Voiceless Message	Vitagraph	35 mm	NFA
Kiddie's Christmas	Lubin	16mm	LoC
My Brother Agostino	Lubin	35 mm	NFA
A Newsboy's Luck	Lubin	35 mm	LoC
[Only a Dream]	Lubin	35 mm	NFA
The Substitute	Lubin	35 mm	NFA
The Two Fathers	Lubin	35 mm	NFA
Captain Brand's Wife	Selig	35 mm	LoC
Captain Kate	Selig	35 mm	NFA
Cinderella	Selig	35 mm/inc	NFA
Curse of the Red Man	Selig	35 mm	NFA
An Indian Vestal	Selig	35 mm	NFA
The Little Widow	Selig	16 mm	LoC
One Hundred Years After	Selig	35 mm/inc	NFA
The Outbreak	Selig	35 mm	NFA
Saved by the Pony Express	Selig	35 mm	LoC
Seminole's Sacrifice	Selig	35 mm	NFA
The Still Alarm	Selig	35 mm	NFA
The Totem Mark	Selig	35 mm	NFA
The Blackfoot Halfbreed	Kalem	35 mm	NFA
By a Woman's Wit	Kalem	35 mm	LoC
By the Aid of the Lariat	Kalem	35 mm	NFA
The Fiddler's Requiem	Kalem	35 mm	NFA
The Little Soldier of '64	Kalem	35 mm	NFA
The Lost Freight Car	Kalem	35 mm	NFA
The Mexican "Joan of Arc"	Kalem	35 mm	NFA
On the War Path	Kalem	35 mm	LoC

1911 (*continued*)

The Plot against Bertie	Kalem	16 mm	LoC
The Railroad Raiders of '62	Kalem	16 mm	LoC
Rory O'Moore	Kalem	35 mm	NFA
Slim Jim's Last Chance	Kalem	35 mm	NFA
A Special Messenger	Kalem	35 mm	NFA
Tangled Lives	Kalem	35 mm	NFA
When the Sun Went Out	Kalem	35 mm	LoC
Alkali Ike's Auto	Essanay	Video	n/a
A Child of the West	Essanay	35 mm	NFA
The Corporation and the Ranch Girl	Essanay	35 mm	NFA
Forgiven in Death	Essanay	35 mm	NFA
The Indian Maiden's Lesson	Essanay	35 mm	NFA
The Loafer	Essanay	35 mm	NFA
The Millionaire Barber	Essanay	16 mm	LoC
The Outlaw and the Child	Essanay	35 mm	NFA
The Rosary	Essanay	35 mm	NFA
Winning an Heiress	Essanay	35 mm	LoC
Artful Kate	IMP	16 mm	LoC
At The Duke's Command	IMP	16 mm	LoC
The Dream	IMP	16 mm	LoC
The Dynamiters	IMP	35 mm	LoC
The Forged Dispatch	IMP	35 mm	LoC
In Old Madrid	IMP	16 mm	LoC
In The Sultan's Garden	IMP	35 mm	LoC
The Lighthouse Keeper	IMP	35 mm	LoC
Maid or Man	IMP	16 mm	MOMA
[Margharita]	IMP	35 mm	LoC
The Penniless Prince	IMP	35 mm	LoC
Sweet Memories	IMP	35 mm	LoC
Through the Air	IMP	35 mm/inc	NFA
'Tween Two Loves	IMP	35 mm	LoC
Uncle Pete's Ruse	IMP	35 mm	LoC
Wise Druggist	IMP	16 mm	LoC
A Range Romance	NYMP/Bison	35 mm	LoC
A Redskin's Bravery	NYMP/Bison	35 mm	LoC
Wenona's Broken Promise	NYMP/Bison	16 mm	MOMA
Cupid's Monkey Wrench	Powers	35 mm	LoC
Dr. Jekyll and Mr. Hyde	Thanhouser	16 mm	WCFTR
Only in the Way	Thanhouser	35 mm	LoC
The Ranchman's Nerve	American	35 mm	LoC

TITLE	PRODUCTION COMPANY	FORMAT	ARCHIVE
1911 (*continued*)			
A Western Dream	American	35 mm	NFA
Her Mother's Fiancé	Yankee	16 mm	LoC
Big Noise Hank	Nestor	16 mm	MOMA
The Blessed Baby	Nestor	16 mm	MOMA
Dippy Advertises for a Pup	Nestor	16 mm	MOMA
Mutt and Jeff Discover a Wonderful Remedy	Nestor	16 mm	MOMA
Mutt and Jeff Join the Opera	Nestor	16 mm	MOMA
Dad's Girl	Reliance	16 mm	LoC
O'er Grim Fields Scarred	Reliance	35 mm	LoC
Greater Love Hath No Man	Solax	35 mm	LoC
His Mother's Hymn	Solax	35 mm	UCLA
The Attempt on the Special	American Kinematograph	35 mm	NFA
Back to the Prairie	American Kinematograph	35 mm	NFA
A Daughter of Dixie	Champion	35 mm	LoC
An Up-to-Date Squaw	Pathé American	35 mm	LoC
The Colonel's Daughter	Rex	35 mm	NFA
The Little Major	Rex	35 mm	NFA
The Girls of Pinetree Branch	Moosehead	35 mm	NFA
1912			
A Baby's Shoe	Edison	35 mm	LoC
"Believe Me, If All Those Endearing Young Charms"	Edison	35 mm	LoC
Bobby's Dream	Edison	16 mm	MOMA
Children Who Labor	Edison	16 mm	MOMA
The Crime of Carelessness	Edison	16 mm	MOMA
The Land beyond the Sunset	Edison	Video	n/a
The Mighty Hunters	Edison	16 mm	MOMA
No Place for a Minister's Son	Edison	16 mm	MOMA
An Old Appointment	Edison	16 mm	MOMA
A Suffragette in Spite of Himself	Edison	35 mm	LoC
Blind Love	Biograph	16 mm	MOMA
Brutality	Biograph	16 mm	MOMA
A Dash through the Clouds	Biograph	Video	n/a
The Girl and Her Trust	Biograph	Video	n/a

1912 (*continued*)

His Lesson	Biograph	Video	n/a
Man's Genesis	Biograph	16 mm	WCFTR
The Musketeers of Pig Alley	Biograph	Video	n/a
Neighbors	Biograph	Video	n/a
The New York Hat	Biograph	Video	n/a
The Painted Lady	Biograph	Video	n/a
The Sands of Dee	Biograph	Video	n/a
A Temporary Truce	Biograph	Video	n/a
Conscience, or the Chamber of Horrors	Vitagraph	35 mm	NFA
The Cross-Roads	Vitagraph	35 mm	LoC
A Cure for Pokeritis	Vitagraph	35 mm	LoC
Father's Hot Toddy	Vitagraph	16 mm	LoC
Her Choice	Vitagraph	16 mm	MOMA
His Official Appointment	Vitagraph	Video	n/a
Love Hath Wrought a Miracle	Vitagraph	35 mm	LoC
The Loyalty of Sylvia	Vitagraph	35 mm	NFA
Mr. Bolter's Infatuation	Vitagraph	35 mm	LoC
Out of the Shadows	Vitagraph	35 mm	NFA
Stenographer Wanted	Vitagraph	16 mm	MOMA
Willie's Sister	Vitagraph	35 mm	LoC
The Bank Cashier	Lubin	35 mm	NFA
Glued	Lubin	35 mm	LoC
In the Service of the State	Lubin	35 mm	NFA
The Missing Finger	Lubin	35 mm	NFA
A Physician's Honor	Lubin	Video	n/a
The Preacher and the Gossips	Lubin	35 mm	LoC
A Romance of the Coast	Lubin	35 mm	NFA
The Samaritan of Coogan's Tenement	Lubin	35 mm	NFA
Satin and Gingham	Lubin	35 mm	NFA
'Twixt Love and Ambition	Lubin	35 mm	LoC
Water Wagon	Lubin	35 mm	LoC
An Assisted Elopement	Selig	35 mm	LoC
Buck's Romance	Selig	35 mm	LoC
The Devil, the Servant and the Man	Selig	35 mm	NFA
Euchered	Selig	35 mm	LoC
The Girl at the Cupola	Selig	35 mm	LoC
Her Bitter Lesson	Selig	16 mm	MOMA
The Last of Her Tribe	Selig	35 mm	NFA
The Ranger and His Horse	Selig	35 mm	NFA
The Trade Gun Bullet	Selig	35 mm	NFA

TITLE	PRODUCTION COMPANY	FORMAT	ARCHIVE
1912 (*continued*)			
Captured by Bedouins	Kalem	35 mm	LoC
Driver of the Deadwood Coach	Kalem	16 mm	MOMA
The Grit of the Girl Telegrapher	Kalem	16 mm	WCFTR
The Gun Smugglers	Kalem	35 mm	LoC
The Heart of John Grimm	Kalem	35 mm	NFA
The Little Wanderer	Kalem	35 mm	NFA
Reconciled by Burglars	Kalem	16 mm	LoC
The Siege of Petersburg	Kalem	35 mm/inc	LoC
The Tide of Battle	Kalem	16 mm	LoC
Winning a Widow	Kalem	35 mm	LoC
Broncho Billy and the Bandits	Essanay	35 mm	LoC
Broncho Billy's Heart	Essanay	35 mm	NFA
Broncho Billy's Love Affair	Essanay	35 mm	NFA
Broncho Billy's Narrow Escape	Essanay	35 mm	NFA
The Cat's Paw	Essanay	35 mm	NFA
The End of the Feud	Essanay	35 mm	NFA
The Loafer's Mother	Essanay	35 mm	NFA
The New Church Organ	Essanay	35 mm	NFA
A Soul Reclaimed	Essanay	35 mm	NFA
The Voice of Conscience	Essanay	35 mm	NFA
A Woman of Arizona	Essanay	35 mm	LoC
A Bad Tangle	IMP	35 mm	LoC
The Bridal Room	IMP	35 mm	LoC
A Bronx Cocktail	IMP	35 mm	LoC
A Foreign Invasion	IMP	35 mm	LoC
Let No Man Put Asunder	IMP	16 mm	LoC
The Long Strike	IMP	35 mm	NFA
The New Fire Chief	IMP	35 mm	LoC
The Tankville Constable	IMP	35 mm	LoC
An Apache Father's Vengeance	NYMP/Bison	35 mm	NFA
At Old Fort Dearborn	NYMP/Bison	35 mm	NFA
The Battle of the Red Men	NYMP/Bison	35 mm	LoC
Blazing the Trail	NYMP/Bison	16 mm	MOMA
Cowboy's Day Off	NYMP/Bison	35 mm	NFA
The Deserter	NYMP/Bison	16 mm	WCFTR
The Empty Water Keg	NYMP/Bison	16 mm	LoC
The Lieutenant's Last Fight	NYMP/Bison	35 mm	LoC

1912 (*continued*)

The Massacre of the Fourth Calvary	NYMP/Bison	16 mm	MOMA
Bangs' Burglar Alarm	Powers	35 mm	LoC
Her Yesterday	Powers	35 mm	NFA
The Jealous Wife	Powers	35 mm	NFA
Wanted, a Practice	Powers	35 mm	LoC
The Cry of the Children	Thanhouser	Video	n/a
For Sale—a Life	Thanhouser	16 mm	LoC
In a Garden	Thanhouser	35 mm	NFA
Petticoat Camp	Thanhouser	Video	n/a
Treasure Trove	Thanhouser	35 mm	NFA
Under Two Flags	Thanhouser	35 mm	NFA
Undine	Thanhouser	35 mm	NFA
With the Mounted Police	Thanhouser	35 mm	LoC
The Borrowed Flat	American	35 mm	LoC
The Distant Relative	American	35 mm	NFA
The Fear	American	35 mm	NFA
Maiden and Men	American	35 mm	LoC
Man's Calling	American	35 mm	LoC
The Reformation of Sierra Smith	American	35 mm	LoC
Saved by an Auto	American	35 mm	LoC
Their Hero Son	American	35 mm	LoC
The Thief's Wife	American	35 mm	LoC
The Vanishing Tribe	American	35 mm	NFA
The Bandit of Tropico	Nestor	35 mm	NFA
Young Wild West Leading a Raid	Nestor	35 mm	NFA
Jealousy	Reliance	35 mm	LoC
Love Is Blind	Reliance	16 mm	LoC
Canned Harmony	Solax	16 mm	LoC
A Comedy of Errors	Solax	35 mm	NFA
The Detective's Dog	Solax	16 mm	LoC
The Girl in the Arm-Chair	Solax	35 mm	LoC
Making an American Citizen	Solax	Video	n/a
Celebrations on the Ranch	American Kinematograph	35 mm	NFA
A Chance Meeting	American Kinematograph	35 mm	NFA
The Coward	American Kinematograph	35 mm	NFA
Kid Canfield, Notorious Gambler	Champion	35 mm	NFA

TITLE	PRODUCTION COMPANY	FORMAT	ARCHIVE
1912 (*continued*)			
An Ill Wind	Rex	35 mm	NFA
A Japanese Idyll	Rex	35 mm	LoC
Leaves in the Storm	Rex	16 mm	LoC
A Prophet without Honor	Rex	35 mm	LoC
Through a Higher Power	Rex	16 mm	LoC
The Simple Life	Majestic	16 mm	LoC
Flo's Discipline	Victor	16 mm	LoC
Not Like Other Girls	Victor	16 mm	LoC
The Army Surgeon	Kay-Bee	35 mm	LoC
The Ball Player and the Bandit	Broncho	35 mm	LoC
Stolen Glory	Keystone	35 mm	NFA
The Water Nymph	Keystone	Video	n/a
Alice's Choice	Méliès	35 mm	NFA
A Frontier Soldier of Fortune	Comet	35 mm	LoC
Smashing a Masher	Criterion	35 mm	NFA
1913			
The Ambassador's Daughter	Edison	16 mm	MOMA
Aunt Elsa's Visit	Edison	16 mm	MOMA
Bragg's New Suit	Edison	16 mm	MOMA
Dances of the Ages	Edison	16 mm	MOMA
Dangers of the Street	Edison	16 mm	MOMA
Jack's Joke	Edison	16 mm	MOMA
The Minister's Temptation	Edison	16 mm	MOMA
The Battle at Elderbush Gulch	Biograph	Video	n/a
By Man's Law	Biograph	Video	n/a
Death's Marathon	Biograph	Video	n/a
Her Mother's Oath	Biograph	Video	n/a
Just Gold	Biograph	Video	n/a
The Lady and the Mouse	Biograph	Video	n/a
The Mothering Heart	Biograph	Video	n/a
Bedelia Becomes a Lady	Vitagraph	16 mm	LoC
The Coming of Gretchen	Vitagraph	35 mm	LoC
Everybody's Doing It	Vitagraph	16 mm	LoC
The Locket	Vitagraph	16 mm	MOMA
Playing with Fire	Vitagraph	35 mm	LoC
Auntie's Affinity	Lubin	Video	n/a
The Guiding Light	Lubin	35 mm	NFA

1913 (*continued*)

The Hidden Bankroll	Lubin	35 mm	LoC
Belle Boyd, a Confederate Spy	Selig	Video	n/a
A Matrimonial Deluge	Selig	35 mm	LoC
The Burglar and the Baby	Kalem	35 mm	LoC
A Female Fagin	Kalem	35 mm	NFA
The Sheriff of Stone Gulch	Kalem	Video	n/a
Broncho Billy's Capture	Essanay	16 mm	LoC
The Death Weight	Essanay	35 mm	NFA
The Making of Broncho Billy	Essanay	Video	n/a
Old Gorman's Gal	Essanay	35 mm	LoC
The Bald Headed Club	IMP	35 mm	NFA
In Peril of the Sea	IMP	35 mm	NFA
Now I Lay Me Down to Sleep	IMP	35mm	NFA
Eph's Dream	Powers	35 mm	LoC
Injuns	Powers	35 mm	LoC
Mammy's Child	Powers	35 mm	LoC
Mother	Powers	35 mm	LoC
While the Children Slept	Powers	35 mm	NFA
The Farmer's Daughters	Thanhouser	35 mm	NFA
The Girl of the Cabaret	Thanhouser	35 mm	NFA
Just a Shabby Doll	Thanhouser	35 mm	NFA
Proposal by Proxy	Thanhouser	16 mm	LoC
Uncle's Namesakes	Thanhouser	35 mm	NFA
When the Studio Burned	Thanhouser	16 mm	LoC
Ashes of Three	American/Flying "A"	35 mm	NFA
The Fugitive	American/Flying "A"	35 mm	NFA
The Trail of Cards	American/Flying "A"	35 mm	LoC
Trapped in a Forest Fire	American/Flying "A"	35 mm	NFA
The Unwritten Law of the West	American/Flying "A"	35 mm	LoC
Mum's the Word	Nestor	35 mm	LoC
Death's Short Cut	Reliance	35 mm	NFA
Dick's Turning	Reliance	35 mm	LoC
A House Divided	Solax	Video	n/a
Matrimony's Speed Limit	Solax	Video	n/a
The Thief	Solax	35 mm	NFA
Suspense	Rex	16 mm	MOMA
The Widow Widower	Rex	35 mm	LoC
Heart of a Fool	Majestic	35 mm	LoC
Pedro's Revenge	Majestic	35 mm	LoC
A Bandit	Keystone	Video	n/a
The Bangville Police	Keystone	Video	n/a

TITLE	PRODUCTION COMPANY	FORMAT	ARCHIVE
1913 (*continued*)			
Barney Oldfield's Race for a Life	Keystone	Video	n/a
Mabel's Dramatic Career	Keystone	16 mm	MOMA
Mabel's New Hero	Keystone	Video	MOMA
A Muddy Romance	Keystone	Video	n/a
Peeping Pete	Keystone	Video	n/a
The Speed Kings	Keystone	Video	n/a
Toplitsky and Co.	Keystone	Video	n/a
St. Joseph's Taper	Méliès	35 mm	NFA
Hand of Providence	Crystal	35 mm	LoC
How Men Proposed	Crystal	Video	n/a
The Innocent Bridegroom	Crystal	16 mm	LoC
A Night in Town	Crystal	16 mm	LoC
Billy's Suicide	Gem	35 mm	LoC
The Ninth Commandment	Gem	16 mm	LoC
Miss Fairweather Out West	Frontier	16 mm	LoC
The Blacksmith's Story	Pilot	16 mm	LoC

WORKS CITED

Abel, Richard. 1987. "Before *Fantomas:* Louis Feuillade and the Development of Early French Cinema." *Post Script* 7, no. 1: 4–26.

Abel, Richard. 1989. "Scenes from Domestic Life in Early French Cinema." *Screen* 30, no. 3: 4–28.

Abel, Richard. 1994. *The Ciné Goes to Town: French Cinema, 1896–1914.* Berkeley: University of California Press.

Abel, Richard. 1999. *The Red Rooster Scare: Making Cinema American, 1900–1910.* Berkeley: University of California Press.

Allen, Robert C. 1979. "Contra the Chaser Theory." *Wide Angle* 3, no. 1: 4–11.

Allen, Robert C. 1984. "Looking at 'Another Look at the "Chaser Theory."'" *Studies in Visual Communication* 10, no. 4: 45–50.

Allen, Robert C. 1996. "Manhattan Myopia; or, Oh! Iowa!" *Cinema Journal* 35, no. 3: 75–103.

Altman, Rick. 1999. *Film/Genre.* London: British Film Institute.

Anderson, Robert. 1979. "The Role of the Western Film Genre in Industry Competition, 1907–1911." *Journal of the University Film Association* 31, no. 2: 19–27.

Andrew, Dudley. 1989. "The Limits of Delight: Robert Ray's Postmodern Film Studies." *Strategies,* no. 2: 158–64.

Ball, Eustace Hale. 1913. *The Art of the Photoplay.* 2d ed. New York: G.W. Dillingham Company.

Balshofer, Fred J., and Arthur C. Miller. 1967. *One Reel a Week.* Berkeley: University of California Press.

Bazin, André. 1967. "The Myth of Total Cinema." In vol. 1 of *What Is Cinema?,* translated by Hugh Gray. Berkeley: University of California Press.

Bitzer, G. W. 1973. *Billy Bitzer: His Story.* New York: Farrar, Straus and Giroux.

Bogdanovich, Peter. 1971. *Allan Dwan: The Last Pioneer.* New York: Praeger Publishers, Inc.

Bordman, Gerald. 1994. *American Theatre: A Chronicle of Comedy and Drama, 1869–1914.* New York: Oxford University Press.

Bordwell, David. 1983. "Lowering the Stakes: Prospects for a Historical Poetics of Cinema." *Iris* 1, no. 1: 5–18.

Bordwell, David. 1985a. "The Classical Hollywood Style, 1917–60." In *The Classical Hollywood Cinema: Film Style and Mode of Production to 1960,* co-authored by David Bordwell, Janet Staiger, and Kristin Thompson. New York: Columbia University Press.

Bordwell, David. 1985b. *Narration and the Fiction Film.* Madison: University of Wisconsin Press.

Bordwell, David. 1988. *Ozu and the Poetics of Cinema.* Princeton, N.J.: Princeton University Press.

Bordwell, David. 1989a. "Historical Poetics of Cinema." In *The Cinematic Text,* edited by R. Barton Palmer. New York: AMS Press.

Bordwell, David. 1989b. *Making Meaning: Inference and Rhetoric in the Interpretation of Cinema.* Cambridge, Mass.: Harvard University Press.

Bordwell, David. 1996. "La Nouvelle Mission de Feuillade; or, What was Mise en Scène?" *Velvet Light Trap,* no. 37: 10–29.

Bordwell, David. 1997. *On the History of Film Style.* Cambridge, Mass.: Harvard University Press.

Bordwell, David, and Kristin Thompson. 1997. *Film Art: An Introduction.* 5th ed. New York: McGraw-Hill.

Bowser, Eileen. 1979. "The Brighton Project: An Introduction." *Quarterly Review of Film Studies* 4, no. 4: 509–38.

Bowser, Eileen. 1983. "Toward Narrative, 1907: *The Mill Girl.*" In *Film before Griffith,* edited by John L. Fell. Berkeley: University of California Press.

Bowser, Eileen. 1985. "Le Coup de téléphone dans les films des premiers temps." In *Les Premiers ans du cinéma français,* edited by Pierre Guibbert. Perpignan: Institut Jean Vigo.

Bowser, Eileen. 1990. *The Transformation of Cinema, 1907–1915.* New York: Charles Scribner's Sons.

Branigan, Edward. 1992. *Narrative Comprehension and Film.* New York: Routledge.

Brewster, Ben. 1982. "A Scene at the 'Movies.'" *Screen* 23, no. 2: 4–15.

Brewster, Ben. 1987. "Frammenti Vitagraph alla Library of Congress." In *Vitagraph Co. of America: Il cinema prima di Hollywood,* edited by Paolo Cherchi Usai. Pordenone: Edizioni Studio Tesi.

Brewster, Ben. 1989. "The Notion of Space in Early Cinema." Paper presented at the Communication Arts Colloquium, University of Wisconsin–Madison.

Brewster, Ben. 1990. Reprint. "Deep Staging in French Films." In *Early Cinema: Space, Frame, Narrative,* edited by Thomas Elsaesser; translated by the author. London: British Film Institute. Original publication 1985.

Brewster, Ben. 1991a. "A Bunch of Violets." Paper presented to the Society for Cinema Studies Conference, Los Angeles.

Brewster, Ben. 1991b. "*Traffic in Souls:* An Experiment in Feature-Length Narrative Construction." *Cinema Journal* 31, no. 1: 37–56.

Brewster, Ben, and Lea Jacobs. 1997. *Theatre to Cinema.* New York: Oxford University Press.

Brownlow, Kevin. 1968. *The Parade's Gone By . . .* New York: Alfred A. Knopf, Inc.

Burch, Noël. 1978/9. "Porter, or Ambivalence." *Screen* 19, no. 4: 91–105.

Burch, Noël. 1986. "Primitivism and the Avant-Gardes: A Dialectical Approach." In *Narrative, Apparatus, Ideology,* edited by Philip Rosen. New York: Columbia University Press.

Burch, Noël. 1990a. "Business Is Business: An Invisible Audience." In *Life to Those Shadows,* edited and translated by Ben Brewster. Berkeley: University of California Press.

Burch, Noël. 1990b. Reprint. "Passions and Chases—A Certain Linearisation." In *Life to Those Shadows,* edited and translated by Ben Brewster. Berkeley: University of California Press. Original publication 1983.

Chatman, Seymour. 1978. *Story and Discourse: Narrative Structure in Fiction and Film.* Ithaca, N.Y.: Cornell University Press.

Crafton, Donald. 1990. *Emile Cohl, Caricature, and Film.* Princeton, N.J.: Princeton University Press.

Crafton, Donald. 1995. Reprint. "Pie and Chase: Gag, Spectacle and Narrative in Slapstick Comedy." In *Classical Hollywood Comedy,* edited by Kristine Brunovska Karnick and Henry Jenkins. New York: Routledge. Original publication 1988.

deCordova, Richard. 1990. *Picture Personalities: The Emergence of the Star System in America, 1907–1922.* Urbana: University of Illinois Press.

Elsaesser, Thomas. 1990. "Introductions." In *Early Cinema: Space, Frame, Narrative,* edited by Thomas Elsaesser. London: British Film Institute.

Fell, John L. 1974. *Film and the Narrative Tradition.* Norman: Oklahoma University Press.

Fell, John L. 1980. "Motive, Mischief, and Melodrama: The State of Film Narrative in 1907." *Film Quarterly* 33, no. 3: 30–37.

Fell, John L. 1986. "Cellulose Nitrate Roots: Popular Entertainments and the Birth of Film Narrative." In *Before Hollywood: Turn-of-the-Century Film from American Archives,* edited by Jay Leyda and Charles Musser. New York: The American Federation of the Arts.

Fuller, Kathryn. 1996. *At the Picture Show: Small Town Audiences and the Creation of Movie Fan Culture.* Washington, D.C.: Smithsonian Institution Press.

Gartenberg, Jon. 1982. "Camera Movement in Edison and Biograph Films: 1900–1906." In *Cinema 1900–1906, An Analytical Study,* edited by Roger Holman. Brussels: Fédération Internationale des Archives du Film.

Gartenberg, Jon. 1984. "Vitagraph before Griffith: Forging Ahead in the Nickelodeon Era." *Studies in Visual Communication* 10, no. 4: 7–23.

Gaudreault, André. 1983. "Temporality and Narrativity in Early Cinema, 1895–1908." In *Film before Griffith,* edited by John Fell. Berkeley: University of California Press.

Gaudreault, André. 1987. "Theatricality, Narrativity, and 'Trickality': Reevaluating the Cinema of Georges Méliès." Translated by Paul Attallah. *Journal of Popular Film and Television* 15, no. 3: 110–19.

Gaudreault, André. 1990. Reprint. "Film, Narrative, Narration: The Cinema of the Lumière Brothers." In *Early Cinema: Space, Frame, Narrative*, edited by Thomas Elsaesser. London: British Film Institute. Original publication 1984.

Genette, Gérard. 1980. *Narrative Discourse: An Essay in Method.* Translated by Jane E. Lewin. Ithaca, N.Y.: Cornell University Press.

Graham, Cooper C., Steven Higgins, Elaine Mancini, and João Luiz Vieira. 1985. *D. W. Griffith and the Biograph Company.* Metuchen, N.J.: The Scarecrow Press, Inc.

Griffith, Linda Arvidson. 1969. Reprint. *When the Movies Were Young.* New York: Dover Publications, Inc. Original publication 1925.

Gunning, Tom. 1981. "Weaving a Narrative: Style and Economic Background in Griffith's Biograph Films." *Quarterly Review of Film Studies* 6, no. 1: 11–25.

Gunning, Tom. 1982. "The Non-Continuous Style of Early Film, 1900–1906." In *Cinema 1900–1906, An Analytical Study*, edited by Roger Holman. Brussels: Fédération Internationale des Archives du Film.

Gunning, Tom. 1983 "An Unseen Energy Swallows Space: The Space in Early Film and Its Relation to American Avant-Garde Film." In *Film before Griffith*, edited by John L. Fell. Berkeley: University of California Press.

Gunning, Tom. 1984. "Non-Continuity, Continuity, Discontinuity: A Theory of Genres in Early Films." *Iris* 2, no. 1: 101–12.

Gunning, Tom. 1986. "D. W. Griffith and the Narrator-System: Narrative Structure and Industry Organization in Biograph Films, 1908–1909." Ph.D. diss., New York University.

Gunning, Tom. 1987. "I film Vitagraph e il cinema dell'integrazione narrativa." In *Vitagraph Co. of America: Il cinema prima di Hollywood*, edited by Paolo Cherchi Usai. Pordenone: Edizioni Studio Tesi.

Gunning, Tom. 1988. "What I Saw from the Rear Window of the Hôtel des Folies-Dramatiques, or The Story Point of View Films Told." In *Ce que je vois de mon ciné . . .* , edited by André Gaudreault. Paris: Méridiens Klincksieck.

Gunning, Tom. 1989. "'Primitive' Cinema—A Frame Up? or The Trick's on Us." *Cinema Journal* 28, no. 2: 3–12.

Gunning, Tom. 1991. *D. W. Griffith and the Origins of American Narrative Film.* Urbana: University of Illinois Press.

Gunning, Tom. 1993a. "Notes and Queries about the Year 1913 and Film Style: National Styles and Deep Staging." *1895*, no. 14: 195–204.

Gunning, Tom. 1993b. "Now You See It, Now You Don't: The Temporality of the Cinema of Attractions." *Velvet Light Trap*, no. 32: 3–12.

Gunning, Tom. 1993c. "Visual Evidence and Mute Testimony." Paper presented to the Society for Cinema Studies Conference, New Orleans. Revised and reprinted as "Tracing the Individual Body: Photography, Detectives and Early Cinema." In *Cinema and the Invention of Modern Life*, edited by Leo Charney and Vanessa Schwartz. Berkeley: University of California Press, 1995.

Gunning, Tom. 1995. "Crazy Machines in the Garden of Forking Paths: Mischief Gags and the Origins of American Film Comedy." In *Classical Hollywood Comedy*, edited by Kristine Brunovska Karnick and Henry Jenkins. New York: Routledge.

Gunning, Tom. 1998. "Early American Film." In *The Oxford Guide to Film Studies*, edited by John Hill and Pamela Church Gibson. New York: Oxford University Press.

Hansen, Miriam. 1991. *Babel and Babylon: Spectatorship in American Silent Film*. Cambridge, Mass.: Harvard University Press.

Heath, Stephen. 1981. *Questions of Cinema*. Bloomington: Indiana University Press.

Higashi, Sumiko. 1996. "Dialogue: Manhattan's Nickelodeons." *Cinema Journal* 35, no. 3: 72–74.

Hulfish, David. 1970. Reprint. *Motion Picture-Work*. New York: Arno Press. Original publication 1915.

Jacobs, Lewis. 1968. Reprint. *The Rise of the American Film: A Critical History*. New York: Teachers College Press. Original publication 1939.

Jesionowski, Joyce. 1987. *Thinking in Pictures: Dramatic Structure in D. W. Griffith's Biograph Films*. Berkeley: University of California Press.

Keil, Charlie. 1989. "Transition through Tension: Stylistic Diversity in the Late Griffith Biographs." *Cinema Journal* 28, no. 3: 22–40.

Keil, Charlie. 1991. "Steel Engines and Cardboard Rockets: The Status of Fiction and Nonfiction in Early Cinema." *Persistence of Vision*, no. 9: 37–45.

Keil, Charlie. 1992. "*From the Manger to the Cross:* The New Testament Narrative and the Question of Stylistic Retardation." In *Une Invention du diable? Cinéma des premiers temps et religion*, edited by Roland Cosandey, André Gaudreault, and Tom Gunning. Sainte-Foy, Que.: Les Presses de l'Université Laval.

Keil, Charlie. 1993. "Advertising Independence: Industrial Performance and Advertising Strategies of the Independent Movement, 1909–10." *Film History* 5, no. 4: 472–88.

Kern, Stephen. 1983. *The Culture of Time and Space, 1880–1918*. Cambridge, Mass.: Harvard University Press.

Kirby, Lynne. 1997. *Parallel Tracks: The Railroad and Silent Cinema*. Durham, N.C.: Duke University Press.

Krämer, Peter. 1988. "Vitagraph, Slapstick and Early Cinema." *Screen* 29, no. 2: 98–104.

Lacassin, Francis. 1972. "The Comic Strip and Film Language." *Film Quarterly* 26, no. 1: 11–23.

Lahue, Kalton C., ed. 1973. *Motion Picture Pioneer: The Selig Polyscope Company.* New York: A. S. Barnes and Company.

Loughney, Patrick. 1984. "In the Beginning Was the Word: Six Pre-Griffith Motion Pictures Scenarios." *Iris* 2, no. 1: 17–31.

Marsh, Mae. 1921. *Screen Acting.* Los Angeles: Photo-Star Publishing.

Merritt, Russell. 1976. "Mr. Griffith, *The Painted Lady,* and the Distractive Frame." *Image* 19, no. 4: 26–30.

Merritt, Russell. 1986. "Dream Visions in Pre-Hollywood Film." In *Before Hollywood: Turn-of-the-Century Film from American Archives,* edited by Jay Leyda and Charles Musser. New York: The American Federation of the Arts.

Münsterberg, Hugo. 1970. Reprint. *The Film: A Psychological Study, the Silent Photoplay in 1916.* New York: Dover Publications, Inc. Original publication 1916 as *The Photoplay: A Psychological Study.*

Musser, Charles. 1979. "The Early Cinema of Edwin Porter." *Cinema Journal* 19, no. 1: 1–38.

Musser, Charles. 1983. "The Nickelodeon Era Begins: Establishing the Framework for Hollywood's Mode of Representation." *Framework,* nos. 22/23: 4–11.

Musser, Charles. 1984a. "Another Look at the 'Chaser Theory.'" *Studies in Visual Communication* 10, no. 4: 24–44.

Musser, Charles. 1984b. "Towards a History of Screen Practice." *Quarterly Review of Film Studies* 3, no. 1: 59–69.

Musser, Charles. 1990. *The Emergence of Cinema: The American Screen to 1907.* New York: Charles Scribner's Sons.

Musser, Charles. 1991a. *Before the Nickelodeon: Edwin S. Porter and the Edison Manufacturing Company.* Berkeley: University of California Press.

Musser, Charles. 1991b. "Pre-Classical American Cinema: Its Changing Modes of Film Production." *Persistence of Vision,* no. 9: 46–65.

Musser, Charles, and Carol Nelson. 1991. *High-Class Moving Pictures: Lyman H. Howe and the Forgotten Era of Traveling Exhibition, 1880–1920.* Princeton, N.J.: Princeton University Press.

Nichols, Bill. 1989. "Form Wars: The Political Unconscious of Formalist Theory." *South Atlantic Quarterly* 88, no. 2: 487–515.

Niver, Kemp. 1968. *The First Twenty Years: A Segment of Film History.* Los Angeles: Locare Research Group.

Parker, John, ed. 1908. *The Green Room Book: or Who's Who on the Stage.* London: T. Sealey Clark & Co.

Pearson, Roberta. 1992. *Eloquent Gestures: The Transformation of Performance Style in the Griffith Biograph Films.* Berkeley: University of California Press.

Pearson, Roberta. 1996. "Transitional Cinema." In *The Oxford History of World Cinema,* edited by Geoffrey Nowell-Smith. Oxford: Oxford University Press.

Pratt, George C. 1973. *Spellbound in Darkness: A History of the Silent Film.* Rev. ed. Greenwich, Conn.: New York Graphic Society Ltd.

Rabinovitz, Lauren. 1998. *For the Love of Pleasure: Women, Movies, and Culture in Turn-of-the-Century Chicago.* New Brunswick, N.J.: Rutgers University Press.

Reynolds, Herbert. 1992. "From the Palette to the Screen: The Tissot Bible as Sourcebook for *From the Manger to the Cross.*" In *Une Invention du diable? Cinéma des premiers temps et religion,* edited by Roland Cosandey, André Gaudreault, and Tom Gunning. Sainte-Foy, Que.: Les Presses de l'Université Laval.

Riblet, Doug. 1991. "Chase Films and Narrativity." Paper presented to the Society for Cinema Studies Conference, Los Angeles.

Riblet, Doug. 1995. "The Keystone Film Company and the Historiography of Early Slapstick." In *Classical Hollywood Comedy,* edited by Kristine Brunovska Karnick and Henry Jenkins. New York: Routledge.

Salt, Barry. 1983. *Film Style and Technology: History and Analysis.* London: Starword.

Salt, Barry. 1984. "What We Can Learn from the First Twenty Years of Cinema." *Iris* 2, no. 1: 83–90.

Salt, Barry. 1987. "Vitagraph, un tocco di classe." In *Vitagraph Co. of America: Il cinema prima di Hollywood,* edited by Paolo Cherchi Usai. Pordenone: Edizioni Studio Tesi.

Salt, Barry. 1992. *Film Style and Technology: History and Analysis.* 2d ed., expanded. London: Starword.

Schivelbusch, Wolfgang. 1986. Reprint. *The Railway Journey: The Industrialization of Time and Space in the 19th Century.* Berkeley: University of California Press. Original publication 1977.

Singer, Ben. 1995. "Manhattan Nickelodeons: New Data on Audiences and Exhibitors." *Cinema Journal* 34, no. 3: 5–35.

Singer, Ben. 1996. "New York, Just Like I Pictured It . . ." *Cinema Journal* 35, no. 3: 104–28.

Singer, Ben. 2001. *Melodrama and Modernity: Early Sensational Cinema and Its Contexts.* New York: Columbia University Press.

Slide, Anthony. 1987. *The Big V: A History of the Vitagraph Company.* Revised ed. Metuchen, N.J.: The Scarecrow Press, Inc.

Slide, Anthony, ed. 1982. *Selected Film Criticism, 1896–1911.* Metuchen, N.J.: The Scarecrow Press, Inc.

Sloan, Kay. 1988. *The Loud Silents: Origins of the Social Problem Film.* Urbana: University of Illinois Press.

Spadoni, Robert. 1999. "The Figure Seen from the Rear, Vitagraph, and the Development of Shot/Reverse Shot." *Film History* 11, no. 4: 319–41.

Staiger, Janet. 1980. "Mass-Produced Photoplays: Economic and Signifying Practices in the First Years of Hollywood." *Wide Angle* 4, no. 3: 12–27.

Staiger, Janet. 1985a. "The Eyes Are Really the Focus: Photoplay Acting and Film Form and Style." *Wide Angle* 6, no. 4: 14–23.

Staiger, Janet. 1985b. "The Hollywood Mode of Production to 1930." In *The Classical Hollywood Cinema: Film Style and Mode of Production to 1960*, co-authored by David Bordwell, Janet Staiger, and Kristin Thompson. New York: Columbia University Press.

Staiger, Janet. 1995. *Bad Women: Regulating Sexuality in Early American Cinema.* Minneapolis: University of Minnesota Press.

Stamp, Shelley. 2000. *Movie-Struck Girls: Women and Motion Picture Culture after the Nickelodeon.* Princeton, N.J.: Princeton University Press.

Sternberg, Meir. 1978. *Expositional Modes and Temporal Ordering in Fiction.* Baltimore: Johns Hopkins University Press.

Thompson, Kristin. 1984. Review. "Cinema 1900/06: An Analytical Study." *Iris* 2, no. 1: 139–43.

Thompson, Kristin. 1985a. *Exporting Entertainment: America in the World Film Market, 1907–34.* London: British Film Institute.

Thompson, Kristin. 1985b. "The Formulation of the Classical Style, 1909–28" and "Initial Standardization of the Basic Technology." In *The Classical Hollywood Cinema: Film Style and Mode of Production to 1960*, co-authored by David Bordwell, Janet Staiger, and Kristin Thompson. New York: Columbia University Press.

Thompson, Kristin. 1988. *Breaking the Glass Armor: Neoformalist Film Analysis.* Princeton, N.J.: Princeton University Press.

Thompson, Kristin. 1997. "Narration in Three Early Teens Vitagraph Films." *Film History* 9, no. 4: 410–34.

Thompson, Kristin. 1998. "Narrative Structure in Early Classical Cinema." In *Celebrating 1895: The Centenary of Cinema*, edited by John Fullerton. Sydney: John Libbey.

Thompson, Kristin, and David Bordwell. 1994. *Film History: An Introduction.* New York: McGraw-Hill, Inc.

Todorov, Tzvetan. 1971. "The Two Principles of Narrative." Translated by Philip E. Lewis. *Diacritics* 1, no. 1: 37–44.

Todorov, Tzvetan. 1977a. "Categories of the Literary Narrative." Translated by Ann Goodman. *Film Reader*, no. 2: 19–37.

Todorov, Tzvetan. 1977b. *The Poetics of Prose.* Translated by Richard Howard. Ithaca, N.Y.: Cornell University Press.

Tsivian, Yuri. 1994. "'Speeding the Bullet Message': Images of 'Elsewhere' in the Age of Electric Media." Paper presented to the Domitor conference, New York City.

Turim, Maureen. 1989. *Flashbacks in Film: Memory and History.* New York: Routledge.

Uricchio, William, and Roberta E. Pearson. 1993. *Reframing Culture: The Case of the Vitagraph Quality Films.* Princeton, N.J.: Princeton University Press.

Uricchio, William, and Roberta E. Pearson. 1994. "Constructing the Audience: Competing Discourses of Morality and Rationalization during the Nickelodeon Period." *Iris*, no. 17: 43–54.

Uricchio, William, Roberta E. Pearson, Judith Thissen, and Ben Singer. 1987. "Dialogue: Manhattan's Melodramas." *Cinema Journal* 36, no. 4: 98–112.

Vardac, A. Nicholas. 1987. Reprint. *Stage to Screen, Theatrical Origins of Early Film: David Garrick to D. W. Griffith.* New York: Da Capo Press. Original publication 1949.

Waller, Gregory. 1995. *Main Street Amusements: Movies and Commercial Entertainment in a Southern City, 1896–1930.* Washington, D.C.: Smithsonian Institution Press.

Wölfflin, Heinrich. 1989. Reprint. "Principles in Art History." In *Modern Perspectives in Western Art History,* edited by W. Eugene Kleinbauer. Toronto: University of Toronto Press. Original publication 1932.

FILM INDEX

An asterisk precedes films appearing in the Filmography of viewed titles. Page numbers in italic type specify illustrations.

GENERAL INDEX